Unions in Court

Law and Society Series

W. Wesley Pue, General Editor

The Law and Society Series explores law as a socially embedded phe-
nomenon. It is premised on the understanding that the conventional division of law from society creates false dichotomies in thinking,
scholarship, educational practice, and social life. Books in the series
treat law and society as mutually constitutive and seek to bridge scholarship emerging from interdisciplinary engagement of law with dis-
ciplines such as politics, social theory, history, political economy, and
gender studies.

A list of recent titles in the series appears at the end of the book.
For a complete list, see the UBC Press website, www.ubcpress.ca/books/
series_law.html.

Unions in Court

Organized Labour and the Charter of Rights and Freedoms

LARRY SAVAGE AND
CHARLES W. SMITH

UBCPress · Vancouver · Toronto

26 25 24 23 22 21 20 19 18 17   5 4 3 2 1

Printed in Canada on FSC-certified ancient-forest-free paper (100% post-consumer recycled) that is processed chlorine- and acid-free.

Library and Archives Canada Cataloguing in Publication

Savage, Larry, author
    Unions in court : organized labour and the Charter of Rights and Freedoms / Larry Savage and Charles W. Smith.

(Law and society series)
Includes bibliographical references and index.
Issued in print and electronic formats.
ISBN 978-0-7748-3538-1 (hardcover). – ISBN 978-0-7748-3539-8 (softcover)
ISBN 978-0-7748-3540-4 (PDF). – ISBN 978-0-7748-3541-1 (EPUB)
ISBN 978-0-7748-3542-8 (Kindle)

    1. Canada. Canadian Charter of Rights and Freedoms. 2. Labor laws and legislation – Canada. 3. Labor unions – Canada. I. Smith, Charles W., author II. Title. III. Series: Law and society series (Vancouver, B.C.)

KE3109.S38 2017   344.7101   C2016-908171-0
KF3320.ZA2S38 2017   C2016-908172-9

Canadä

UBC Press gratefully acknowledges the financial support for our publishing program of the Government of Canada (through the Canada Book Fund), the Canada Council for the Arts, and the British Columbia Arts Council.

This book has been published with the help of a grant from the Canadian Federation for the Humanities and Social Sciences, through the Awards to Scholarly Publications Program, using funds provided by the Social Sciences and Humanities Research Council of Canada.

Printed and bound in Canada by Friesens
Set in Sabon and Myriad by Marquis Interscript
Copy editor: Joyce Hildebrand
Indexer: Margaret de Boer
Cover designer: David Drummond

UBC Press
The University of British Columbia
2029 West Mall
Vancouver, BC V6T 1Z2
www.ubcpress.ca

Contents

Acknowledgments

When we set out to write this book in 2012, the idea that the Supreme Court of Canada would declare a constitutional right to strike a few years later seemed nothing more than a fanciful hope for many union activists. The Supreme Court's decision to turn a labour movement pipe dream into constitutional reality, however, challenged us in ways we had not originally anticipated. Labour-related constitutional cases have become so prevalent in recent years that the biggest quandary we faced as authors was which Charter case to use as a bookend for our analysis. Canada's Supreme Court justices certainly kept us guessing over the course of the writing process, and the court's historic decisions certainly extended the timeline for writing this book. In the end, however, we think the analysis is richer for it.

We have plenty of people to thank for helping us to see this book through to completion. First and foremost, we owe a debt of gratitude to Beth Bilson, Stephanie Ross, and the anonymous reviewers at UBC Press for reading and making helpful suggestions on how to improve the manuscript, in whole or in part. Their thoughtful insights and comments proved invaluable.

We also owe a giant thank you to family, friends, and colleagues, all of whom have been encouraging and supportive. Charles would like to thank Allison Smith for her patience in dutifully listening to ongoing discussions about this book over the past several years. Both Dylan and Jonah Smith have provided ongoing inspiration and are a constant source of happiness. Larry would like to thank his Labour Studies colleagues at Brock University, particularly Carmela Patrias, Kendra Coulter, Simon Black, Jonah Butovsky, June Corman, and Michelle Webber for helping to sustain a highly collegial and supportive work environment.

We would also like to thank Dennis Pilon, Larry Hubich, Bryan Palmer, and Stephen McBride. They all contributed to the successful completion of this book in their own way.

We were lucky to work with excellent research assistants on this project. Jane Basinski, Heather Franklin, Aleida Oberholzer, and Alexandra Turcotte at the University of Saskatchewan; and Matthew Skubel and Nick Ruhloff-Queiruga at Brock University all did an amazing job and made the task of the writing the book so much easier.

Randy Schmidt and Megan Brand at UBC Press were a pleasure to work with and the financial support of the Social Sciences and Humanities Research Council of Canada was greatly appreciated.

A special thank you is reserved for our students who, over the years, have challenged our own perceptions, ideas, and attitudes about work, labour, and the law. We hope the arguments and perspectives put forward in this book will inspire lively debate that extends well beyond university lecture halls into workplaces, union halls, and workers' centres.

Finally, we thank those labour movement activists, past and present, who've shown a willingness to bend, break, and challenge unjust laws. Their continued struggles to achieve dignity and fairness at work are truly inspiring.

Abbreviations

These are all the abbreviations (acronyms) used in the text, excluding those for legislative acts.

ACCL	All-Canadian Congress of Labour
AFL	Alberta Federation of Labour
AUN	Alberta Union of Nurses
AUPE	Alberta Union of Provincial Employees
BCFL	BC Federation of Labour
BCLRB	BC Labour Relations Board
BCTF	BC Teachers' Federation
CAPE	Canadian Association of Professional Employees
CAW	Canadian Auto Workers
CBRT	Canadian Brotherhood of Railway, Transport, and General Workers
CCCL	Canadian and Catholic Confederation of Labour
CCF	Co-operative Commonwealth Federation
CCL	Canadian Congress of Labour
CIO	Congress of Industrial Organizing
CLC	Canadian Labour Congress
CMA	Canadian Manufacturers' Association
CUPE	Canadian Union of Public Employees

CUPW	Canadian Union of Postal Workers
HEU	Hospital Employees' Union
ILO	International Labour Organization
JCPC	Judicial Committee of the Privy Council
LICC	Labour Issues Coordinating Committee
NAPE	Newfoundland and Labrador Association of Public and Private Employees
NAWL	National Association of Women and the Law
NCC	National Citizens Coalition
NDP	New Democratic Party
NLRB	National Labor Relations Board
NUPGE	National Union of Public and General Employees
NWLRB	National War Labour Relations Board
NWTPSA	North West Territories Public Service Association
OFL	Ontario Federation of Labour
OPSEU	Ontario Public Service Employees Union
OTF	Ontario Teachers' Federation
PIPSC	Professional Institute of the Public Service of Canada
PSAC	Public Service Alliance of Canada
PQ	Parti Québécois
QFL	Québec Federation of Labour
RCMP	Royal Canadian Mounted Police
RWDSU	Retail, Wholesale, and Department Store Union
SEIU	Service Employees International Union
SFL	Saskatchewan Federation of Labour
SGEU	Saskatchewan Government and General Employees Union
SLRB	Saskatchewan Labour Relations Board
SUN	Saskatchewan Union of Nurses
TLC	Trades and Labour Congress
UAW	United Auto Workers
UEW	United Electrical, Radio, and Machine Workers of Canada
UFCW	United Food and Commercial Workers
UNA	United Nurses of Alberta
USWA	United Steelworkers of America

Unions in Court

Introduction
Law, Workers, and Courts

On 9 April 1987, the Supreme Court of Canada ruled in a series of cases dubbed the "labour trilogy." At the centre of the labour trilogy was the Canadian labour movement's attempt to breathe life into the *collective* nature of the guarantee of associational freedoms enshrined in the Charter of Rights and Freedoms. Much to the labour movement's dismay, however, the Supreme Court ruled that freedom of association was an individual freedom; therefore, workers had no constitutional right to strike. Fresh from that stinging defeat, the leadership of the Canadian Labour Congress (CLC) told a parliamentary committee examining the Meech Lake proposals on constitutional reform that the country's largest labour organization was not interested in seeing workers' rights to bargain collectively or to strike enshrined in the Charter. Constitutionalized labour rights, they argued, would become subject to uncertain legal interpretation by a conservative judiciary. Instead, they reasoned, the labour movement was far better positioned to secure workers' rights in the political arena (Special Joint Committee 1987, 12–17).

The Supreme Court's refusal to recognize a constitutional right to strike seemed to close the door on the potential for the constitution to protect the collective rights of workers. As Peter McCormick recently observed, the "heavy lifting" in this area of Charter jurisprudence seemed to be over and the most that labour could expect from future

litigation would be a tinkering of the "subtle details" over minor constitutional principles (McCormick 2015, xx). McCormick's observation,
however, may have been premature. Between 2001 and 2015, the Supreme Court of Canada slowly shifted its thinking on freedom of association and the constitutional rights of workers, becoming far more
hospitable to the labour movement than most provincial and federal
governments. In late 2001, the court ruled in *Dunmore v. Ontario* (2001,
para. 48) that it was now reasonable to conclude that the exclusion of a
particular subset of vulnerable agricultural workers from legislative protection "substantially interferes with their fundamental freedom to organize" as guaranteed by freedom of association protection in the Charter.

Building on the confined but important *Dunmore* precedent, the
Supreme Court stunned the country's political establishment in 2007 by
constitutionalizing the right to collective bargaining as part of its landmark decision in *Health Services and Support – Facilities Subsector Bargaining Assn. v. British Columbia (BC Health Services)*. The court then
departed completely from its labour trilogy jurisprudence, extending
constitutional protection for the right to strike in *Saskatchewan Federation
of Labour v. Saskatchewan* (2015). Union leaders and activists, who had
warmed up considerably to the idea of constitutionalized labour rights
during the preceding decades, were ecstatic with the court's decisions.
Speaking at a celebratory conference immediately following the *SFL*
decision, James Clancy, president of the National Union of Public and
General Employees (NUPGE), declared, "Our chief justices have clearly
affirmed that unions matter to our country and our communities. They
have once again recognized the importance of labour rights as a cornerstone of Canada's democracy" (Canadian Foundation for Labour Rights
2015, 1).

How did Canada's labour movement, within the span of three decades, go from being indifferent, if not openly hostile, to the prospect of
constitutionally protected labour rights in the 1980s to being strong
proponents – and in some cases, champions – of constitutionally protected collective rights for workers? The story of the evolving relationship between the Charter of Rights, the Supreme Court, and the
Canadian labour movement is the subject of this book.

While organized labour played a key role in advancing human rights protections in the immediate postwar era and was an early supporter of a constitutional bill of rights (Patrias 2011), unions were late to embrace the Charter revolution of the 1980s. The enactment of the Canadian Charter of Rights and Freedoms in 1982 fundamentally altered Canada's judicial landscape and ushered in a political and legal tidal wave of rights claims from a wide range of social movements (M. Smith 1999, 2005, 2014). Canada's labour movement initially treated the Charter very cautiously, fearing its impact on the country's labour relations regime and casting doubt on its progressive potential to defend, let alone strengthen, the legal rights and freedoms of workers. In the late 1980s and throughout the 1990s, however, the rise of neoliberal political parties and policy frameworks ushered in an unprecedented rolling back of the postwar statutory and regulatory protections of Canada's labour law regime (Panitch and Swartz 2003). These changes severely undermined the relative power and influence of organized labour, forcing unions to reconsider their relationship to the courts and governments, and to politics more generally (Smith 2012). That response was very much a defensive strategy, initiated to maintain and protect the well-established postwar labour relations regime created in the 1940s in the face of an increasingly hostile political and economic environment. Labour's strategic reorientation towards Charter-based politics has led the labour movement to gradually embrace both the Charter and rights discourse as part of a political and legal project to transform labour rights into more concrete and inalienable human rights.

The primary objective of this book is to document this evolution of the labour movement's engagement with the Charter of Rights and Freedoms. To that end, we set out to explain why the labour movement, historically hostile to judicial involvement in labour relations, has come to embrace constitutionalized labour rights and Charter-based litigation. Our secondary objective is to explain how and why that evolution took place, all with a view to making sense of the union movement's strategic shift in the realm of judicial politics. We take the position that while constitutional protections for workers' collective rights undoubtedly expand the zone of legal tolerance for organized labour, legitimizing certain collective actions within the existing regime of labour relations, such constitutional protections also come with tightened boundaries of legal constraint which demand that labour act responsibility in order to receive legal protection. Thus, while unions may win legal challenges at the Supreme Court from time to time, the balance of class forces within contemporary capitalism is hardly disrupted, and our system of labour relations continues to fail most workers seeking a modicum of workplace justice. Our final objective is geared towards answering a more fundamental question of strategy: If Charter-based litigation is not an effective tool for achieving social transformation, what are workers' options in the current era of neoliberalism? While the answer to this question is complex, it must begin with a reintroduction of labour's historical recognition that the law and judicial interpretation rarely advance workers' collective rights when those rights challenge the dominant class relations in society.

Law, Workers, and Courts in Liberal Capitalist Societies

Any analysis of workers' rights within a capitalist society must begin with an examination of the social relations embedded within the workplace. In their earliest stages, laws regulating labour relations emerged as a form of contractual relations between individual workers, who sell their labour for a wage, and individual employers, who purchase that labour power. As the law developed alongside the transition to capitalism in the nineteenth century, first in England and later in Canada, workers entered into contracts of employment freely and without legal constraint. Under early capitalist labour relations, the contract was not simply a declaration of ownership (or property) but rather "an instrument for protecting against changes in supply and price in a market economy" (Horwitz 1974, 937). Recognizing the centrality of the contract in early employment relations, Harry Glasbeek (1985, 282–301) argues that the sovereignty of the individual worker was at the centre of the contractual employment relationship and was thus closely tied to the liberal values of individual freedom. In liberal society, rights, privileges, and duties of the individual are not dependent on historical privilege. Rather, these rights arise from the capacity of sovereign individuals to maximize their potential in a competitive labour market

free from government interference. In other words, workplace rights at the centre of capitalist labour relations are secured through individual contracts of employment and characterized by the normative claim that there is structural "inequality of bargaining power" between individual employees and individual employers (Langille 2011, 106). Although the individual employment contract promised liberty through a free exchange of labour, it also reinforced the power of employers to shape, control, and demand specific output from human labour. The state reinforced these unequal bargaining relationships by severely restricting collective forms of worker resistance. In short, individual market freedom took precedence over any form of collective workplace justice.

Viewed historically, the tension between workers' associational rights and the labour movement's collective hostility towards judicial intervention in labour relations reveals the class nature of legal interpretation and demonstrates the fact that power within the institutions that administer and apply the law in liberal capitalist societies – namely, courts, judges, and administrative tribunals – is political, and thus contested (Fudge and Tucker 2001; Hutchinson and Monahan 1984). The contested nature of law allows us to explain the alleged contrast between the ideological character of legal decision-making and claims to judicial impartiality in the realm of workplace relations. Such an approach to the law and workers' rights seeks to "reconstruct the ideological content and political and institutional implications of collective rights" by examining them in their social and historical setting (Klare 1981, 451). In our view, adopting these assumptions with respect to the law in liberal capitalist democracies implies that the Supreme Court's interpretation of constitutional associational rights cannot be divorced from the law's historical relationship to workplace regulation.

The entire history of capitalism is intertwined with a variety of legal constructs, including individual rights of property, ownership, tort, contract, criminality, conspiracy. Indeed, it would be impossible for a capitalist economy to function without such state-imposed legal instruments defending the rights of capital (Teeple 2004). Given that both capital and labour will lay claim to specific human rights within different phases of capitalism, both groups inevitably "seek to establish their interests, ideologically and legally in terms of rights the state recognizes: the [individual] rights of property and managerial prerogative on the one hand, and on the other, the [collective] right of association and the right to strike" (Panitch and Swartz 2003, 10). Therefore, structural tensions between workers and employers are contested through all levels of the state, including courts, legislatures, and the formal content of the law itself. Acknowledging the interconnections among the state, law, and capitalist social relations, however, does not suggest that the law is a simple instrument protecting the power of the ruling classes. Rather, we take the position that the law is, as Bryan Palmer (2003, 466) has argued, "a malleable construct, a changing set of understandings that demands to be appreciated historically."

Describing the law as a "malleable construct" suggests that it is not fixed but rather a broader reflection of class forces. In its nineteenth-century form, the rule of law was premised on "limited" government, the creation of a private sphere of individual market liberty, and the rigorous defence of private property (Hutchinson and Monahan 2001, 344). Throughout this period, the law constructed rigid boundaries of constraint that limited workers' ability to collectively challenge employer power (Tucker 1991b). By the middle of the twentieth century, however, the law's social and legal zones of toleration had changed to support workers' collective rights to organize, bargain, and strike. Yet in accepting this new legal regime, workers also had to respect the boundaries of constraint that prioritized the employer's individual right to manage the workplace free from industrial conflict (Fudge and Tucker 2001). Tracing this history, we find that resistance to what the law tolerated (the zone of toleration) and what it did not (the boundaries of constraint) was very much defined by workers' collective challenges to the form, content, and structure of the law. These often occurred through broad and collective forms of civil disobedience, which included violating existing legal norms. Inasmuch as these struggles about the nature and content of the law are actually over economic and political power, workers' challenges to the law's limitations should be understood as "both imposed and internalized; [as] a wall of silence and an articulation of political economy's material and hierarchical ordering of society around its concepts or property and propriety, and expression of cultures that have, from antiquity to the present day, valued rank whatever the evolving rhetoric of equality" (Palmer 2003, 466). In this way, the "cobweb-like confinements" of the law (475) act as barriers to furthering the collective rights of workers because they challenge society's core values of individual market rights. Nevertheless, in specific instances, the law can be expanded, stretched, and broken by challenging the boundaries of constraint that are equally structured around ideological and legal means.

While Canadian courts may recognize certain rights of labour, those rights are typically constrained by the institutional limits of Canada's version of postwar industrial pluralism. As we demonstrate in Chapter 1, Canada's Wagner/PC 1003 model of labour relations both outlined the ability of workers to act collectively and limited those rights, especially with regard to strike action. In critically examining the interconnection between Canada's system of labour relations and workers' collective constitutional rights, we argue in this book that elevating Canada's system of labour relations to the Charter's protection of associational rights ignores the real boundaries of constraint that the system already places on workers' collective freedom. Those limitations include severe restrictions on the ability of workers to strike and impose internal demands on the union leadership to construct conditions necessary for "responsible unionism" to flourish. Since the mid-1940s, responsible unionism has become a cornerstone of Canada's system of labour relations, one that requires unions to police the negotiated collective agreement while discouraging responses to workplace disputes that fall outside of the narrow confines of the law.

While the Wagner/PC 1003 model of labour relations imposes strict limitations on the collective rights of workers, liberal legal discourse and the politics of constitutional rights impose others. Too often, for instance, arguments surrounding liberal human rights are co-opted by business and the political Right. While those on the Right tend to conceptualize rights differently than do those on the Left, their judicially based claims to liberal individual rights will often find greater sympathy in the courts than will arguments seeking collective rights protection (Petter 2010, 93–94). We maintain that the flood of researchers who are now promoting the "labour rights as human rights" legal agenda have all but ignored the tension between individual and collective rights in Canada's liberal constitutional regime. We conclude that a liberal human rights–based approach to understanding workers' rights threatens to depoliticize and ultimately undermine traditional collective and class-based strategies for advancing labour rights that are premised on the notion that rights flow from power, and not vice versa. In this age of neoliberalism, rights-based litigation alone does not offer the labour movement the kind of transformative political power it needs to assert its enduring demands for class-based economic equality and social justice. Rather, to be transformative, labour's strategies must take seriously those historical moments of struggle and civil disobedience when the law was stretched, broken, and reworked through collective forms of struggle.

While a wide variety of academics have written about these issues, there has been very little dialogue between labour law scholars, political scientists, and labour studies researchers studying the Charter of Rights and Freedoms. In fact, unlike other sections of the Charter, legal scholars have dominated the discussion of labour rights. Within this area, scholars have largely maintained a strict institutional focus on how Charter interpretation benefits or weakens Canada's Wagner/PC 1003 model of labour relations. Labour law scholars generally fall within three broad categories: Charter romantics, pragmatic pluralists, and realist skeptics (Etherington 1991, 1992). For Charter romantics, the possibility of constitutional protection for Canada's system of labour relations affords a counterweight to neoliberal forces attempting to restructure legislative protections related to collective bargaining (Adams 2003, 2006, 2008, 2009a; Beatty 1987; Bilson 2009; Doorey 2013). Pragmatic pluralists believe that labour relations is best left to the actors and institutions of postwar industrial pluralism, including labour relations boards, labour board chairs, and other experts in the complex labour policy field (J. Weiler 1986; P. Weiler 1990).

In contrast, traditional Charter skeptics suggest that constitutional protection of the labour relations system offers little hope for altering the balance of power in the workplace (Langille 2010a, 2010b) and cannot offer workers long-term protection (Arthurs 2009). More radical skeptics suggest that judicial decision-making in this area offers little hope for workers because Charter jurisprudence is rooted in a liberal notion of individual rights that is inherently antagonistic to collective rights in particular and to workers' interests more generally (Fudge 2008a; Mandel 1994; Tucker 2008). In our view, the sometimes highly technical legalistic nature of these debates – while essential for under-standing the long-term trajectories in legal decision-making – have not adequately explained the historical, political, and economic contexts surrounding the labour movement's interaction with the Canadian legal system.[1] Organized labour's renewed interest in constitutional rights raises a series of important questions that go far beyond technical disputes over legal reasoning. For instance, can legal institutions pro-mote the type of social transformation that organized labour is seek-ing? Do legal institutions exist independently of the social struggle in the workplace, or are they influenced by such struggles? Moreover, how does a labour movement that is ontologically connected to a collective sense of rights and freedoms engage with legal institutions that have historically served capitalist notions of individual economic and polit-ical freedoms?

Critical Institutionalism

The historical tension between how workers and unions understand the law, on the one hand, and how it is interpreted by courts and judges, on the other, both reflects and reproduces important social struggles revolving around disputes concerning the common law, the primacy of individual rights of property, and the nature of workplace regulation. To fully explain the nature of these tensions, including their emergence and their evolution over time, requires a critical institutionalist analy-sis. Critical institutionalism is an interdisciplinary theoretical approach that draws on strands of critical legal and historical institutional theory to focus on the dialectical interplay between institutional structures and social dynamics over time (Pilon 2013, 26).

Critical institutionalism views judicial interpretations of workers' rights as inseparable from the political struggles and class tensions that underpin Canadian society. In other words, applying this approach allows us to analyze "the interrelationships between the particular capitalist relations and attributes of civil society in Canada, on the one hand, and its law and legal institutions, on the other" (Bartholomew and Boyd 1987, 213). As part of her historical research on Canada's judicial system, Miriam Smith (2002, 20) persuasively argues that "decisions of courts (and the work of judges in making judicial decisions) must be placed within a broader sociological context that takes into account the economic, political and social environment in which litigation occurs." Institutions are not static. Rather, they are shaped and transformed by broader political and economic forces and by the social relations that they both reflect and reproduce. Unlike various strands of conventional institutional analysis, critical institutionalism does not necessarily privilege structure over agency, or vice versa, but rather maps institutions and institutional relationships themselves as sites of social struggle. In the words of Dennis Pilon (2015b, 6), it is critical institutionalism's "focus on relations – and the power inequities they embody – that allows us to explore why things are happening, why critical junctures are emerging when they do, or why paths remain dependent for various actors."

Consistent with this approach, and specific to the field of legal studies, H.C. Pentland (1979, 9) encourages us to reach beneath the "letter of the law" in order to examine how "interpretation and enforcement by public authorities and judicial actors shapes the system of industrial relations" and, in turn, shapes the broader political environment in which actors themselves respond politically. In short, a critical institutionalist approach allows us to focus on the courts as a terrain of class struggle itself (Panitch 1995, 166). At the centre of this analysis is the realization that

> class power is not independent of institutions, but neither are institutions independent of class power. Workers and employers struggle to shape the institutional and legal environment in which their relations will be conducted. Once established, this environment has, to varying degrees, a life of its own that mediates the effect of future shifts in the balance of economic and political power between labour and capital. (Tucker and Fudge 1996, 82–83)

Applying a critical institutionalist lens to the study of the relationship between organized labour and the courts therefore allows us to carefully assess the broader contextual evolution without losing sight of the conflict-laden social dynamics that colour and give life to the relationship.

More concretely, critical institutionalism allows us to demonstrate how labour's strategic orientation vis-à-vis the courts is not only shaped by broader economic and political forces but also deeply intertwined with struggles to expand the zone of legal toleration and the very nature of workers' rights in a capitalist democracy. Such an analysis, which Colin Hay terms the "strategic-relational" approach to political analysis, moves beyond the structure-agency debates within orthodox institutionalism and focuses instead on "strategic actors and the strategic context in which they find themselves" (2002, 128). This approach

> acknowledges that agents both internalize perceptions of the context and consciously orient themselves towards that context in choosing between potential courses of action. Strategy is intentional conduct oriented towards the environment in which it is to occur. It is the intention to realize certain outcomes and objectives which motivates action. Yet for that action to have any chance of realizing such intentions, it must be informed by a strategic assessment of the relevant context in which strategy occurs and upon which it subsequently impinges. (129)

Hay's strategic-relational analytical approach provides us with the tools to explain why different labour movement actors approached the question of constitutionalized labour rights in different ways and in different contexts over several different periods. Consistent with a critical institutionalist theoretical framework, labour movement actors were pushed and pulled in different strategic directions by a combination of three factors: political and economic pressures and opportunities, internal social dynamics, and, most importantly, the relationship of those actors to the judicial system – specifically, to judicial outcomes, which sometimes expanded the zone of legal toleration or reinforced the boundaries of legal constraint.

Labour Politics and Strategy

Contextualizing the labour movement's strategic shift towards rights-based legal activism also requires a discussion of organized labour's strategic approach to politics in Canada more generally. Labour strategy is often examined in connection with a set of frames, repertoires, and internal organizational practices associated with two broad categories of union orientation: business unionism and social unionism (Ross 2012).

Business unionism, or what is typically referred to as pure and simple unionism, is narrowly concerned with securing the best possible economic deal for workers through collective bargaining and workplace representation. This orientation is widely associated with Samuel Gompers, the founding president of the American Federation of Labor. While Gompers conceded that capitalists and workers do have some conflicting interests, he was well known for his political pragmatism; he rejected outright suggestions that the capitalist system needs to be replaced or that workers need an independent labour party to promote their interests more effectively (Hoxie 1914; Reed 1966). In the realm of electoral politics, Gompers argued that labour could strengthen its economic clout in the workplace by employing a strategy of "rewarding friends and punishing enemies" (Ross et al. 2015, 11). In the words of Stephanie Ross (2012, 37), Gomperists, or "business unionists will mobilize their members to support politicians with a labour-friendly record, but will work to shift that support if those politicians do not deliver for labour." Generally, Gomperist political strategy is geared towards the narrow interests of a specific group of union members rather than towards social justice issues with broader implications for the working class as a whole (Ross 2012). Although business unionist strategies did unquestionably result in real material gains for some unionized segments of the construction, craft, and industrial working class in the immediate postwar period, the economic and political conditions that made such advances possible – namely, rapid economic growth and the postwar "compromise" – have altered the strategic terrain for unions (Ross et al. 2015, 177). Today's unions operate in an economic and political system that has abandoned Keynesian-inspired economic planning in favour of neoliberal policy measures designed to reduce the power of organized labour and strengthen the profit-making potential of capitalist interests, leading to widening income inequality and growing economic uncertainty.

A significantly altered political and economic terrain has led some researchers and many union activists to offer up social unionism as an alternative orientation to business unionism. Social unionism offers a much broader understanding of the labour movement's goals, purpose, and politics. As Sam Gindin (1995, 268) points out, while collective bargaining and workplace representation are central labour activities, unions can also act as vehicles to lead "the fight for everything that affects working people in their communities." In other words, because the challenges facing workers cannot always be resolved at the bargaining table, unions must be politically engaged beyond the workplace. For example, affordable housing and climate change are not direct bargaining issues, but both have a tremendous impact on workers' quality of life. Advocates of social unionism typically argue that unions have an important political role to play in organizing, educating, and mobilizing working-class people around social justice issues that transcend the workplace (Kumar and Murray 2006; Ross 2012).

While some of the literature on labour politics, in part, equates social unionist political activism with partisan electoral support for social democratic parties like the New Democratic Party (NDP) (Kumar and Murray 2006, 28; Robinson 2000, 114), social unionist political strategy has, in fact, been much broader and can often take on a more radical tone. Social unionists routinely engage in extraparliamentary activities like direct actions, demonstrations, civil disobedience, public awareness campaigns, and coalitions with social movement organizations, all in an effort to pressure governments and employers (Black 2012; Coulter 2012). Because social unionist frames tend to be conceived around issues of social justice and economic equality, it is not uncommon to see social unionists take up causes ranging from anti-racism to homelessness. These campaigns often intersect with the agendas and priorities of social democratic parties, but one is certainly not dependent on the other.

Against the backdrop of the ascendency of neoliberal public policy frameworks in the early 1980s and 1990s, a general consensus has emerged among labour movement researchers that social unionist strategies are necessary "both to contest policies that harm working-class people and to bring into existence the political economic arrange-ments that will sustain a socially just and equitable society" (Ross et al. 2015, 177). As such, they have become central to debates concern-ing union renewal in general and labour strategy specifically (Kumar and Schenk 2006).

For its part, as a particular political strategy for the labour move-ment, legal activism does not fit clearly within either social unionism or business unionism, the two broad categories of union orientation. In much the same way that electoral political engagement can take on both social unionist and business unionist dimensions (Savage 2012), so too can judicial-based political action. On the one hand, legal activ-ism shares much in common with business unionism in terms of inter-nal organizational practices insofar as legal activism does not rely on mobilizing or activating rank-and-file union members. Instead, this ap-proach relies heavily on outside experts (i.e., lawyers) who are hired to defend the membership's interests in court. On the other hand, the call for the courts to embrace a "labour rights as human rights" approach to judicial decision-making clearly frames union struggles in social union-ist terms. Moreover, depending on the nature of the legal battle itself, legal activism may achieve one of the central goals of social unionism – namely, extending greater rights and freedoms to the labour move-ment or working-class people as a whole. The point here, following Ross, is to highlight the fact that established conceptual dichotomies typically fail to appreciate the degree to which labour unions are "com-plicated hybrids" (Ross 2007, 22).

If the business unionist/social unionist typology can only get us so far in understanding union strategies, how then do we conceptualize legal activism as a particular strategic repertoire for the labour move-ment? Applying the critical social movement theory concept of political opportunity structures is useful here insofar as it allows us to account for shifts in strategic orientation in specific directions and in specific periods (McAdam, McCarthy, and Zald 1996; Tarrow 1998). Sidney Tarrow argues that the relative success or failure of social movements is significantly determined by political opportunity structures, which he defines as "consistent – but not necessarily formal, permanent, or na-tional – dimensions of the political struggle that encourage people to engage in contentious politics" (1998, 19–20). Conceptualizing union strategy in this way helps to reveal both the strategic constraints faced by unions and the opportunities made available at key moments during the Charter era. Taken together with Hay's strategic-relational analytical approach to political analysis, this conceptualization helps to clarify why the Canadian labour movement abandoned its critique of legal-ized politics and instead embraced a Charter-based rights discourse.

In short, the Canadian labour movement changed its strategic think-ing in relation to legal activism as a result of shifting political oppor-tunity structures, which narrowed a number of traditionally viable strategic routes while opening up opportunities on the judicial front. Specifically, the crisis of social democratic electoral politics in the 1990s – combined with the rise of neoliberalism, so-called Charter values, and human rights discourse – helped to push unions back into the legal arena as a last resort, despite the movement's long-standing distrust of the courts. Once that defensive strategic choice was validated with a ser-ies of nominally pro-union Charter decisions, culminating with the *Dunmore* decision in 2001, the ideological apparatus to support labour-led legal activism was marshalled, along with the language of "labour rights as human rights," to justify the new strategic approach. Over this period, the courts became a virtue rather than a last resort in the eyes of many union leaders and activists, and the union movement's well-established distrust of the judicial system increasingly fell by the way-side with each Charter victory.

It is clear that since the turn of the twenty-first century, Charter-based legal activism has emerged as a significant political strategy with-in the Canadian labour movement. Political scientists, however, have not been able to explain effectively the labour movement's embrace of Charter-based activism, partly because the labour movement has been largely absent from scholarly examinations of the Charter of Rights and Freedoms (see for instance the absence of labour unions in MacIvor 2013, discussion of social movements and the Charter, 179–98).[2] Given the voluminous scholarship on social movements' interactions with the Charter, the lack of a detailed examination of labour's constitutional challenges is surprising for several reasons. First, labour unions have, more or less, monopolized legal debates surrounding the Charter's guarantee of freedom of association (Sharpe and Roach 2009, 183–93). Second, organized labour was among the first groups to challenge the substantive meaning of association and equality rights in the Charter. The movement's judicial losses in the 1980s led many Charter skeptics to argue that the constitution as a legal institution was incapable of challenging private power structures within capitalist society (Mandel 1994; Petter 2010, 102). Third, few social movements have the organizational and financial reach of the Canadian labour movement. Although the movement's political influence has waned in recent decades, labour continues to help shape political discourse in most provinces while also maintaining a steady stream of membership dues to organize, bargain, and agitate. Organized labour's resource capacity has allowed unions to go to court frequently to test the institutional boundaries of Canada's legal rights protection.

Organization of the Book

We have organized the book chronologically. Labour's tense relationship with the law and legal institutions prior to the enactment of the Charter in 1982 is the subject of Chapter 1. This chapter examines how the construction of modern labour law – and particularly the Wagner/PC 1003 model of labour relations – was itself contested by both labour unions and employers. Through an overview of the injunction battles in the late 1950s and 1960s and the anti-inflation fight in the 1970s, we explain why organized labour, despite its strong leadership in the realm of human rights, developed a deep mistrust of the Canadian judicial system.

Chapter 2 tells the story of the labour movement's decision to disengage from the process used to create and shape the content of the proposed Charter of Rights and Freedoms in the early 1980s. Here, we challenge long-held assumptions about why the Canadian labour movement seemingly turned its back on years of human rights advocacy. A historical investigation of the relevant constitutional episodes demonstrates that organized labour was acutely aware that the Charter could have an important impact on collective bargaining, and on labour rights more generally, but strategically decided to sit on the sidelines for fear of alienating its allies in the federal NDP (which strongly favoured the Charter) and the Quebec Federation of Labour (which strongly opposed the Charter). This strategic decision was, of course, made easier by the labour movement's long-standing distrust of the courts.

Chapter 3 reviews the first era of Charter decisions related to organized labour, paying specific attention to the political and economic climate that framed the Supreme Court's interpretation of the Charter's guarantee of freedom of association. This chapter demonstrates how the first era of Charter challenges seemingly confirmed the labour movement's worst fears about the judiciary's perceived anti-union bias, thus preventing organized labour from becoming swept up in the "Charter revolution" of the period.

In Chapter 4, we document the labour movement's change of heart about Charter litigation around the turn of the twenty-first century. We detail organized labour's newfound judicial success, beginning with an easing of the limits on secondary picketing and increased support for the rights of agricultural workers to organize into associations. Our case summaries, which chronicle the evolving relationship between labour and the courts, are embedded within a broader political analysis. More specifically, the ascendency of neoliberalism and the elevation of "rights consciousness" among social movements in Canada are offered as key explanatory variables for why unions' traditional class-based critiques of the courts dissolved during this period.

Chapter 5 details the Supreme Court's landmark 2007 decision in *BC Health Services*, which extended constitutional protection to collective bargaining and, in the process, virtually evaporated the labour movement's long-lived critique of the Canadian judiciary. We criticize the mainstream labour movement's euphoric reaction to *BC Health Services*, detailing the ways in which the labour movement overstated the court's finding that freedom of association included a right to collective bargaining. The chapter goes on to review a number of Charter cases that followed on the heels of *BC Health Services*, cases that revealed both unresolved tensions in the Court's legal reasoning and the legal limits and possibilities of the union movement's judicial push to transform labour rights into human rights.

Chapter 6 focuses on the landmark *Saskatchewan Federation of Labour v. Saskatchewan* (2015) case, in which the Supreme Court constitution-alized the right to strike. We examine this watershed moment in Canadian labour history in detail with a view to making sense of this new era of constitutional labour rights. Specifically, we argue that by tying a constitutional right to strike to a legalistic collective bargaining process, the court reinforced important boundaries of constraint while simultaneously expanding the zone of legal toleration for workers. In the book's conclusion, we summarize our research findings and critique the use of recent pro-union Charter decisions to justify greater emphasis on judicial-based strategies to build union power in the future. After reviewing some of the cases that have made their way through the courts since the ground-breaking *SFL* decision, we argue that the Canadian judiciary is unlikely to ever interpret the Charter in a way that facilitates transformational political change for organized labour. We ultimately conclude that narrow efforts to advance labour's interests via the courtroom are not only ineffective but also potentially harmful to the union movement in the long term insofar as they can serve to demobilize rank-and-file workers.

While the focus of this book is on the labour movement and the Charter of Rights and Freedoms, our findings have broader implications for a host of social movements and for the politics of rights discourse more generally. The book demonstrates how rights-based claims can serve to both empower and undermine organizations seeking constitutional protection. Moreover, we show that while social movements are certainly shaped by politics and the law, the relationship is reciprocal. As Simeon and Robinson (1990, 159) remind us, "the evolution of the Canadian state has always been shaped by the changing balance of class power." Class is often ignored in discussions of rights, but the two are intrinsically linked in capitalist democracies. The case of the Canadian labour movement's engagement with the Charter demonstrates how this relationship works to consolidate and entrench elite power even while seemingly expanding workers' rights, in the same way that an expanded zone of legal toleration brings with it new and more powerful boundaries of constraint.

Labour Rights in the Pre-Charter Era   1

Any conception of the so-called rights of working people in the pre-Charter era has to be understood within the broader context of class and class struggle in Canada (Palmer 1992). Historically, workers' organizations of all political persuasions recognized that rights were not freely granted by the state or employers but were themselves the product of political and economic power. To be sure, workers and their unions were acutely aware of the coercive nature of the Canadian state, which routinely interfered with, provoked, and subverted the civil liberties of working-class people and their organizations (Leier 2013; Whitaker, Kealey, and Parnaby 2012, 60–89). In part, state and employer coercion in this period explains why labour unions throughout the twentieth century often lobbied for a constitutional bill of rights to protect individual rights of speech and assembly (James 2000). Unions, however, did not see their own collective power as enshrined in the law, nor in constitutional decisions made by judges or constitutional amendments crafted by political elites.

From the perspective of employers and government, the zone of toleration for labour's collective freedoms was inescapably narrow and could be enacted, altered, or withdrawn through simple legislative action. For their part, prior to World War II (and for some time after), judges and the court system were openly hostile to workers' movements and their collective freedoms, more often than not siding with employers and their common law private property rights, even as the early system of what has been defined as "liberal voluntarism" evolved into a system of what labour law scholars now call "industrial pluralism" (Fudge and Tucker 2001). Even after the institutionalization of the so-called postwar compromise between business, labour, and the state, courts and judges continued to play an active role in containing workplace conflict. The history of judicial hostility towards labour's collective rights created enduring tensions between unions and the courts, fomenting distrust and skepticism about judges having any interest in advancing the rights of workers.

This chapter examines labour rights in the pre-Charter era with a view to demonstrating the contested nature of Canada's evolving regime of labour law and its tense relationship to the courts and the judiciary. We also investigate briefly the labour movement's human rights activism in the pre-Charter era. In exploring this history, we seek to illuminate the evolution and complexity of organized labour's view of workers' collective freedoms, class conflict, and human rights over time. This history demonstrates that workers' organizations did not view their own freedoms and power as falling easily within the narrative of justiciable "human rights." Rather, throughout most of Canadian history, workers and their unions have largely understood their collective freedoms as the byproduct of a more naked class power to be won through conflict with employers and the state. To be sure, the nature of class conflict changed after World War II. In the postwar period, class struggle was filtered through the new institutions of the Wagner/PC 1003 model of labour relations, with workers and their unions often seeking to preserve their newfound collective legal freedoms from open attacks by hostile governments, judges, and employers.

Nineteenth-Century Canada and the Non-rights of Labour

Throughout the late nineteenth and early twentieth centuries, the state's unwillingness to recognize (legally or otherwise) workers' collective ability to associate formed the foundation of many industrial conflicts. For workers to engage in any form of collective bargaining, they more often than not had to engage in strike actions. In this period, collective bargaining was rooted in a system of voluntarism wherein the employer only recognized workers' collective organizations if workers themselves were willing to put their livelihood (and often their bodies) on the line through militant strike action. Even when workers were able to engage in collective action to obtain bargaining rights, workers and employers rarely met as equals. Rather, the state usually intervened on the side of employers – either through direct picket-line conflict or through a legal system eager to use injunctions to severely constrict workers' collective actions (Fudge and Tucker 2001).

Inasmuch as the nineteenth-century version of labour law can be defined as a "system," it emerged at the same time that Canada's particular version of industrial capitalism began to expand. While agriculture and small artisan shops still dominated local economies across the country, the intensification of industrial production in southern Ontario and Quebec altered workplace relations as labour moved away from skilled craft work towards mass industrial production (Kealey 1980). Given the changing social conditions, workers' power was increasingly defined by their collective abilities to resist employer control over the workplace. Before the *Trade Union Act* of 1872, however, the simple act of engaging in collective activities (or in combination) represented a challenge to traditional master-and-servant notions of employment and was generally considered an illegal criminal conspiracy to restrain trade (D'Aoust and Delorme 1981; Fudge and Tucker 2010; Tucker 1991b). The objection of government and the courts to workers resisting employer power through combination was firmly rooted in liberal economic doctrine, which sought to protect the capitalist market's iron laws of supply and demand against so-called price-fixing.

Yet many workers resisted the idea that their labour was simply a commodity to be regulated by the forces of supply and demand in the capitalist market place. In the early 1870s, workers across Ontario, in an impressive display of solidarity, challenged Dominion law restricting collective activities by withdrawing their labour in a struggle to achieve the nine-hour workday (Kealey 1980; Palmer 1992; Ostry 1960). The most well-known and widely studied of these struggles occurred between Toronto typographical workers and former Liberal leader George

Brown. As publisher of the *Globe* newspaper and leading spokesperson of the typographical employers' association, Brown opposed the workers on both ideological and legal grounds. Although the Dominion's law regulating employment was in flux and uneven (Craven 1984; but see Tucker's response in Tucker 1991b), Brown published a legal opinion regarding what many believed to be the state of labour rights in the Dominion:

> While the law to the fullest extent provides for the protection and preservation of individual or personal liberty, it is equally against combinations for the purposes of raising or affecting wages. A man may, by his own individual efforts, raise or attempt to raise his wages. But that which is lawful for the individual to do, or as an individual, is not lawful for individuals to do as a body, or in combination. A combination on the part of workmen, either to raise their wages or shorten the hours of labour, is I think, by the Common Law of England, and therefore by the law of Canada, an indictable conspiracy. (Harrison 1872)

Put simply, the law acted as a perceived barrier to the collective rights of workers in the Dominion. Yet numerous workers (mostly in the skilled craft trades) continued to engage in collective challenges to those restrictions through illegal action, including strikes, secondary boycotts, and organizing (Palmer 1992).

One of the state's responses to worker militancy in this period was the passage of the *Trade Union Act* of 1872, designed to remove criminal sanctions on labour union organizing. The act expanded the zone of legal toleration for workers by stating that unions were in fact legal institutions. On the same day, the *Criminal Law Amendment Act* expanded and clarified the criminal sanctions for illegal behaviour during labour disputes and simplified sanctions available for employers for any damage to property during a strike. Unions were also required to register with the federal government in order to receive the limited protections set down in the act; given the widespread perception, however, that the balance of power between workers and employers was not dramatically altered by the new law, few unions actually registered.

Thus, while the acts opened a small window for workers' freedoms, the law also enacted limitations on the collective freedoms of workers during labour disputes (D'Aoust and Delorme 1981). Ultimately, while the Canadian state legalized the act of forming a labour union, it did nothing to promote or protect the collective actions of workers to challenge the power of employers. It was these tensions – both in the law and in the workplace – that formed the basis of workplace conflict throughout the late nineteenth and early twentieth centuries.

In the early decades of the twentieth century, Canada underwent a significant transformation in workplace relations. Between 1900 and 1914, Canada experienced what some scholars have termed its second industrial revolution, altering the system of production to include new technologies in the workplace and the adoption of so-called scientific management, which mechanized the labour process in almost all industries. Not only did the forces of production alter the landscape of towns and cities throughout central and western Canada; they created new pools of workers divorced from the skilled craft unions of the nineteenth century. Under these conditions, workplace conflict intensified, with Canada experiencing a marked increase in strike activity (Cruikshank and Kealey 1987). For many skilled and craft unions in the Trades and Labor Congress (TLC) the strike was a means to protect the workers' craft and to resist employers' attempts to undermine the rarity of their skills. Often, these workplace conflicts were defensive, and sometimes, they were waged against other (often unskilled) workers (Craven 1980, 111–22).

In response to craft union strikes, employers increasingly turned to the courts to contain spontaneous worker outbursts. By the early 1890s, judges had begun responding to employers' requests to constrain workers' collective action through civil torts law that effectively limited such action. According to Fudge and Tucker (2001, 19), these relatively new civil torts took many forms, but they were all designed to have union strike activity "stopped quickly." Judges routinely issued injunctions that were designed to preserve the pre-strike state of affairs until such time that the courts were able to hear a complaint of a civil wrong (which were routinely dropped by employers once the picket line came down). By applying for civil remedies, employers effectively constrained strike activity through the "nominate" or "economic" torts. Nominate torts include nuisance, trespass, assault, property damage, and defamation, while economic torts are civil violations based on charges as varied as conspiracy, intimidation, and inducing breach of contract (Adell 2003, 418). In the context of strikes, alleged violations of torts allowed employers to apply for injunctive relief in order to end illegal strikes or to limit the effectiveness of picketing during strikes. Until the 1970s, judges and the courts proved all too willing to assist employers in using the law to limit or altogether thwart union-initiated boycotts or strike action (Fudge and Tucker 2001).

For workers on the margins or those performing unskilled, tedious industrial work, collective actions were even more constrained. When this growing number of unskilled industrial workers took similar strike actions, the heavy hand of the state often intervened to end the dispute by force. These dual forms of court and government coercion against the working classes, according to Fudge and Tucker (2001, 18), "smacked of class bias, [thus] undermining the appearance of neutrality essential to the liberal state." Under these conditions, the federal government was under immense pressure to respond to the so-called labour problem of the period (Kealey 1995, 419–40; Palmer 1992, 156–58).

Even after the passage of the *Trade Union Act* in 1872, labour relations continued to be structured so as to contain workplace conflict (Craven 1980). In 1900, the federal government passed the *Conciliation Act*, and in 1903, the *Railway Labour Disputes Act*. These were later amalgamated into the 1907 *Industrial Disputes Investigation Act* (*IDIA*). Created by Canada's first deputy minister of labour and future Liberal prime minister, William Lyon Mackenzie King, the *IDIA* attempted to promote co-operation between responsible (i.e., non-militant) unions and employers in the mining, transportation, communications, and public utility sectors. At the centre of the *IDIA* was the federal government's commitment to use the law to limit the duration and frequency of strikes without offering parallel protection for mandatory union recognition or collective bargaining (Fudge and Tucker 2001; Russell 1990). The *IDIA* played this role by offering state-sponsored conciliation for those unions that acted responsibly – that is, those that agreed to "cooling off periods" and delayed strike activity before a report from a conciliation board – before commencing a strike. According to Stuart Jamieson (1973, 122), the limitations on workers' collective freedoms contained in the *IDIA* aggravated many of the unions (especially outside of the skilled crafts) because the act "put additional curbs and delays on unions' freedom of action without giving them effective protection from employers." The *IDIA* was particularly hostile to legally protected free collective bargaining because it left union recognition entirely in the hands of employers. The act was also silent on numerous employer tactics used to break a strike or avoid unionization, including stockpiling, union blacklisting, creating company unions, or using "yellow-dog contracts."[1] Employers were also free to continue using private strikebreakers or firing union organizers or sympathizers outright (Morton 1998, 89). For unions that stepped outside of the act and exerted their collective capacities to strike – most prominently in Winnipeg in 1919 and during the Oshawa sit-down strikes in the 1930s, but also exemplified by strike strategies in company towns across the country – the heavy hand of the *Criminal Code* (including the nefarious s. 98), court injunctions, deportation, and the police were used to end disputes by force (Endicott 2012).[2]

Despite the perceived shortcomings of the *IDIA*, if the unions accepted the conditions imposed by the act, they were entitled to third-party intervention through conciliation. For many of the craft unions, conciliation offered a legal tool to offset some of the raw employer power that could fall on organized workers prior to the commencement of a strike or lockout. In this way, the *IDIA* laid the foundation for a liberal regime of industrial regulation that imposed constraints on workers' collective rights of association in return for legislative protection from the state (Russell 1990, 105; Tucker 1991a). Recognizing this, labour groups felt compelled to defend the act when, in 1925, the British Judicial Committee of the Privy Council (JCPC) ruled in *Toronto Electric Commissioners v. Snider* (1925) that labour relations fell under the power of the provincial governments' "property and civil rights" provisions under section 92 of the *British North America Act*. The British JCPC was the court of final appeal for Canada until 1949, when ultimate appellant jurisdiction transferred to the Supreme Court of Canada. The *Snider* case dealt with the Toronto Electric Commission's refusal to recognize a federally appointed conciliation board to mediate a labour dispute between the commission and its workers. The conciliation board, which drew its authority from the *IDIA*, was illegitimate, according to the commission, because the federal government did not have the constitutional authority to pass laws affecting employers under provincial jurisdiction.

The JCPC agreed with the commission and declared the *IDIA* unconstitutional on the grounds that it exceeded federal jurisdiction. Shortly thereafter, the federal government reworked the act to reflect that it only applied to areas of federal jurisdiction, and the provinces moved to create their own distinct regulatory labour regimes. This event served to fragment an already divided labour movement by creating a multitude of jurisdictions relating to labour relations in Canada. In response, many labour organizations began actively lobbying the federal government for constitutional reform in an effort to facilitate the development of stronger national protections for unions. At the 1925 TLC convention, delegates supported an executive report recommendation, which stated:

> The time has arrived when amendments to the *British North America Act* should be secured which would give greater authority to the Dominion Parliament and bring about more centralization of our laws which vitally affect the conditions of wage earners in this country, and that it is only by such a step that any essential social reform can be brought about and made equally applicable to all citizens of Canada. (Canada, Department of Labour 1925, 894)

The TLC's recommended changes to the *BNA Act* included the abolition of appeals to the JCPC and of the Senate, as well as the shift of complete responsibility for social and labour legislation to the federal government (Canada, Department of Labour 1926, 338). The TLC made the same request, more or less, to the federal cabinet for the rest of the decade and throughout the 1930s. In 1929, the Quebec Provincial Council of Carpenters went one step further by successfully presenting a resolution to the TLC's convention that called on the federal government to request amendments to the *BNA Act* in order to accommodate the labour movement's demand for an eight-hour workday and a forty-hour work week (Canada, Department of Labour 1929a, 1014). Soon after its creation in 1927, the All-Canadian Congress of Labour (ACCL) joined the TLC in calling for constitutional amendments (Canada, Department of Labour 1929b, 1365). However, the federal government ignored union requests for constitutional change.

Labour unions renewed their efforts to amend the *BNA Act* after 1931, the year Canada became a sovereign dominion within the British Commonwealth under the terms of the Statute of Westminster. In the new political climate created by the Statute of Westminster, there were calls for a new constitutional order that would strengthen the central government. For labour unions, the call to amend the constitution was primarily driven by two factors. First, many of the provinces (especially in the regions) were tied directly to specific capitalist enterprises in a way that made it very difficult for the subnational state to create labour relations acts that promoted *bona fide* collective bargaining regimes. Second, unions saw a stronger national government as part of a larger left-wing political project to transform Canadian society into one that could more effectively engage in central planning and more meaningfully pursue policy measures to improve the level of economic and social equality between citizens. The labour movement's penchant for centralization was consistent with the political objectives of the newly formed Co-operative Commonwealth Federation (CCF), which called for the *BNA Act* to be amended in order to facilitate the creation of a national labour code (Black 1975, 47–48). The CCF argued that Canada's regional and linguistic divisions, exacerbated by the country's federal system of government, "are unnecessary and are the result of the inherent contradictions of capitalism" (Lewis and Scott 1943, 104).

In 1937, the JCPC dealt another blow to the labour movement by ruling that the federal government did not have the constitutional authority to implement laws regarding basic employment standards that Canada had agreed to in international treaties. In the *Labour Conventions* (1937) case, *Canada (A.G.) v. Ontario (A.G.)*, the JCPC required that implementation of international treaties respect the constitutional division of powers – thus preventing the federal government from fulfilling its obligations under international law (Stevenson 2004, 268–69).

Between 1937 and 1940, the TLC, the ACCL, and the Railway Transportation Brotherhood all pressed unsuccessfully, once again, for constitutional reform. In a 1939 memorandum submitted to the Quebec provincial cabinet, even the independent Canadian and Catholic Confederation of Labour (CCCL) known for its provincial orientation, argued in favour of greater centralization (Canada, Department of Labour 1940, 549).[3] Despite these failed attempts to spur reforms, James (2000, 51) argues that "constitutional politics appealed to workers' organizations as a forum for advocating courses of action that Canadian governments had hitherto been able to avoid." More than this, however, organized labour clearly saw constitutional reform as a means to bolster the influence of the union movement, but unions would have to wait until World War II to see any progress on this front.

Canada's System of Industrial Pluralism and Labour Rights

In 1940, the Royal Commission on Dominion-Provincial Relations (also known as the Rowell-Sirois Commission) recommended, among other things, that the federal government assume control over unemployment insurance. Union activists from across the political spectrum had fought specifically for this recommendation and had used the commission as a platform to fight for greater centralization of power in general, all in an effort to secure New Deal–like legislation in Canada. Part of that effort was to secure a Canadian version of the American *National Labour Relations Act,* also known as the *Wagner Act,* passed in 1935. The *Wagner Act* grew out of Democratic President Franklin Delano Roosevelt's New Deal initiatives, which sought to lift the United States out of the Great Depression by, among other things, facilitating the redistribution of wealth through the statutory duty for employers to recognize and engage in collective bargaining with *bona fide* labour unions. The American government adopted this position because of growing labour strife in several industries; American capitalism was under direct threat due to collapsing industry, skyrocketing unemployment, and increased worker (and poor people's) activism (Bernstein 1970, 217–23). The *Wagner Act* sought to address this crisis by removing labour regulation from the jurisdiction of individual states while also limiting the judiciary in its imposition of common law doctrines protecting individually owned private property. These doctrines limited the ability of workers to engage in meaningful collective bargaining because of their constraint on private trade.

The *Wagner Act* created a set of institutions that placed restrictions on the rights of employers to unilaterally dictate the terms of employment. It entrusted workers with a much-needed voice in the governance of the workplace and protected unions in order to facilitate the resolution of workplace grievances (Lichtenstein 2002, 35–39). It also guaranteed workers the right to select their own union through a majority vote and protected the rights of workers to strike, to participate in secondary boycotts, and to picket. Equally important, the new labour framework enumerated a list of unfair labour practices, a list that eliminated employers' ability to resist unionization through establishing company-dominated unions, blacklisting union activists, or intimidating and firing union organizers. The act also banned such subversive tactics as employing industrial spies or hiring strikebreakers. In order to protect these new regulations, the *Wagner Act* created the National Labor Relations Board (NLRB), an independent federal body with the authority to adjudicate disputes arising from the act. By any account, the changes associated with the *Wagner Act* were the most far-reaching component of the American New Deal, since it gave workers a significant legal means to protect and expand their collective freedoms.

The passage of the *Wagner Act* in the United States created a distinct model of state regulation for labour union certification. Since the leadership of the Canadian Congress of Labour (CCL) had ties to the American Congress of Industrial Organizations (CIO) and the TLC was affiliated with the American Federation of Labor, the *Wagner Act* had a great deal of influence on Canadian workers and their union leaders (Sefton-MacDowell 1978, 177–78). For labour leaders and many social democratic (and even some communist) political activists, the legal reforms to promote a statutory duty for employers to engage in collective bargaining and *bona fide* labour unionism provided a far more democratic model for the recognition of workers' rights than anything that existed in Canada. It also provided a legislative framework that curtailed (but certainly did not eliminate) the power of employers to resist unions in the workplace. Yet, notwithstanding the *Wagner Act* model, legislators in Canada continued to resist legislation supporting collective bargaining and mandatory union recognition. The social, economic, and political changes that emerged out of the country's participation in World War II, however, slightly altered the balance of class power in Canada and opened the space for significant legal reform to occur.

When the war began, the federal government was content to maintain the institutions of industrial voluntarism. In 1939, Prime Minister King extended the *IDIA* to all industries deemed essential to the war, which led to the federal government imposing a wage ceiling, job freezes, and an appropriation of the right to transfer any human labour to what government deemed essential industries (Jamieson 1973, 122–23). Moreover, in order to curb outright dissent and labour unrest during the war, the government imposed the *War Measures Act*, limiting the civil liberties of Canadian workers in an effort to eliminate what the government believed were subversive labour agitators. These decisions led to a series of conflicts with the burgeoning and more militant industrial labour unions in heavy industries. For many industrial workers, controls on labour mobility, wages, and benefits without corresponding restraints on corporate war profits demonstrated that the time was ripe for substantive collective bargaining and mandatory union recognition legislation. Faced with intense employer opposition, however, the King government only introduced incremental changes to the *IDIA*. These piecemeal reforms allowed for certain forms of union recognition and a strengthened wage conciliation procedure through the National War Labour Relations Board (NWLRB). These legislative modifications changed the way the government intervened in wage disputes (Order-in-Council PC 2685) and introduced mandatory strike votes before a strike could take place (Order-in-Council PC 7307). The government also continued to use the *IDIA*'s mandatory conciliation procedure as a way to delay potential strike action (Webber 1986, 142).[4]

The federal government's opposition to collective bargaining did not stop industrial unions from launching aggressive organizing campaigns during the war. In fact, the labour shortages associated with wartime production gave workers a new structural power to recover economic and political gains lost during the Depression years. Workers were thus eager to sign union cards despite the continued anti-union tactics used by employers. Between 1940 and 1944, Canadian labour union membership doubled, reaching 724,000 members, or 25 percent of the non-agricultural workforce (Panitch and Swartz 2003, 12). The willingness of workers to protect their livelihoods and their unions was demonstrated by the increased level of strike activity during the war. Strikes in the mines, steel, auto, coal, aircraft, and lumber sectors directly challenged wartime wage controls and pushed for Wagner-inspired collective bargaining reforms (Fudge and Tucker 2001, 265–66). This unrest was intensified by the refusal of most employers to recognize labour unions in their workplaces. Recognition strikes were so intense that by the summer of 1943, one out of every three Canadian workers was engaged in some form of strike action (Sefton-MacDowell 1978). Faced with this opposition, members of King's own NWLRB were advising the government to adopt *bona fide* collective bargaining legislation (Cameron and Young 1960, 65).

The Liberal government also felt pressure from the rising popularity of industrial labour's political ally, the CCF. In September 1943, national polls showed the federal CCF ahead of the Liberals and the Progressive Conservatives for the first time in history. In vote-rich Ontario, the CCF registered 32 percent of the vote, trailing the Tories at 40 percent but well ahead of the Liberals at 26 percent support (Caplan 1973, 110–11). The dual pressures of strikes and increased social democratic electoral support culminated in the federal Liberal government passing the Wartime Labour Relations Privy Council Order 1003 (PC 1003) on 17 February 1944. Borrowing language from the *IDIA*, PC 1003 had as its objective "the maintenance of industrial peace" but also guaranteed Wagner-like protections to promote collective bargaining "satisfactory both to employers and to employees" (Logan 1956, 26–27). This exercise in balancing worker and employer freedoms was advanced by creating a permanent administrative structure to rule on the certification of unions. Under the order, employers had a legal duty to recognize unions and bargain in good faith once state-sponsored certification had been granted. Like the *Wagner Act,* PC 1003 made it illegal for employers to discriminate against employees for participating in labour union activity while also limiting the ability of employers to create company unions (or employee associations) to thwart unionization drives. Most importantly, PC 1003 expanded the legal zone within which labour unions operated by drafting new rules for meaningful collective bargaining in a unionized workplace, mandating a workplace grievance procedure, and removing some of the restrictions on the right to strike.

Notwithstanding the economic and political benefits of the new Wagner/PC 1003 model, class tensions remained. The 1945 strike at Ford Motor Company in Windsor aptly demonstrates this point. This strike was significant because it tested the government's commitment to collective bargaining against the company's desire to use the inevitable postwar economic downturn to crush the United Auto Workers (UAW). The conflict began in response to Ford Motor Company's decision to lay off fourteen thousand workers as it scaled down wartime production. UAW members walked off the job on 12 September 1945 and remained on the picket line until 20 December of that year. In order to protect its members, the union packaged its demands as a fight for job security, union security, and a living wage.

Given that the UAW was responding to what was feared to be the first in a massive wave of layoffs, the strike had the potential to escalate into a national confrontation between Canadian labour and business (Fudge and Tucker 2001, 283–85; Moulton 1974, 136–37). While the strike enjoyed wide community support, the federal and provincial governments were under immense pressure from the company's Canadian director, Wallace Campbell, to end the conflict through direct legal or police intervention. The company argued that the state should act forcefully, but Liberal MP Paul Martin (who represented the consitutency of Essex East, encompassing parts of Windsor) convinced the union and the company to agree to binding arbitration, conducted by Supreme Court Justice Ivan Rand (Fudge and Tucker 2001, 284; Moulton 1974, 147). Rand's subsequent decision, which provided the UAW with a legal form of union financial security, seemed to capture – according to liberal labour historians – the spirit of the pluralist compromise evolving between labour, business, and the state immediately following the end of the war (Kaplan 2009, 165–220).

Rand premised his ruling on the notion that "capital must in the long run be looked upon as occupying a dominant position," adding that "it is in some respects at greater risk than labour; but as industry becomes established, these risks change inversely" (Canada, Department of Labour 1946, 124). In analyzing these risks, Rand acknowledged that the power of organized labour had grown exponentially in the previous decade. In order to protect the interests of both parties, Rand reasoned that labour had to be accepted as a legitimate partner in the managing of industry. Yet he qualified his support for labour freedoms, ruling that only a certain ideal type of labour union merited such protection. In fact, he demanded that union leaders "bring maturity of judgment and of conduct" to the affairs of labour relations. He condemned the "abuse of striking power" by the UAW in conducting the rather militant strike but recognized that the unfettered demand of management to control workplace regulation contributed to the intensity of the dispute (126). Having come to this conclusion, Rand's new "formula" demanded that unions had to have

> enlightened leadership at the top and democratic control at the bottom, similarly as to capital. The absolutist notion of property like national sovereignty must be modified and the social involvement of industry must be the setting in which reconciliation with the interests of labour and public takes place. (125)

Abandoning purely voluntarist notions of labour relations, Rand coupled his demand for union responsibility with the new legal instrument protecting union financial security. Yet he balanced that decision against the rights of the individual not to join a union. Rand thus attempted to eliminate the problem of "free riders" by ruling that all workers should benefit from collective bargaining and suggested that every member share in the cost of maintaining the local union; these members, however, were not required to join the union (Cako 1971, 137–40). Rand's decision meant that union leaders no longer had to rely on voluntary agreements with individual workers to maintain the financial health of the union.

In order to sustain union security, unions were required to act responsibly through what Rand called "enlightened leadership." While workers were forbidden to strike during the life of a contract by PC 1003 (and later the *Industrial Relations and Disputes Investigations Act*

[IRDIA 1948]), Rand reasoned that responsible union leadership had a legal obligation to limit collective outbursts from workers. Rand believed that if a group of workers did strike illegally, employers should be able to appeal to a labour relations board to declare the strike illegal. If the strike continued, both the government and the courts would be able to intervene in order to demand a resumption of work. Often, the declaration of an illegal strike would lead to crippling fines imposed on the union and, in rare instances, jail time for union leaders. In this new environment of legalized collective bargaining and union security, it was in the best interest of union leaders to constrain militant outbursts by rank-and-file members. Moreover, responsibility also implied that certain forms of union political action were illegitimate. Under the guise of union responsibility, communist-affiliated unions were raided while communist union members were purged or absorbed into burgeoning union bureaucracies (Abella 1973; Whitaker and Marcuse 1994, 313–63), thus helping to consolidate social democracy as the primary political orientation of Canada's labour movement.

For workers and their unions, the new "Rand formula," as it came to be called, institutionally secured their place in industry and in society more broadly. In exchange, unions were required to take responsibility for maintaining steady and uninterrupted flows of production.[5] The implementation of union security clauses became a key component of the postwar regime of Canada's Wagner/PC 1003 model of industrial relations (Canada, Department of Labour 1951, 1360; 1954, 1140–41). After Rand's decision, the basic foundations of Canada's system of labour relations functioned within an institutional framework guaranteeing union recognition, collective bargaining, and legally protected union security agreements. All of these provisions were protected through a Wagner-inspired board that had the administrative discretion to protect labour's newly won labour rights.

Notwithstanding the collective benefits to workers and their unions, the acceptance of the new labour relations model placed additional restrictions on workers' control over their unions (Heron 1996). Prior to Rand's union security agreement, union leadership, in order to support the union financially, had to go through the rather prolonged exercise of reaching out to individual workers. While that process was certainly cumbersome, it created a close connection between workers' daily work-place struggles and their union leadership. After Rand, the interpersonal process that tied the union directly to the social relations of production was weakened. Increasingly, union leaders and staff were integrated within management structures responsible for enforcing collective agreements (McInnis 2002). Workplace discipline also tightened with the development of a formalized grievance system, often placing the adjudication of workplace disputes into the hands of third parties (usually labour lawyers) chosen jointly by union leaders and employers. As contracts became more technical and legally complex, workers were increasingly distanced from their own representatives (Matheson 1989). Whereas past disciplinary action had sometimes led to spontaneous strikes in order to proclaim a collective cause with fellow workers, the new model of industrial relations imposed strict disciplinary measures on workers who stepped outside of the contract, and thus the law (Palmer 1992, 284). In short, the new Rand formula was a legal instrument that expanded the zones of toleration in which postwar unions operated while also erecting new boundaries of constraint on workers' collective freedoms.

The Wagner/PC 1003 and Rand compromises between labour, business, and the state were later codified in federal law with the passage of the *IRDIA* in 1948. In the years that followed, control over labour relations – following the *Snider* precedent – was slowly returned to provincial governments, where similar Wagner-type legislation quickly followed. For workers who had suffered through the years when federal and provincial legislation had openly legitimized union repression, blacklisting, company unionism, and limited health and safety regulations, the significance of the freedoms outlined in these new legislative protections cannot be overstated. For the first time, the federal government (and later the provinces) recognized that labour legislation had to constrain the rights of employers to unilaterally dictate the conditions of employment.

In Canada's version of industrial pluralism, governments adopted the principles of "exclusivity" and "majoritarianism," awarding unions the absolute right to bargain collectively and to represent workers once legally recognized certification had been obtained by a majority of workers on individual job sites (Carter et al. 2002; *Fraser v. Ontario (Attorney*

General) 2008). In return for this legal protection, unions were required to respect employers' right to manage the workplace free from strikes during the life of a collective agreement. For governments, the institutions of the Wagner/PC 1003 model allowed for protection of the broader public interest because the model sought to limit the frequency, intensity, and violence associated with strikes (Carrothers, Palmer, and Rayner 1986, 63–64; Peirce 2003, 339). Recognizing that the Wagner/PC 1003 model sought to balance workers' collective freedoms with limits on workers' ability to use those freedoms, the new regime of labour law was centred on

> the belief that industrial conflict in democratic capitalist societies is best dealt with through routinized procedures of negotiation and compromise leading to agreements formalized in contracts. Its adherents conceive of management and labour as self-governing equals who, through collective bargaining, jointly determine the terms and conditions of sale of labor power; and they see the historic purpose of labor relations law as nothing more than the facilitation of this process. (Tomlins 1985, 19)

Arguably, for governments and employers, the implementation of the Wagner/PC 1003 model had significant political and economic benefits. By limiting the ability of workers to strike during a collective agreement, employers had little reason to fear that industrial unrest would interrupt production or profit. By institutionalizing the conditions to foster long-term labour peace, the government was also able to divorce workers' collective power from political objectives, recognizing that strikes would only occur at specific times and generally over narrow economic interests (Arthurs 1985; Hollander 2001; McInnis 2002; Russell 1995; Sefton-MacDowell 1978).

Within the postwar Keynesian economic framework, the new model of industrial pluralism worked to stabilize the labour process in crucial sectors of the economy, including secondary manufacturing, transportation, shipping, and natural resources. Supporters of this new era of "free" collective bargaining believed that the Wagner/PC 1003 model heralded a new era of "industrial democracy" in which mass production and natural resource industries (and later the public sector) worked in partnership with strong labour unions to mediate class tensions (Canada 1968; Carrothers, Palmer, and Rayner 1986, 57). As Daniel Drache and Harry Glasbeek (1992) have argued, the mediation of class conflict was at the centre of the new regime, representing a reformist compromise and creating institutions that acted autonomously from the tensions at the point of production. Over the long term, McBride (2001, 41) argues this "tacit class compromise" between unions, the state, and employers was designed to integrate the industrial working class into a sphere of consumption that provided the necessary pillars for the postwar economy to expand. The new model of labour relations opened legitimate space for responsible unions in the Keynesian model of capitalism. If unions acted "irresponsibly" by, for example, stepping outside of the law and striking in mid-contract, they faced coercive measures such as fines or jail time (Drache and Glasbeek 1992, 10–11).

As the new Keynesian model of employment took hold, work in labour-intensive goods (and later service) production was also transformed. The power of the collective agreement – always at the centre of regulation in unionized workplaces – became the lifeline for workers seeking redress for employment injustices. If there were not specific limitations to employer controls in the contract, management rights clauses transferred all additional workplace powers to employers. Similar forces changed the culture of union organizing, as highly trained staff carried out campaigns and legal representatives prevailed over the more militant and class-oriented unionism of the 1930s and the 1940s (Wells 1995). Stephanie Ross has argued convincingly that the limitations demanded by the new workplace rules had long-term ideological implications for workers' notion of collective labour rights because they reinforced the "legitimacy of employers' rights of ownership and interests in profitability and workers' subordinate place in the labour process and economy in general" (Ross 2005, 72–73).

The restrictions imposed by the courts on the new institutions of labour relations were most noticeable when class antagonism broke into open conflict. When workers withdrew their labour, they now did so in a legal context that set conditions on how unions could "legitimately" strike (Fudge and Tucker 2001, 10–15). These new rules regulating the strike shifted much workplace conflict from the picket lines, controlled by rank-and-file workers, to labour boards and the courts, where union staff, employers, government personnel, lawyers, and judges were central decision-makers. Ultimately, the embrace of the Wagner/PC 1003 model of industrial relations integrated important components of the working class into a legal system that promoted industrial stability as the central means to foster long-term capital accumulation.

Meanwhile, as unions became more bureaucratic and legally accountable to the state and employers, unions continued to push for more national controls over the labour relations regime. In its 1950 brief to the federal cabinet, for instance, the CCL pressed for a national labour code, which would establish "uniformity in the legislation governing labour relations, particularly with respect to industries of national scope" (Canada, Department of Labour 1950, 639). In its brief of the same year, the TLC went one step further by urging that "all jurisdiction over matters of health, social welfare and labour relations be placed under the Federal Government and the Parliament of Canada" (639). While labour had little success in pushing for macro-constitutional reforms, it did manage to secure smaller scale victories in individual provinces by successfully demanding that the institutions associated with the new regime of the Wagner/PC 1003 model of industrial relations – especially labour relations boards – remain free from "legalization."

In fact, throughout the 1950s and 1960s, one of the ongoing struggles related to the new system of labour law was over whether it should be administered by sympathetic labour policy experts within government bureaucracies and in administrative tribunals, as proposed by the unions, or whether decision-making should rest with the more conservative judiciary, as proposed by employers (Smith 2009). That conflict broke out into the open in early 1947, when steelworkers in Saskatchewan launched an organizing drive at the John East Iron Works Ltd. Company. In an attempt to break the organizing campaign, the company fired six lead organizers. At the hearing before the Saskatchewan Labour Relations Board (SLRB) on 8 July 1947, the board ruled that the actions of the company were in violation of Saskatchewan's *Trade Union Act* and ordered that John East Iron Works reinstate the fired workers.

Failing to oblige, the company filed a notice of motion in the Court of Appeal for Saskatchewan seeking to overturn the SLRB's decision because the board was *ultra vires* (outside the constitutional jurisdiction) of the legislature of Saskatchewan (*Saskatchewan (Labour Relations Board) v. John East Iron Works Ltd.*, 1948.

Before the Saskatchewan Court of Appeal, the company argued that Saskatchewan's *Trade Union Act* delegated unconstitutional authority to the SLRB because it gave the board remedial powers similar to a court. Company lawyers successfully argued that the board's ability to review contracts of hiring and breaches of those conditions had always fallen to the courts. Since the act delegated such authority to the board, it stood to reason, the company argued, that provinces were unable to to create such bodies under section 96 of the *British North America Act*. On this basis, the Court of Appeal reversed the decision of the board.[6] The Canadian Supreme Court later adopted this decision on 15 December 1947.

On appeal, the British JCPC overturned the Saskatchewan Court and ruled that Saskatchewan's *Trade Union Act* and the SLRB's remedial powers were constitutional. The JCPC reasoned that the board did not perform judicial functions but rather was created to administer government policy. In other words, the board's primary purpose "is the means by which labour practices regarded as unfair are frustrated and the policy of collective bargaining as a road to industrial peace is secured" (*Saskatchewan (Labour Relations Board) v. John East Iron Works Ltd.*, 1948, para. 27).

While the JCPC admitted that the board did perform quasi-judicial functions, it suggested that the board's tripartite nature (not being entirely staffed from members of the Bar of Saskatchewan) made it institutionally distinct from the courts. The JCPC concluded that the jurisdiction exercised by the board was not such that it constituted a court within section 96 of the *BNA Act* and thus reversed the decisions of the lower courts. Recognizing the constitutionality of the powers of the board opened space for these institutions to slowly administer the new system of industrial relations over the next several decades. Yet the JCPC was also cautious in its ruling, assuring dissenters that

> [the board's] immunity from *certiorari* [judicial review] or other proceedings [should not] be pressed too far. It does not fall to their Lordships upon the present appeal to determine the scope of that provision but it seems clear that it would not avail the tribunal if it purported to exercise a jurisdiction wider than that specifically entrusted to it by the Act. (*Saskatchewan [Labour Relations Board] v. John East Iron Works Ltd*, [1948] 2 W.W.R., para. 30)

With that broad stroke, the JCPC ruled that the powers delegated to the SLRB, while constitutional, were still subject to close judicial scrutiny (Strayer 1963, 162).[7]

John East Iron Work's strategy of challenging the power of the new administrative apparatuses of the Wagner/PC 1003 institutions was quickly taken up by other employer organizations. For example, the Canadian Manufacturers' Association (CMA) was extremely critical of the institutions associated with the new regime of industrial relations. Throughout the 1950s and 1960s, the association interpreted any government recommendation to strengthen labour boards as promoting unionization (Smith 2008). Those involved with business believed that any conflict arising from the employment contract or from collective agreements should be finalized in the courts. In essence, the only way to preserve the power of capital in this new system of labour relations was to have disputes over certification, bargaining, and strikes returned to "the courts, and never [again] left in the hands of an administrative body."[8] For its part, the labour movement strongly opposed transferring power from labour relations boards to the courts. For example, the Ontario Federation of Labour, in its 1957 submission to the Select Committee on Labour Relations, argued that employer challenges placed labour relations boards

> into the position where they had to tailor their operations, sometimes, we suggest, not with a view of the trade unions or their problems in mind, but rather in how were they going to make out once they got to court-and this has brought about a development of the Board where more and more courtroom atmosphere, lawyers, and what have you, and trade unionists today say that this is semi-judicial,

more courtroom atmosphere Board than a board dealing with labour relations and human relations problems.[9]

Business deference to the courts was an important reason why labour unions were hostile to judicial involvement in labour disputes.

This long-standing hostility towards judicial power broke wide open in the 1960s. In this period, the constraints imposed by the postwar model of labour relations were readily challenged by rank-and-file militancy directed not just at capital and courts but also at labour leaders and the union bureaucracy (McInnis 2012; Palmer 1992, 2009; Sangster 2004). Indeed, the disputes over the constraints imposed by the industrial relations models in the provinces and at the federal level intensified intra- and inter-union conflict as young workers challenged entrenched older workers for control over their unions. In addition, women workers confronted both well-established male unionists and powerful capital interests while struggling for just wages and for workplaces (and societies) free of sexual discrimination (Sangster 2010). The rise in workplace conflict exposed an unprecedented level of working-class unrest, and an increasingly large percentage of all strikes were illegal (Jamieson 1968, 398–403). The explosion of wildcat strikes in the 1960s cannot easily be dismissed. In fact, the 1960s strike wave was a rebellion against established authority that proved to be a direct challenge to the law itself. In particular, these acts of illegality challenged the industrial system's framing of "legal" versus "illegal" strikes. As Palmer (2009, 220) has noted, "If the legal strike is about securing a contract, the wildcat strike can either be about skirting the contract, or alternatively, present itself as a forceful statement from the shop floor that workers are tired of waiting for one." For thousands of workers, pent-up frustration with the institutional grievance system, entrenched union bureaucracies, and management sparked illegal civil disobedience. Oftentimes, this resistance was simple anger over a lengthy workday or a simple act of rebellion against work itself. In any event, the wildcat wave represented a collective response to the institutions of the Wagner/PC 1003 model of industrial relations and the institutional limits of the postwar economy.

Labour unions, business, and the state all responded to the 1960s wildcat wave in different ways. One response by business and the state was to clamp down on illegal strikes through court-ordered injunctions – court orders that compelled unions to refrain from strike and picket activity under threat of facing criminal and possibly civil legal penalties, including imprisonment. In the 1960s, injunctions were often granted without strikers' knowledge, and once they were granted, the law ended the strike.

The entire labour movement's hostility towards injunctions and the judiciary's approach to labour law more generally was most apparent before the Ontario government's Royal Commission Inquiry into Labour Disputes, also know as the Rand Commission, in 1967 and 1968 (Ontario 1968). The commission was established by the Ontario government in order to address the growing wave of wildcat strikes, but it grew out of a particularly violent strike in Peterborough, Ontario (Sangster 2004). In testimony before the Rand Commission, union leaders complained about inherent biases in the legal system. When strikes occurred, the unions argued, there was "an added adversary, [because] the company has been joined in their contest by the courts [and then] it's a 'what is the law for a poor man' sort of thing."[10] For many labour unions, the pro-employer biases in the legal system had both legal and ideological implications for Canada's system of labour relations. Leaders from the CLC forewarned that the open biases of "courts have intervened on the side of management, or so it seems. It is the old axiom that justice must not only be done but it must be seen to be done."[11] For labour unions, the overarching concern was that "not too many of the judges are experts, and perhaps should not be, in the labour relations field. I think there is a difference between law itself and labour relations."[12]

Labour and Human Rights
While the new Wagner/PC 1003 model of labour relations placed constraints on union capacities to challenge capital and governments through collective action, it also legitimized workers' collective rights in those workplaces where workers opted for unionization. Labour's institutional legitimization, in turn, gave unions greater clout around broader political issues. For example, in the wake of World War II, some union groups turned their attention to combatting racial and religious discrimination, laying bare the hypocrisy of a Canadian government

that fought against racism in Europe but actively supported racist and discriminatory policies at home (Patrias 2011). As part of this campaign, the CCL came out in favour of a national bill of rights as early as 1947, and the TLC did the same in 1948 (Clément 2008, 21). At the 1950 Special Senate Committee on Human Rights and Fundamental Freedoms, both the TLC and CCL made presentations calling on the federal government to implement a national bill of rights to protect minority groups from discriminatory employers and government officials (James 2000, 143–44).

While labour's primary concern was with ending racial and religious discrimination (although, oddly, not gender-based discrimination), unionists also raised with the committee the importance of preserving newly achieved collective bargaining rights for workers. Both the CCL and TLC insisted that court injunctions and police intervention were being used to violate workers' freedom of association. However, unlike other groups – such as the National Japanese-Canadian Citizens' Association and the National Council of Women of Canada, who called for a symbolic bill of rights – labour organizations, in the words of Matt James (2000, 146), "displayed no interest in using official symbolism to impress the civic worthiness of workers upon other Canadians." Rather, union groups saw working-class militancy and struggle, especially the strike weapon, as the primary method of preserving their rights in the face of hostile employers and governments. It is worth noting that while some unionists played an important role in the fight for human rights legislation to stop racial, religious, and, later, gender-based discrimination both within and beyond the workplace in the immediate postwar period, those same activists never claimed that collective bargaining was a human right worthy of constitutional protection. On the contrary, labour movement activists drew a sharp distinction between the role of courts in the realm of human rights and the role of the courts in the realm of labour relations. George Burt, president of the UAW in the 1950s and 1960s, for instance, was adamant that in the field of industrial relations, "the further we stay away from the courts the better we are in the labour relations process." He went on to declare, "I think I have the backing of all of the Labour in the land ... [that] unions do not want to go to court to defend [their] rights."[13] Instead, unions continued to fight for constitutional changes in order to protect the civil liberties of workers long denied basic liberal freedoms by the state.

In 1960, at a meeting of the House of Commons Special Committee on Human Rights and Fundamental Freedoms, which was established to consider the Diefenbaker government's proposed Bill of Rights, the CLC argued that the proposed legislation fell far short of labour's expectations. Specifically, the Congress argued that the bill was toothless in that it would not apply to provincial governments or "provide any protection against violation of rights or freedoms by a future parliament or even this parliament at its very next session" (CLC 1960, 192). Congress representatives argued for a strengthened bill of rights that would put the "rights it seeks to protect beyond the power of both parliament and the provincial legislatures"; interestingly, they did not push for specific constitutional protection for collective bargaining, strike activity, or any sort of economic rights (194). They did, however, argue for a "right to access" to be added to the list of enumerated rights and freedoms, citing examples where union organizers or union representatives were denied access to company property for the purposes of furthering legitimate union activity (196–97).

When questioned by MPs Deschatelets and Martin about what the Congress thought about the lack of positive economic and social rights enumerated in the bill, CLC president Jodoin wavered before punting the question over to Eugene Forsey, the CLC's research director. Forsey argued that such rights, although popular in international declarations like those of the United Nations, were the product of entirely different legal traditions that would not necessarily apply to Canada, where common law reigned supreme (CLC 1960, 209–11). The CLC's counter-intuitive position on positive social and economic rights was deeply rooted in the principle of parliamentary supremacy and the British tradition of civil liberties. While the committee hearing presented an opportunity for the Congress to advance a rights-based agenda that would challenge parliamentary supremacy and the British tradition of civil liberties and common law, the Congress chose instead to reflect those conservative traditions in its own submission. This is probably due to the strong influence of Forsey, a recognized constitutional expert who worked as research director for the CCL from 1942 to 1956 and for the

CLC from 1956 to 1966. Forsey was known to use his position within the Canadian labour movement to promote his views on Canada's constitutional questions. In summarizing Forsey's preoccupation with the constitution, J.E. Hodgetts (2000, 6) notes, "One gets the impression that his colleagues in the CCL sometimes thought he misspent his time chasing constitutional exotica ... Forsey, ever the independent, was always more comfortable speaking on his own account, even though he might be signing a letter in one of his many official capacities." In previous years, Forsey, a strong centralist, had used his position to advocate for the common use of disallowance, drafting detailed labour memorandums calling for the centralization of labour law and social policy in Canada.[14] His legalistic dismissal of international human rights declarations in the context of a Canadian bill of rights at the 1960 committee hearings added an additional dimension to the labour movement's antipathy towards constitutionalized rights for core labour union activities. Labour's antipathy towards such rights, and towards the judicial system more broadly, was reinforced once again with a common law judicial decision in the landmark *Hersees* case of 1963.

The *Hersees* Case

In *Hersees v. Goldstein* (1963), a secondary picketing case, the Ontario Court of Appeal was asked to consider the legality of the Amalgamated Clothing Workers of America's decision to leaflet outside Hersees, a third-party business in Woodstock, Ontario, in order to place pressure on its primary employer, Deacon Brothers, to conclude a collective agreement. The union's leafleting campaign, which encouraged the public to purchase only union-made clothing at Hersees, was designed to place pressure indirectly on Hersees for continuing a business relationship with Deacon, notwithstanding the ongoing labour dispute (Tucker 2010). In response, Hersees applied for an injunction to restrain the union on the basis that secondary picketing was illegal and therefore violated the right to trade.

In siding with Hersees, the Ontario Court of Appeal found several civil tort violations, including breach of contract (between Hersees and Deacon) and conspiracy to injure the retailer in conducting trade. It is worth noting that Justice John Aylesworth, the senior member of the

Ontario Court of Appeal who authored the *Hersees* decision, was a former management-side labour lawyer who had plenty of experience representing auto companies and other heavy manufacturers. Aylesworth had been leading counsel for the auto companies during the famous Windsor strike in 1945 (Tucker 2010, 234). In applying decades-old civil law remedies to questions of labour law, the court, clearly out of step with postwar labour legislation sympathized with the right of the individual business owner to conduct trade free from collective action, even if that action was peaceful (Arthurs 1963, 579). In applying these traditional tort doctrines, however limiting, the court decided to go one step further by maintaining that *all* secondary picketing was "illegal *per se*" (*Hersees v. Goldstein* 1963, 88). In the court's view, all secondary picketing would cause or would be *likely* to cause damage to business interests. Therefore, a right to secondary picketing "must give way ... to the retailer's right to trade which is a more fundamental right for the benefit of the community at large than the right of secondary picketing which is exercised for the benefit of a particular class only" (87). Although critiqued by leading labour law scholars as grossly out of step with Canada's constitutional tradition of government (Arthurs 1963, 581), the court's "illegal *per se*" doctrine clamped down on the ability of workers to use their collective pressure to challenge employers through the use of secondary picketing or consumer boycotts. The court's decision only confirmed organized labour's worst suspicions about the judicial system's ability to protect workers' rights.

Labour, the Courts, and the Politics of Inflation
The labour movement's hostility towards the legal system continued throughout the 1970s and 1980s. By the beginning of the 1970s, there was a general consensus among unions and labour-side lawyers that judicial intervention in labour disputes was detrimental to economic and political stability (Weiler 1971). Within the broad field of administrative and labour law, the growing expertise of arbitrators, grievance officers, and legal personnel contributed to courts' slow acquiescence of labour relations jurisdiction to labour relations boards, with the exception of tortious issues arising out of strikes and lockouts (Weiler 1980).

The Supreme Court's thinking on the expertise of industrial relations experts resulted in a 1986 ruling in *St. Anne Nackawic Pulp and Paper v. CPU* (1986) where the court ruled that it had little jurisdiction to intervene in decisions arising out of a collective agreement (including decisions from labour boards and arbitrators). Paradoxically, this judicial transfer of supervisory power in industrial relations to more sympathetic labour relations boards and other experts coincided with the long decline in the postwar system of industrial relations. In fact, by the middle of the 1970s, the dual pressures of high unemployment and rising prices had weakened Canada's version of postwar Capitalism. As government and capital blamed the high wages of unionized workers for fuelling inflation, governments increasingly responded with coercive actions to limit labour's collective ability to bargain and to strike (Panitch and Swartz 2003).

The struggle between unions, business, and the state increased as the federal government's macroeconomic response to the crisis of stagflation turned towards neoliberalism, with an emphasis on monetarism. Monetarism is concerned with controlling the money supply in order to combat high rates of inflation at the expense of full employment. For monetarists, an important component of reducing inflation is to address labour market "rigidities" that stand in the way of full competition by weakening labour unions and collective bargaining. A second and more coercive strategy introduced by the federal and, later, provincial governments to address the inflationary crisis was to limit directly the purchasing power of unionized workers. In 1975, the federal government passed the *Anti-inflation Act*, which introduced wage (and price) controls in both the private and public sectors. The wage controls were controversial, not only because of their economic impact but also because they raised important constitutional questions about the federal government's ability to regulate economic relations in areas of provincial jurisdiction.

In order to address the immediate threat that wage controls posed to the material well-being of workers, the CLC temporarily abandoned its time-honoured support for central economic planning and centralization in constitutional affairs by lining up beside Alberta's provincial government in arguing that the *Anti-inflation Act* was unconstitutional on the basis that it fell outside of the federal government's jurisdiction (Russell 1977, 652).

In the case of Ontario, the union representing Renfrew secondary school teachers challenged the legality of the province's anti-inflation arrangement with the federal government at the Divisional Court of the Supreme Court of Ontario after the teachers' agreed-upon wage increases were virtually wiped out by the Anti-inflation Board. The union argued that the province's arrangement with the federal government was invalid because it was enacted through an order-in-council rather than through legislation. At around the same time, a provincial board of arbitration ruled that the province was not bound by the terms of the federal government's anti-inflation law. These events prompted Ontario's Attorney General to ask the federal minister of justice to refer the legislation to the Supreme Court of Canada (Russell 1977, 643).

In a proactive effort to rebuff the federal government's inevitable argument that Ottawa's emergency powers under the *British North America Act* gave it the constitutional authority to enact the law, labour unions enlisted the support of Queen's University economist Richard G. Lipsey and thirty-eight of his academic peers, who argued that there was no case to be made that Canada was experiencing, or about to experience, an economic crisis at the time the *Anti-Inflation Act* was introduced (Russell 1977, 648). On 12 July 1976, the Supreme Court rendered a split decision (7–2) upholding the federal government's wage controls legislation, with Chief Justice Bora Laskin arguing that the law "was temporarily necessary to meet a situation of economic crisis" that required "stern intervention in the interests of the country as a whole" (*Re: Anti-Inflation Act* 1976, 425). The court did rule, however, that the Province of Ontario had acted wrongly in using an order-in-council rather than legislation to impose wage controls on the province's public sector, and the Ontario government moved swiftly to pass a law to bring the province into compliance with the ruling. Unions reacted angrily to the Supreme Court decision, which validated the federal government's ability to intervene in the collective bargaining process in the name of a questionable national economic emergency. The decision also fuelled the organization of a one-day nation-wide illegal strike in October 1976 (Mosher 1976).

The continued use of injunctions and the increased use of back-to-work legislation in the 1970s further demonstrated the extent to which governments and the judiciary would tolerate the collective right to strike when it conflicted with the political or economic objectives of the country's leaders. As Gregory Hein observed, in more general terms,

> For more than a century, few organizations entered the courtroom to affect public policy. It was possible to have a complete understanding of Canadian politics without ever thinking about interest group litigation. The labour movement concentrated on the party system because courts did little to help workers; relying on the assumptions of classical liberalism, judges allowed market forces to settle most issues. (Hein 2001, 222)

While governments at all levels and of all political stripes began clamping down on workers' rights in the mid- to late 1970s, support for legislation protecting human rights was growing by leaps and bounds as part of a broader human rights revolution (Clément 2008). In Quebec, the provincial government passed the *Quebec Charter of Human Rights and Freedoms* in 1975. The federal government followed soon after with the adoption of the *Canadian Human Rights Act* in 1977. While organized labour had played a leading role in advancing human rights legislation in the immediate postwar period, by the 1970s, the CLC, Canada's largest labour organization, increasingly "deferred to rights associations with regard to leading human rights campaigns" (Clément 2008, 138). Although a number of smaller labour groups and non-governmental organizations called for the inclusion of positive social and economic rights in a bill of rights during this period, most progressive organizations remained ambivalent. The Canadian Bar Association, for example, reflected the mainstream view of the Canadian labour movement in arguing that "most economic rights, such as the right to a basic standard of living or the right to work, can best be protected by positive state action by legislatures ... A Bill of Rights should be carefully drafted so as to minimize the possibilities of judicial interference in economic and social welfare policy" (Canadian Bar Association 1978, 16–17).

The long-standing tension between organized labour and the courts in the pre-Charter era was the product of nearly a century of judicial anti-unionism in Canada. The use of injunctions and common law to preserve private property rights at the expense of workers' collective rights contributed to a growing sentiment among union leaders and activists that courts were elitist and pro-employer, that they could not possibly be trusted to defend workers' collective interests. Moreover, dominant labour movement thinking about rights in this period was characterized by a clear distinction between human rights (which included the right to be free from discrimination based on race, religion, ethnicity, and later gender) and labour rights as an extension of working-class power (expressed in terms of civil liberties, with rights to association, collective bargaining, organizing, and strike action). While the labour movement certainly fought for the advancement of both human rights and labour rights in the pre-Charter era, unions rarely conflated the two. Indeed, while labour proposed that human rights be enshrined in a constitutionally recognized bill of rights, it did not seriously pursue constitutional protection for core union activities like collective bargaining or strikes.

Disorganized Labour and the Charter of Rights

2

The tension between labour's distrust of the courts and its interest in constitutional reform was in full display during the constitutional debates of the early 1980s. In 1980–81, the Special Joint Committee on the Canadian Constitution heard submissions from more than one thousand individuals and groups attempting to shape the content of Prime Minister Trudeau's "magnificent obsession" over an entrenched Charter of Rights and Freedoms (Harder and Patten 2015, 13–14). Women's groups, civil liberties associations, Aboriginal organizations, ethnocultural groups, and the business lobby all made their presence felt; the committee even heard from a group of British Columbians who wanted the right to use hallucinogenic mushrooms entrenched in the Constitution (Sheppard and Valpy 1982, 137). Given the labour movement's enduring interest in constitutional issues, the Canadian Labour Congress (CLC) was conspicuously absent from the deliberations surrounding the new constitution. Before the Special Committee began hearing submissions, the CLC did take the time to write a symbolic letter in support of Aboriginal rights, but after the committee began its work, the CLC and the vast majority of its affiliates decided against making any formal written or oral submissions (CLC 1980b). Instead, the Canadian labour movement refused to take a public position on the new constitution.

This chapter explains why the CLC excluded itself from the national debate over patriation of the constitution. Using a strategic-relational analytical approach to examine and explain workers' political and constitutional strategies, we argue that the CLC's non-involvement was influenced by its desire to neither alienate its Quebec section, the pé-quiste Quebec Federation of Labour (QFL), nor exacerbate the internal dissension over the Charter within the NDP, labour's long-standing political ally. Underlying this strategic decision was the labour movement's age-old distrust of courts and the judicial system. In particular, many activists in the labour movement adopted the position that a judicially enforced Charter of Rights would actually threaten the collective democratic freedoms that labour had won in the postwar period. In particular, there was concern that the Charter would emphasize negative individual rights at the expense of collective economic rights. Some union leaders and rank-and-file activists were particularly concerned that a constitutional document emphasizing individual rights would help employers or anti-union workers to weaken or destroy unions. Given these divisions, the CLC encouraged affiliates to exclude themselves from discussions or debates concerning the shape, content, or character of the Charter.

Québécois Nationalism and the CLC

As demonstrated in Chapter 1, labour unions in Canada had been pronouncing on constitutional questions since the late nineteenth century. Indeed, the Trades and Labor Congress (TLC) was among the first organizations in Canada to call for a Charter of Rights as part of its 1938 submission to the Rowell-Sirois Commission on Dominion-Provincial Relations (James 2000, 52). However, in the decade leading up to patriation of the constitution in 1982, the CLC had been noticeably absent from pronouncing on constitutional questions. As noted in Chapter 1, during this period the Congress largely retreated from direct engagement with constitutional issues as they pertained to human rights, in deference to the growing number of organizations specializing in that area of the law (Clément 2008, 138). Moreover, as has been well documented, with the rise of Quebec nationalism in the 1960s, constitutional issues shifted focus somewhat towards national unity (McRoberts

1997; Russell 2004). Despite the rise of "French power" in Ottawa, key components of Quebec's nationalist movement embraced an explicitly sovereigntist political project. In response, the Trudeau government prioritized the implementation of a Charter of Rights, which the Liberals believed would play a central role in building a pan-Canadian sense of citizenship (based largely on individual rights and freedoms) while simultaneously serving to undermine Quebec nationalism.

In contrast, this period saw a dramatic shift within the CLC in terms of its own positions on constitutional issues, with the Congress drifting away from a politics of fierce centralization towards an approach that was much more accommodating of Quebec's nationalist aspirations. This shift was no doubt influenced by the retirement of CLC researcher and constitutional expert Eugene Forsey, who passionately defended national unity and the British constitutional tradition from the separatists and provincialists who began to make waves towards the end of his career at the CLC (Milligan 2004, chaps. 8 and 9). While Forsey's views continued to hold sway with much of the CLC's old guard, they were certainly at odds with the nationalist aspirations of an increasingly militant and radical Quebec labour movement. Amid growing nationalist and linguistic tensions between the CLC and the QFL, the Congress refrained from participating in the Molgat-McGuigan committee on constitutional reform that sat from 1970 to 1972. Unthinkable only a decade earlier, the CLC's decision to keep quiet in the constitutional debate reflected a strategic desire to keep the peace with its QFL affiliate in a period of social upheaval in Quebec.

Constitutional issues were further thrust into the spotlight when René Lévesque's Parti Québécois (PQ) swept to power in the 1976 provincial election on a promise to hold a referendum on sovereignty-association. The QFL's official support for the PQ during the election campaign was certainly reciprocated once the party was elected to power. Lévesque's first government could easily be described as social democratic and thus labour friendly (McGrane 2014; Rouillard 2004, 195). In the government's first year in office, the PQ put an end to the province's anti-inflation program, reformed the province's labour code to ban replacement workers, and made it easier for unions to win certification votes. The government also improved health and safety legislation, much to the satisfaction of the province's labour leaders. In addition to its union-friendly labour law reforms, the PQ impressed its allies in organized labour by introducing a system of public automobile insurance; nationalizing the Asbestos Corporation; expanding the public sector; implementing campaign finance reform; and introducing the controversial Bill 101, the Charter of the French Language, which made French the common public language in virtually every facet of Quebec society, including the province's workplaces. At a QFL conference in March 1977, the Federation's president, Louis Laberge, introduced René Lévesque as "our" premier (Leclerc 1978), and in 1978, the PQ adopted a program calling for the establishment of "an economic system that eliminates all forms of worker exploitation and meets the needs of all of Quebec's citizens, rather than the demands of a privileged economic minority" (Parti Québécois 1978).

A year after the PQ's stunning election victory, pan-Canadian unions like the United Steelworkers of America (USWA), United Auto Workers (UAW), Canadian Union of Public Employees (CUPE), and Canadian Union of Postal Workers (CUPW) all endorsed Quebec's right to self-determination in order to appease their increasingly pro-sovereigntist Quebec memberships (List 1977, 5). UAW president Dennis McDermott, who also served as a member of the CLC executive, defended this controversial decision:

> If I were a French Canadian living in Quebec, I would probably call myself a Quebecker rather than a Canadian. I most certainly would have voted PQ because I think that the word separation is in our vocabulary because there has been 100 years of g-dd--n inequity, of real persecution, and certainly of exploitation, economic and otherwise. And I understand what is happening there. I have no problem with the Quebeckers, because they understand instinctively that I am a soul brother. (List 1978, 10)

At the CLC's 1978 convention, eleven resolutions calling for patriation of a new constitution or some sort of fundamental constitutional reform were submitted by various union locals representing the UAW; the USWA; the Fishermen's Union; the United Electrical, Radio and

Machine Workers of America; the Canadian Brotherhood of Rail and Transport Workers; and the United Brotherhood of Carpenters and Joiners of America (CLC 1978a). At the behest of the CLC leadership, none of these resolutions managed to make it to the convention floor, for fear of dividing delegates along linguistic lines. Instead, on the eve of the convention, a backroom deal between leaders of the QFL and leaders of the Congress was struck in order to ensure the successful passage of a proposed statement on national solidarity. After the compromise position was reached, outgoing CLC president Joe Morris, a hard-line federalist, told the media, "If we take an unequivocal position on unity we are in effect destroying the solidarity of the workers. And that solidarity is more important to preserve in framing our document than the question of Canadian unity" (List 1978, 10). The statement – which, in Laberge's words, was "negotiated from the first word of the first paragraph to the last word of the last paragraph, including every comma and period" (Hoogers 1978, 19) – also contained the following statements about the possibility of Quebec separation:

> We, the workers of Quebec, who are members of the Canadian Labour Congress, assert the right to determine our political and constitutional future. This is fundamental; an essential prerequisite to establish the balance for future negotiations. It is an important right, and we have a full appreciation of the importance inherent in our responsibility if we choose to exercise that right.
>
> We, the workers in other parts of Canada, who are members of the Canadian Labour Congress, respect the fundamental right of Quebec workers to exercise that responsibility. In so doing, we express the hope that a continuing dialogue will lead to the restructuring of the relationship between us which will serve the interests of our two communities of people in a vibrant and new Canadian society.
>
> Collectively, we in the Canadian Labour Congress, in making these declarations, embrace the universal principle which guides the democratic structure of our own labour movement. We have confidence that reasoned support for this principle ultimately will serve the best interests of our communities of people ...

... Without presuming the outcome of the search for new constitutional and political relationships, we the workers of both French-speaking and English-speaking Canada, reassert our commitment to maintain powerful bonds of solidarity in our unions. (CLC 1978b)

The CLC's statement on national solidarity was adopted by convention delegates without much controversy and allowed the leadership to breathe a sigh of relief over the fact that the labour movement had managed to avoid a direct constitutional collision. Attaining widespread support for a particular constitutional option would have been virtually impossible given the wide gap between union activists in English Canada and their counterparts in Quebec. Torn between respective national attachments to Canada and Quebec, on one hand, and the need for self-preservation, on the other, the CLC leadership chose the option that would meet the least resistance on the convention floor.

Unlike his predecessors, newly elected Congress president Dennis McDermott, who replaced Morris as head of the CLC at the 1978 convention, did not see the point of combatting separatists in the labour movement. He felt that their demands had to be accommodated in order to maintain solidarity in the House of Labour. McDermott was by no means a champion for Quebec, but he differed significantly from his predecessors in that he did not actively combat Quebec nationalism by promoting a unified pan-Canadian vision for the CLC. Instead, as president, he preferred to remain silent on constitutional questions. Indeed, one year after his election, the CLC decided to skip hearings being held by the Task Force on Canadian Unity again in an effort to avoid a confrontation with the QFL.

It is important to recognize that while the CLC refrained from entering constitutional debates during this period, many of its affiliates refused to follow suit. About a dozen labour organizations made presentations to the 1970 Molgat-McGuigan committee on constitutional reform, including Local 444 of the UAW (Windsor), who called on the federal government to guarantee every Canadian the right to a job (UAW Local 444 1970, 8). The Task Force on Canadian Unity also received a number of submissions from labour organizations. The Manitoba Federation of Labour, the Labour Council of Metropolitan

Toronto, the USWA, the Alberta Federation of Labour, and the Nova Scotia Federation of Labour all stressed the economic dimension of constitutional instability in their submissions to the Task Force, showing concern for the ultimate impact on workers and their families (Canada, Task Force on Canadian Unity 1979).

After the victory of federalist forces in the 1980 Quebec referendum on sovereignty-association, federal justice minister Jean Chrétien was dispatched to the provincial capitals to test the waters for a new round of constitutional reform. His efforts resulted in the establishment of the 1980–81 Special Joint Committee on the Canadian Constitution, which was tasked with gathering citizens' views on patriation of the constitution with a proposed Charter of Rights and Freedoms. By the time the Special Joint Committee convened in 1980, the CLC's strategic ambivalence towards constitutional issues was well-established, and several competing forces, including the CLC's ties to the NDP and its relationship with the QFL, were working very hard to sustain it.

The CLC and Constitutional Paralysis

In commenting on the role of organized labour in the patriation process, Michael Mandel (1994, 260–61) argues that labour's non-involvement stemmed from its belief that the Charter was of no consequence to Canadian unions. Similarly, Joseph Weiler contends,

> The union movement's refusal to attend the Special Committee hearings was not intended to be seen as a boycott or protest against the process of constitutional reform or the entrenchment of human rights in the Canadian Constitution. Rather, the leadership of the Canadian Labour Congress (CLC) decided that the unemployment rate at the time was so high that the unions could not use their limited resources to appear in front of another panel of politicians who were talking about the arcane issues of constitutional reform and human rights. (Weiler 1986, 213)

Although it is accurate to suggest that the CLC was not an active participant in the process of constitutional reform, inactivity should not be confused with disinterest. While it is probably true that union leadership was more concerned about fighting unemployment than engaging in constitutional battles, it is incorrect to assert that organized labour considered constitutional reform or human rights to be "arcane issues." On the contrary, the CLC's own constitutional battles with its Quebec affiliate, the QFL, made the union leadership very attentive to the constitutional tensions between the Province of Quebec and the federal government (Savage 2008).

Moreover, the labour movement had not fallen "asleep at the switch" with regard to the Charter, as Mandel (1994, 261) suggests. It is clear from the evidence that the Congress made a strategic political decision to exclude itself from the patriation debate in order to avoid an internal battle between its political allies in the NDP and its union allies in the QFL. Underlying that strategic decision was the union movement's long-standing anti-judicial bias. The CLC understood very clearly that a Charter of Rights had the potential either to expand workers' rights or to undermine them, but following its historical recognition that courts and judges most often deferred to employers, many labour movement insiders worried that a Charter would be used as a weapon by employers or anti-union employees to weaken union interests. This view is supported by the content of a report delivered at a September 1980 CLC Executive Council meeting. The report, authored by Pat Kerwin, head of the CLC Political Action Department, noted that "the Charter of Rights may come up in the next few months which could inevitably threaten collective bargaining rights" (CLC 1980a). After weighing the various options, the CLC made a very conscious effort to stay away from the constitutional battles on Parliament Hill in the early 1980s. This self-imposed neutrality was partially sustained by organized labour's suspicion of the judicial system and, more specifically, by the Supreme Court's controversial 1976 decision in the anti-inflation reference. Given this reality, it becomes more evident why some within the CLC were feeling quite pessimistic about the idea of a justiciable Charter of Rights, notwithstanding the internal organizational struggles between the Congress and the QFL.

Within Quebec, labour organizations, to varying degrees, closed ranks around PQ premier René Lévesque, who vigorously opposed the Charter and the patriated constitution on the basis that it did not adequately recognize collective rights for Quebec. The QFL, in a December 1980 memorandum to the provincial government, unleashed a blistering attack on the Trudeau government's patriation scheme (QFL 1980, 2) and followed up, in February 1981, with a detailed brief criticizing the specific content of the proposed constitutional package (QFL 1981). The QFL argued that unilateral patriation of the constitution was unnecessary, undemocratic, and part of a strategy to increase the power of Ontario and the federal government at the expense of Quebec. The Federation also argued that the proposed Charter of Rights and Freedoms threatened the rights of workers and that the proposed amending formula was unacceptable because it did not give a veto to Quebec (QFL 1981).

The Quebec government, along with the governments of Manitoba and Newfoundland, challenged the federal government's authority to proceed with unilateral patriation. Amid the legal deliberations on the constitutionality of such a move, the Quebec provincial Liberal Party joined with Premier Lévesque's PQ government in voicing opposition to the Trudeau government's plan for unilateral patriation (Denis and Denis 1992, 131). The Quebec government's position was also endorsed by organized labour in Quebec. Indeed, the Quebec labour movement's opposition to the patriation process was so intense that the province's labour union centrals actually toyed with the idea of appealing to the British Trade Union Congress for support in preventing a new constitution from being adopted in London. The QFL eventually joined a group known as Solidarité-Québec, which gathered 700,000 signatures on a petition calling on Queen Elizabeth II to protect Quebec from unilateral patriation of the constitution (131).

National unity debates and constitutional battles aside, the CLC could not afford to alienate its Quebec affiliate. At the CLC's 1974 convention, the QFL won jurisdiction over union education and organizing in Quebec and over local and regional labour councils; it also gained the transfer of both human and financial resources from the CLC to the QFL. These organizational changes made the QFL first among equals compared to other provincial federations of labour, bolstering its influence within the CLC and guaranteeing that the federation's political positions could not be ignored. Furthermore, the CLC president was in an awkward political position personally given his unpopularity in Quebec at the time. McDermott's failure to back CUPW president Jean-Claude Parrot when he encouraged his members to defy a federal back-to-work order during the 1978 postal strike enraged rank-and-file union activists, especially in Quebec (Parrot 2005). Prior to being confronted with the issue of patriation of the constitution, McDermotts' presidency had barely survived a spring CLC convention in 1980, where the QFL, Quebec locals of CUPE, and the CUPW roundly condemned him for the Parrot incident. These same unions mused openly about finding a replacement for McDermott as CLC president (Canadian Press 1980, 4). Given this political context, McDermott was not interested in further alienating the CLC's Quebec affiliate.

While the CLC's neutrality on the constitution was unquestionably driven by the practical need to retain the allegiance of the QFL, it was further reinforced by the fact that the CLC's political ally, the NDP, was itself internally divided over the constitution. Despite the fact that the party and its forerunner, the Co-operative Commonwealth Federation (CCF), had long advocated the adoption of a patriated constitution, the party's strong provincial sections, particularly the NDP government in Saskatchewan, were expressing strong reservations.

Further Divisions: The CLC, the NDP, and the Special Joint Committee

When Prime Minister Trudeau announced in October 1980 that his government was prepared to move forward with unilateral patriation of the constitution without provincial consent, federal NDP leader Ed Broadbent gave his cautious approval but demanded the inclusion of rights for women, the disabled, and Aboriginal peoples as a condition of his party's support (Steed 1989, 245). Content with the government's commitment to consider appropriate amendments, Broadbent enthusiastically endorsed Trudeau's plan. This raised the ire of many inside the NDP, particularly in Western Canada, who complained that Broadbent had not adequately consulted various constituencies within the party before hatching a deal with a prime minister who had become a *persona non grata* in the West. To complicate matters, Saskatchewan premier Allan Blakeney, the only NDP premier in Canada at the time, opposed entrenching a Charter of Rights in the constitution because he felt it would shift power away from democratically elected legislators to un-accountable judges (Blakeney 2008, 196–203; see also Campbell 1984). The difference of opinion between Broadbent and Blakeney caused a major rift in the federal caucus and nearly ripped the NDP apart in the early 1980s (Steed 1989, 242). Alberta NDP leader Grant Notley initially sided with Blakeney, arguing that provincial agreement was necessary in order for patriation to take place. The two western NDP leaders were no doubt concerned about maintaining provincial control over resource revenues as well. From within Broadbent's own caucus, a group of four Saskatchewan MPs (Nystrom, De Jong, Anguish, and Hovdebo) publicly broke ranks with their leader and sided with Blakeney instead. Saskatchewan MP Les Benjamin, who supported Broadbent, described the political tension as follows: "I was as popular as a skunk at a garden party in my own province. Close friends told me they'd never again put my sign on their lawn; they said I was a traitor to Saskatchewan. It was traumatic" (quoted in Steed 1989, 250).

The CLC was effectively experiencing a severe case of constitutional paralysis: it was unable to advance any position, let alone any meaningful of position, on the proposed Charter of Rights. According to CLC Executive Council minutes of September 1980, "President [Dennis] McDermott explained that he was of the view that we should not get involved in the [constitutional] 'circus' ... especially because the nature of our organization would not lend itself to us having a consensus even within our Council" (CLC 1980a). After a brief discussion, it was generally agreed that the Congress should "stay out of the issue of the Constitutional Talks as much as possible at this time."

The CLC's September 1980 decision to stay out of the constitutional debate was not immune from internal opposition. At the December 1980 Executive Council meeting, Alberta Federation of Labour president Harry Kostiuk appealed "for support in making representation to the federal government on the question of the patriated constitution and the entrenchment of the workers' rights in that constitution" (CLC 1980b). Kostiuk was supported by BC Federation of Labour president Jim Kinnaird and by Dick Martin, president of the Manitoba Federation of Labour: "It was expressed by Brother Martin that in Western Canada there is tremendous pressure being applied by the affiliates to say something about workers' rights, and he would rather see the Congress say something as a body, by reversing the decision made at the last meeting" (CLC 1980b). McDermott clearly did not want to reopen the issue: "If Brother Laberge were here," he said, "he would be speaking very strongly in disagreement of voicing our opinion" (CLC 1980b). The CLC president was supported by his colleague Bob White, "who felt we have no choice at this time but to reaffirm our position or we will be opening serious wounds we thought had been solved long ago" (CLC 1980b). McDermott's view prevailed and the original position of the September 1980 meeting was upheld.

In early 1981, the highest courts in Quebec and Manitoba upheld the position of the federal government on unilateral patriation. However, Newfoundland's Court of Appeal ruled that unilateral patriation of the constitution would constitute a violation of constitutional convention. These contradictory rulings prompted the prime minister to refer the matter to the Supreme Court of Canada. While the court prepared to hear the case, the Special Joint Committee continued its work, meeting with Canadians concerned with shaping the content of the Charter of Rights.

It could certainly be argued that the advent of a Charter of Rights provided organized labour's allies in Parliament and on the Special Joint Committee with an ideal opportunity to push for constitutional-ized workers' rights. After all, it was widely accepted that the NDP was in a position to win certain concessions from the government in exchange for the party's support (Sheppard and Valpy 1982, 114). However, the BC Federation of Labour (BCFL) was the only labour organization in English Canada that bothered to submit a written brief to the committee that addressed the immediate interests of the union movement. Taking up the mantle of previous generations of Canadian labour leaders who had fought for decades to convince government to constitu-tionalize workers' rights, the BCFL complained about the exclusion of social and economic rights from the proposed Charter:

> Nowhere does one find reference to a general right to employment, the right to the enjoyment of just and favourable conditions of work, the right to form trade unions, the right to social security, the

right to protection of the family, the right to an adequate standard of living, the right to the enjoyment of the highest attainable standard of physical and mental health, or a general right to education. It is our opinion that the failure of the Charter to make provision for this category of rights is its single most important shortcoming. (BCFL 1981, 10)

With the overwhelming majority of the labour movement in English Canada sitting on the sidelines, there was no pressure whatsoever on the NDP, let alone the Special Joint Committee, to make union rights a priority in constitutional discussions; as a result, the prospect of consti-tutionalized workers' rights almost fell off the radar completely.

The Ontario and Alberta sections of the NDP both made long, de-tailed presentations to the Special Joint Committee that dealt with a myriad of different issues, but both neglected to mention the absence of specifically categorized labour rights in the Charter. Garth Stevenson, the Alberta NDP's constitutional adviser, explained that the party sup-ported "the principle of entrenching Human Rights in the Constitution" but failed to include workers' rights alongside demands for collective rights for Aboriginals and linguistic minorities (Canada 1981, 110). After the new constitution was proclaimed in 1982, British Columbia NDP leader Dave Barrett confessed, "The constitution on a scale of ten was never more than one and a half to me. The whole debate was a gross waste of time" (Sheppard and Valpy 1982, 219).

Despite the labour movement's noticeable absence from the Special Joint Committee and the NDP's apparent ambivalence towards priori-tizing union rights and freedoms, the party's representatives on the committee did ultimately take up the cause of workers' rights by mov-ing a modest amendment to what would become section 2(d) (freedom of association) of the Charter; the amendment, had it passed, would have explicitly protected the right to organize and bargain collectively but not the right to strike. Although consensus had emerged on the Special Committee that the right of association should include the ability of individuals to organize into various associations, there was sharp disagreement over the notion that freedom of association should be interpreted as extending constitutional protection to labour unions.

MP Svend Robinson, the NDP member of the committee who intro-duced the motion to include constitutional support for workers to or-ganize and bargain collectively (Canada 1981, 43:69), argued that such rights reflected the most "fundamental values in Canadian society" and that the Government of Canada had already tangibly recognized these rights in its ratification of the International Labour Organization (ILO) constitution, the UN Declaration, and the UN Treaty on International and Civil Rights. Robinson's colleague, NDP MP Lorne Nystrom, add-ed that the motion would "give society perhaps a bit of direction, which will underline a basic and fundamental value in our society ... [and] signals to employers that this right is a very important right" (43:72–73). On the surface, Robinson and Nystrom's attempt to include the right to organize and bargain was premised on their understanding of rights that had long been accepted in Canadian legislation and inter-national law and that should therefore be reflected in the constitution. Notably, however, the NDP MPs did not make a case for an explicit constitutional right to strike.

Liberal and Conservative members defeated the NDP's motion. The Liberal minister of justice, Robert Kaplan, argued that rights to organ-ize and bargain were integrated within the definition of "association." Therefore, to enumerate rights for labour unions specifically with a spe-cial subsection in the Charter would "diminish all the other forms of association which are contemplated ... If one tears apart the general freedom of association it may diminish the general meaning – freedom to associate" (Canada 1981, 43:70). Along the same lines, former labour minister and Liberal MP Bryce Mackasey suggested that the real prob-lem for the unions "comes not from their freedom of association, but to be recognized legally for another particular purpose; for instance the right to bargain" (43:72). In Mackasey's view, the constitution should not reflect esoteric principles integrated in modern labour law; rather, it should protect broad democratic values.

Notwithstanding the partisan division between the NDP and the other parties, the debate over the inclusion of labour rights and freedoms in the Charter actually reflected a narrow interpretation of collective rights for workers. Robinson and Nystrom's rationale for the inclusion of collective bargaining and the right to organize was restricted to societal values and already existing legal (and international) norms. The NDP's motion explicitly excluded the right to strike, which Robinson did not see as "the fundamental incidence of freedom of association" (Canada 1981, 43:69). It is unclear why the right to strike was not considered an equally "fundamental" incidence of freedom of association, given that unions had long demonstrated that collective bargaining was superfluous if it did not include a credible threat by workers to withdraw their labour. The NDP's motion did not even go so far as to recommend constitutionalizing the existing zone of toleration for workers' collective rights, let alone address the constraints surrounding state-imposed "responsibility." It is equally important that Liberal and Conservative members did not consider Robinson's motion to be reflective of "essential freedoms." To be sure, Kaplan's insistence that freedom of association already included these rights both pacified his supporters on the committee and gave hope to some that Charter guarantee would form the basis of a constitutional labour code (Beatty 1987, 121–24). Yet, the broad definition that the framers gave to associational rights, coupled with the committee's outright rejection of the NDP's motion on collective bargaining, made clear that it would be the courts who would ultimately determine the constitutional status of workers' rights.

Meanwhile, internal dissent within the CLC over the entire constitutional package continued to mount. McDermott and Blakeney met in March 1981. According to Robert Sheppard and Michael Valpy (1982, 132), "The strongest message he [Blakeney] received from Dennis McDermott was that the CLC president wished the constitution issue would go away so that the politicians could talk about unemployment, inflation and patriation – as he put it – of the economy." McDermott opened the 9 March 1981 CLC Executive Committee meeting by expressing his concern over "the continued harassment of Ed Broadbent by the Saskatchewan people with respect to the Constitution." The CLC president's message was clear: "Quit attacking the federal Party; they made a political deal and they cannot now walk away from it" (CLC 1981). At the CLC Executive Council meeting that followed, Nadine Hunt of the Saskatchewan Federation of Labour (SFL) further frustrated McDermott by urging the CLC to adopt a similar resolution on the constitution to the one adopted previously by the SFL executive, which called for, among other thing, a campaign to ensure that "the Charter of Rights does not infringe on trade union rights such as compulsory membership in legitimate trade unions, compulsory check-off, and the right of workers to organize into the union of their choice" (CLC 1981).

The CLC president ruled Hunt's resolution out of order, stating that the CLC Executive Council had previously agreed to take a neutral position. McDermott went on to express his disappointment over the fact that the SFL wanted to enter into the constitutional debate and "appealed to Sister Hunt to exercise restraint" (CLC 1981). Hunt's retort that the CLC was "doing a disservice to the workers of this country" did not sway the head of the Congress. As the minutes report, "President McDermott said that whether our remaining quiet turns out to be right or wrong, it was a decision made by this Council" (CLC 1981).

Meanwhile, delegates to the NDP's 1981 policy convention voted roughly two-to-one in favour of Broadbent's position, and in September 1981, the Supreme Court of Canada ruled in split decisions that although the federal government did have the authority to patriate the constitution unilaterally, in doing so, it would be violating a constitutional convention requiring substantial provincial consent. The Supreme Court's decision, articulated in the Patriation Reference (*Re: Resolution to Amend the Constitution* 1981), prompted a new round of constitutional consultation between Ottawa and the provinces. In November 1981, the federal government succeeded in gaining the support it needed from the provinces, excluding Quebec. During the "Night of the Long Knives," as Quebec premier René Lévesque later dubbed the events of November 1981, Justice Minister Chrétien and the nine premiers from English Canada hammered out a final agreement while Lévesque was sleeping. The agreement included a "notwithstanding clause" to allay the worries of people like Allan Blakeney who feared judicial supremacy under the new Charter of Rights. Upon learning that the other premiers had accepted Trudeau's patriation scheme, Lévesque claimed that Quebec would neither sign nor recognize the new constitution.

On 17 April 1982, Queen Elizabeth II proclaimed Canada's new *Constitution Act.* A few months later, the Supreme Court of Canada ruled that Quebec did not have a veto over constitutional amendments (*Re: Objection by Quebec to a Resolution to Amend the Constitution,* 1982). In the aftermath of the Supreme Court decision, the Quebec labour movement joined the Société Saint Jean-Baptiste and released a joint statement asserting that "this Constitution ... is not, cannot, and will never be ours" (Déclaration Conjointe 1982).[1] Unions in English Canada, however, had already turned their attention to figuring out how to navigate the uncertain future of labour relations under Canada's new Charter of Rights and Freedoms.

CUPE, Canada's leading public sector union, for instance, encouraged its members to proceed with "prudence and caution," arguing that "no one can predict with any certainty the impact the Charter will have on unions, collective agreements, and working conditions." The union worried openly that employers would use the Charter to attack compulsory union membership and the Rand formula (CUPE 1985, 8).

At an April 1985 meeting of the Saskatchewan Government and General Employees Union (SGEU), Larry Brown, the union's chief executive officer, summed up perfectly the union movement's historical antipathy towards the courts when he warned members of his own union that the Charter would not be a panacea for public sector workers, pointing out that "working people have made their progress in the streets and on picket lines, in meetings and demonstrations, in struggle and confrontation ... not in the halls of justice" (SGEU 1985, 3). Brown's message was clear: labour could not rely on the courts to advance workers' interests.

Despite Brown's misgivings about the Charter, National Union of Public and General Employees (NUPGE) president John Fryer encouraged SGEU members to accept the Charter as a political reality that could not be ignored, arguing, "It is the duty of the trade union movement to do all we can to use the Charter and its provisions to protect and expand the existing rights of our membership" (SGEU 1985, 47). Fryer believed that the Canadian labour movement had to develop a strategic plan to deal with the Charter in order to ensure that it did indeed "protect and expand" the rights of workers. Along the same lines, CUPE argued that Charter-based legal strategies should "be undertaken in coordination with other unions" and assured its members that CUPE would work "to have the Charter amended so as to provide for a right to employment and so as to protect collective rights," including the rights to organize, bargain collectively, and strike (CUPE 1985, 9). To be sure, CUPE and other unions had had the opportunity to press for such rights as part of the Special Joint Committee hearing on the Charter just a few years earlier but decided to abstain from the process.

The CLC's neutrality on the Charter – triangulated as the Congress was by its political loyalties to the federal NDP, its close political connections to powerful provincial sections of the party, and the practical need to retain the allegiance of the QFL – made the labour movement look tremendously disorganized in its approach towards constitutional issues. This disorganization, combined with grumblings from the business community about the potential of using the Charter as a weapon against organized labour, had many in the union movement second-guessing the CLC's strategy of non-involvement.

Canadian Labour and the First Era of Charter Challenges

3

It is no small irony that the adoption of the Charter of Rights and Freedoms in 1982 coincided with a severe economic recession that resulted in state-led austerity programs and a new round of restrictions on the rights and freedoms of unionized workers. Canada's postwar Keynesian economic model was clearly falling out of favour with federal and provincial governments. In an effort to address high levels of inflation, the Trudeau government introduced its "6 and 5" program, which incensed the labour movement by capping wage increases at 6 percent in 1982 and 1983 and 5 percent for the following year. The Liberals also denied the right to strike to the federal public service by legislatively extending collective agreements for two years (Rose 2004; Swimmer 1984). The landslide election of Brian Mulroney and the Progressive Conservatives in 1984 simply intensified state-led attacks on workers' rights. Emboldened by the Mulroney government's blatantly anti-union approach, provincial governments followed suit with their own "temporary" measures aimed at reducing the power of organized labour, including the increased use of back-to-work legislation and other coercive measures designed to undermine the capacity of unions to effectively resist neoliberal restructuring by governments and employers (Panitch and Swartz 2003, 85–142). Panitch and Swartz (2003, 29–25) characterize these types of government responses as "permanent exceptionalism," arguing that temporary restrictive measures on labour rights had become a permanent fixture in Canadian labour relations.

With labour's most trusted political ally – the NDP – stuck on the opposition benches in Ottawa and in every provincial legislature but Manitoba, the union movement was forced to reconsider how it could most effectively challenge incursions on workers' rights and freedoms. Despite the fact that organized labour excluded itself from the process of developing the Charter of Rights, labour unions could not ignore the Charter's potential impact on the Canadian labour relations regime. For some, the new constitution offered the real possibility of reshaping the power imbalances in the workplace by radically rewriting the Canadian labour law regime in favour of organized labour. Perhaps not surprisingly, many of the strongest supporters of Charter action included union-side labour lawyers who were eager to rework the postwar collective bargaining framework. David Beatty, for example, argued that the Charter allowed workers to "insist that the places in which they work be democratized and regulated by legal rules and procedures which parallel those we use to regulate other environments of our community in which we live" (Beatty 1987, 6). Labour lawyer Paul Cavalluzzo was equally optimistic: because "trade unions advance democratic values in Canada," he argued, they represent "the kind of association which should be protected by the fundamental freedom guaranteed by section 2 (d) of the Charter" (Cavalluzzo 1986, 206). According to Charter optimists like Beatty and Cavalluzzo, the Charter offered the possibility of sweeping new collective freedoms that could deepen and expand Canada's regime of industrial legality.

Labour leaders waded into the Charter arena with far less enthusiasm. Incoming Canadian Labour Congress (CLC) president Shirley Carr argued that the judiciary were acting as "jealous guardians of individual rights against collective interference, whereas workers rely on collective strength to carry out their activities" (Crosariol 1985, 1). As mentioned in the previous chapter, Saskatchewan Government and General Employees Union (SGEU) president Larry Brown offered a similar critique, highlighting the structural barriers to social advancement through the courts. Brown cautioned labour leaders to be suspicious of the Charter and not to forget labour's long struggles *against* the law:

Throughout its history, the labour movement has known, or has to re-learn, that the courts and the legal system are not labour's allies. This is not because the personal biases of the judges, but because the whole foundation of the law and the legal system is the protection of those with political and economic power. The rights of property and property holders form the cornerstones of our common law. (SGEU 1985, 3)

Embedded within Brown's critique was the realization that labour had little to gain from the Charter primarily because judges were incapable of lifting the the veil of property rights shrouding Canadian common law. Moreover, such an observation reflected a general skepticism about constitutional law having the potential to expand the zone in which labour unions operated legitimately. In fact, the opposite was true: many union leaders believed that pro-employer biases of Canadian judges would undermine hard-fought workers' rights, such as those addressed by the Rand formula, that were predicated on balancing individual rights with broader notions of collective freedom.

This notion was reinforced by Ontario union activists and labour lawyers who met at a "Charter of Wrongs" conference to strengthen left-wing Charter critiques just a few weeks prior to the release of the labour trilogy decisions (Makin 1987). At that conference, there was a general consensus that the elevation of "individual" rights in the Charter was predicated on the notion that collectivities represented a personification of the classic liberal ideology of the tyranny of the majority.

Notwithstanding the labour movement's overall suspicions, some unions were hopeful that the Charter's seemingly positive embrace of collective rights in its freedom of association and equality provisions could yield benefits for workers. For example, National Union of Public and General Employees (NUPGE) president John Fryer expressed the view that the Charter had the potential to advance the cause of unions (especially the equality provisions), but he was cautious in his overall endorsement of constitutional litigation strategies (SGEU 1985, 29–48). Fryer believed that the Charter had the potential to limit government in its attempt to undermine public sector bargaining. Yet, like his fellow labour leaders, he also worried that a hostile judiciary could undermine many of labour's hard-won collective gains. Fryer's solution was that the Canadian labour movement should take a coordinated approach to the Charter, targeting Charter challenges that were likely to produce positive outcomes. This coordination, Fryer believed, had to come from the CLC rather than from individual locals or unions (48). His call for a coordinated strategy, however, was ultimately doomed to failure given the decentralized and fragmented nature of the Canadian labour movement in the 1980s. Moreover, Charter litigation was ultimately reactive, only occurring after a government or employer eroded the collective rights of labour. As Fryer feared, individual unions, increasingly on the defensive, began launching Charter challenges on a case-by-case basis beginning in the mid-1980s. Once the cases started to make their way through the judicial system, the labour movement's worst fears about the court's long-held anti-union bias were seemingly being realized. By the end of the 1980s, it was becoming crystal clear that the Charter of Rights had very little to offer working people in their struggles against government and employers.

Dolphin Delivery and Secondary Picketing

Organized labour's first experience with the Charter tested the extent to which the constitutional right of expression protected the collective right of workers to secondary picketing. As demonstrated in our discussion of *Hersees v. Goldstein* (1963) in Chapter 1, secondary picketing had long been restricted in Canada on the basis that the action violated the rights of "innocent" third parties to trade during a labour dispute. Picketing itself had always presented a dilemma for governments. While most jurisdictions had created numerous legal obstacles to prevent strikes from occurring, few had actually implemented a legislative regime to govern workers' actions on the picket line. Therefore, the regulation of picketing continued to fall largely to the common law as interpreted by courts and judges. One of the enduring questions for labour unions was the extent to which the new Charter of Rights would challenge common law rules restricting union acts of expression, including existing legal restrictions on picketing. *Retail, Wholesale and Department Store Union v. Dolphin Delivery* (1986) was the first labour-related Charter case heard by the Supreme Court.

The dispute arose out of a 1984 conflict between the Retail Wholesale Department Store Union (RWDSU), Purolator Inc./Supercourier, and a third-party shipping company named Dolphin Delivery. In the course of a legal strike, the RWDSU attempted to convince the court to overturn a *quia timet* injunction.[1] The injunction limited the ability of the union to picket outside Dolphin Delivery, a shipping company to which a struck Purolator/Supercourier location was contracting out its work. Since the dispute involved a federally regulated industry, the issue fell to the *Canada Labour Code*, which was silent on the issue of secondary picketing. The code's silence pushed the dispute to common law rules that, as described above, had long restricted secondary picketing in Canada. While the BC Court of Appeal acknowledged that some elements of picketing reflected legitimate freedom of expression, it also ruled that the primary goal of secondary picketing was to damage third-party employers. The court was thus unwilling to elevate secondary picketing to constitutionally protected speech because it constituted a tortious breach of contract. The justices therefore concluded that even if secondary picketing *was* considered constitutionally protected speech, limiting such actions was entirely justifiable under section 1 because it protected "innocent third parties" (*Dolphin Delivery v. Retail, Wholesale and Department Store Union* 1984). Undeterred, the RWDSU appealed the decision to the Supreme Court.

On the surface, the RWDSU's Charter challenge was simply an attempt to overturn the decades-old "illegal *per se*" doctrine and therefore to constitutionalize an important tool for labour unions to use in pressuring employers during a strike. Yet the RWDSU was also attempting to expand the scope of Charter jurisprudence to move beyond simple government action as stated in section 32 and apply it to the common law. Section 32 is the provision in the Charter stating that the constitution applies "to the Parliament and government of Canada" and "to legislature and government of each province." For many early Charter observers, the exact meaning of section 32 was unclear, especially when coupled with section 52 of the constitution, which states that the constitution is the "supreme law of Canada, and any law that is inconsistent with the provisions of the Constitution is, to the extent of the inconsistency, of no force or effect." Recognizing that the constitution requires all law to be consistent with the Charter embeds a structural tension between section 32 and section 52, because the "law" is not limited to statutes passed by the federal and provincial governments. Private law governing contracts, civil wrongs, torts, and all other common laws arguably has just as much potential to erode the human rights of individuals (Bateman 1998, 4–6; Sharpe and Roach 2009, 97–98). The tension between these two provisions in the constitution provided the RWDSU with an opening to argue that the Charter's fundamental freedoms could be used to alter the balance of power in the private sector. More concretely, the union sought to limit the ability of employers to use the common law to undermine workers' collective actions.

The union's strategy to use the Charter to challenge the common law was unorthodox. As previously discussed, the common law consisted, in its simplest form, of centuries of judge-made law, much of which was hostile to workers' collective action. In making the argument that the Charter should eclipse the common law, the union was attempting to use the Charter to shine a light on the many restrictions that Canadian (and British) judges had constructed to limit or weaken workers' collective action (Fudge and Tucker 2001). Taken to its logical conclusion, the attempt to expand the Charter's reach to the common law was a radical move since the union was asking the court to consider "the social, political, and economic setting from which the new Charter emerges" (*RWDSU v. Dolphin Delivery* 1986, RWDSU Appellant Factum, 7). On this point, the union's rationale was simple enough: the right to strike had been severely limited by the common law and by government's use of back-to-work legislation in the 1970s and 1980s. The union argued that the "Charter is a political as well as legal document" and that the court should provide a broad, liberal, and progressive interpretation of the new constitution in order to offset common legal principles that violate workers' expression (8).

In demanding an "activist and liberal interpretation of the Charter," the RWDSU argued that the Charter delegitimized the use of common law torts to limit core labour freedoms to strike and picket. To use the torts in the current environment, the union argued, would be "akin to trying to bring back the stone axe" in an age when we "have learned to live and work with the laser beam" (*RWDSU v. Dolphin Delivery* 1986,

RWDSU Appellant Factum,23). Underlying this argument was the union's position that section 32 of the Charter applied to all areas shaped by state power, including the preservation of property rights, private litigation, contracts, and private sector disputes between workers and employers. At the centre of the union's argument was the claim that the Charter imposed new societal values that transcended decades of judge-made law favouring employers. In pre-Charter days,

> the common law recognition of the employees' right to free speech took second place to the preservation of the plaintiff's trade and property rights. The introduction of the Charter, however, has fundamentally altered this relationship: free speech has been elevated to the status of constitutional, supreme law; the drafters of the constitution did not see fit to elevate property rights in general or the right to trade in particular ... [i]n short the new constitution sweeps away the predominance of the plaintiff's right to trade as a basis for restricting picketing. (27–28)

In the eyes of the union, therefore, picketing had become much more than a simple action to protect the economic interests of workers. Rather, picketing had been elevated to a fundamental act of expression that "contributes to the central economic debate within the community" (20). Indeed, as workers' struggles in the nineteenth and early twentieth century demonstrate, one of the central struggles in liberal capitalist democracies is that concerning the extent to which workers are free to debate and challenge employers over the distribution of the economic surplus. To deny the right of workers to picket restricts their ability to communicate information to union members, like-minded workers, and the broader public. The union's central position was that denying this most fundamental right to union members would contradict the very freedoms the Charter was created to protect.

By contrast, the employer's argument reached back to a pre-industrial, nineteenth-century interpretation of the common law. Dolphin Delivery claimed that picketing was not a constitutional act of expression because it constituted a signal to "commence economic action against the Respondent and not as a means of discourse or discussion" (*RWDSU v.*

Dolphin Delivery 1986, Dolphin Delivery Respondent Factum, 12). From the company's perspective, picketing (especially secondary picketing) was the equivalent of violent or coercive intimidation, which could not be described as legitimate expression. Comparing secondary picketing to acts of extortion, the company argued that

> to give freedom of expression the widest possible scope would be to give equal constitutional recognition to all imaginable forms of expression no matter how trivial or undesirable these forms of expression might be. For example, an attempt to blackmail or extort would be given the same Constitutional status as the delivery of a campaign speech during a federal or provincial election. (6)

The company believed that there existed a natural hierarchy of expression within liberal societies, with only specific categories deserving constitutional protection. Accordingly, the only speech worthy of protection was that which (1) protected and advanced the democratic process directly; (2) promoted individual self-fulfillment; and (3) promoted the social good by testing new ideas in the "marketplace of ideas" (*RWDSU v. Dolphin Delivery* 1986, Dolphin Delivery Respondent Factum, 8). This minimalist interpretation of expression reinforced the corporate belief that rights were justifiable when questioning public power but had no place when addressing power imbalances within private economic relations. The company concluded by arguing that picketing did nothing to contribute to the democratic process or to promote the overall social good.

As became common in union disputes involving constitutional questions, several governments intervened on the side of business. The governments of Alberta, British Columbia, Newfoundland, and Canada all adopted the employer's argument that picketing was not constitutionally protected speech. Alberta and British Columbia maintained that legislation suppressing secondary picketing (including their own labour relations acts) did not violate the Charter because these actions impose irreparable harm or injury to third-party businesses (*RWDSU v. Dolphin Delivery* 1986, Government of Alberta Intervener Factum, 6–7;

Government of British Columbia Interver Factum). In its simplest form, any secondary action that is designed to harm or "injure the Plaintiff" cannot be elevated to constitutionally protected speech.

The governments of Canada and Newfoundland were equally critical of the union's call for a broader interpretation of section 32 to include the common law. On the surface, it seems somewhat strange for a government to argue that the restrictions in the Charter should only apply to itself. Yet the federal government warned that if the common law applied to the actions of private agents or the courts, it would undermine the scope and purpose of the Charter. The federal government thus concluded that tools such as court injunctions are not

> action[s] taken by the state, in the sense of the executive of the Government of Canada or persons acting on its behalf. What is impugned is a court decision in a dispute between private parties based on the common law relating to picketing. It is submitted that, except for limited purposes specifically enunciated by the Charter, the courts do not form part of the Government for purposes of s. 32 and hence are not caught by the scope of the Charter (*RWDSU v. Dolphin Delivery* 1986, Government of Canada Intervener Factum, 12).

Michael Mandel (1994, 284–85) challenged this rationale, arguing that it was difficult to understand the position that judges, whose authority is reinforced and defended by the state, are somehow divorced from actions of government when applying the common law. Nevertheless, the federal government took the position that the Charter should be limited in its application to actions taken by the executive and legislative branches of the state.

The Supreme Court's eventual decision set the stage for a series of union defeats before the court. In agreeing with the central arguments of the employers and the intervening governments, the court argued that the Charter's guarantee of expression did not protect the right of workers to secondary picketing. In writing for the majority, Justice McIntyre recognized that some forms of picketing – while representing an unfortunate breakdown in the collective bargaining process – do constitute an act of expression (*RWDSU v. Dolphin Delivery* 1986, paras. 20–23). Yet McIntyre, essentially adopting the position of the employer, further reasoned that secondary picketing exposes the company to irreparable harm and thus must be subjected to limitations. He concluded:

> It is therefore necessary in the general social interest that picketing be regulated and sometimes limited. It is reasonable to restrain picketing so that the conflict will not escalate beyond the actual parties. While picketing is, no doubt, a legislative weapon to be employed in a labour dispute by the employees against their employer, it should not be permitted to harm others. (para. 23)

For McIntyre, elevating secondary picketing to constitutionally protected speech would have undoubtedly bestowed economic harm on the company. While picketing may be a form of expression, he reasoned, restrictions on the collective right of workers to challenge employer power represented a reasonable restriction on union freedoms. In other words, the Charter could not be used to override the contractual rights of a private company. Based on this rationale, McIntyre maintained that court injunctions and the subsequent use of torts in labour disputes (inducing breach of contract) effectively balanced the right of expression with broader societal interests (para. 24).

Having concluded that secondary picketing was inevitably linked to harm, the court took an equally narrow view on the question of the Charter and the common law, ultimately ruling that the Charter did not apply to disputes between private parties even when those disputes ended up before the courts. Accepting the argument of the intervening governments, McIntyre contended that Charter freedoms only adhered to a strict definition of "public power"; he essentially ignored any pretext of private power that is buttressed through the application of the common law.

McIntyre's reasoning on the public/private distinction of the Charter was the subject of several critiques. There was a general consensus among orthodox constitutional scholars that divorcing courts from the application of government was an extremely narrow interpretation of section 32 of the Charter, applying it to actions of the executive and the public sector but not to the full extent of all state action (Hogg 1987, 275). Others argued that McIntyre's interpretation of the section 32 trigger was unsustainable given the multiple intersections of governments, private actors, and third parties within capitalist society (Bateman 1998; Slattery 1987). For more critical scholars, the court's line dividing "public" from "private" action seemed arbitrary and thus overtly ideological, in that it recognized the erosion of civil liberties by governments but ignored abuses of human rights everywhere else (Hutchinson and Petter 1988; Petter 2010). While many argued that the Charter had redrawn Canada's political realities based on the values of equality and social justice (Greene 2014; Sigurdson 1993), *Dolphin Delivery* reinforced the notion that for workers, the Charter represented nothing more than a nineteenth-century liberal rights document that ignored the power relations inherent in modern capitalist economies and thus offered little for the traditionally excluded and less powerful (Fudge 1988; Mandel 1994; Petter 1986).

The overall critique of the Supreme Court's reasoning in *Dolphin Delivery* suggested that the labour movement had an uphill battle ahead if it expected substantive gains from the Charter's protection of expression. That opinion was given further credence when the court upheld two lower court decisions that virtually banned courthouse workers from legally picketing outside of courthouses (*B.C.G.E.U. v. British Columbia (Attorney General)* 1988; *Newfoundland (Attorney General) v. N.A.P.E.* 1988). In *McKinney v. University of Guelph* (1990), the Supreme Court developed its rationale on section 32, further arguing that to "open up all private and public action to judicial review could strangle the operation of society" (232). The decisions in *Dolphin Delivery*, *BCGEU*, and *NAPE* exposed a serious problem for advocates of judicially enforced rights for workers. The court's arbitrary line between public and private power suggested that the Charter was not able to rewrite common law restrictions on workers' collective action, let alone challenge the private property rights of employers. On the surface, this was probably not surprising, since courts had long been hostile to workers' collective action, especially when workers challenged the power of employers through strikes (Fudge and Tucker 2001). Even so, there were still many unanswered questions: How would the court rule when direct government action restricted union rights? And how would the court interpret the Charter's right of association?

The Labour Trilogy and the Right to Strike

Notwithstanding the setback in *Dolphin Delivery*, many legal commentators believed that the real questions surrounding labour rights would be answered by section 2(d), which covered freedom of association (Cotler 1981). *Dolphin* highlighted the weakness of pursuing labour rights through the Charter's guarantee of expression, since there was judicial reluctance to define strikes as a legitimate or a democratic form of expression. The belief that unions might find greater success through section 2(d) was based on the ambiguous discussion surrounding freedom of association and labour relations in the 1980–81 parliamentary hearings. While the framers of the Charter chose not to include in the constitution an explicit right to organize, bargain collectively, or strike, they did leave the door ajar for a judicial interpretation favourable to labour rights by preserving the term "association," in its broadest meaning possible, in section 2(d).

Before discussing the three Supreme Court cases in 1987 that became known as the labour trilogy, we step back a few years to several lower court decisions in the early 1980s in which opinions over a constitutional right to strike, in particular, were clearly mixed. In the first labour-related Charter case before any court in Canada, several unions challenged the Ontario government's *Inflation Restraint Act, 1982.* The act unilaterally extended the life of an existing collective agreement, thus eliminating the ability of public sector workers to bargain or go on strike (*Re Service Employees' International Union* 1983, 231). In the Ontario Divisional Court, the justices agreed that section 2(d) of the Charter included a right to bargain and to strike. They also agreed, however, that only one section of the act violated section 2(d) and that the act stood up to the scrutiny of the Charter's reasonable limits clause in section 1. The Ontario Court of Appeal then sidestepped the Charter issue altogether, finding that the Ontario government had the constitutional jurisdiction to create an inflation restraint board to control expenditures in the public service, even if it ruled against union gains at the bargaining table *(Re Service Employees' International Union* 1983, 225). A more concrete victory occurred in Saskatchewan when four unions challenged government legislation restricting their ability to strike in the province's dairy industry *(Retail, Wholesale and Department Store Union, Local 544 v. Saskatchewan* 1985). In that case, the Saskatchewan Court of Appeal ruled in a 2–1 decision that the Charter included a right to strike and that the government's actions eroded the association-al rights of workers. Saskatchewan premier Grant Devine's government announced that it would appeal the decision and, in the interim, imple-mented the notwithstanding clause to keep workers from striking.

Although governments continued to use a heavy legislative hand to deal with union-led challenges to restrictions on workers' rights, *RWDSU v. Saskatchewan* (1985) suggested that there was some judicial sympathy for the right-to-strike provisions embedded within Canada's regime of labour relations. That support, however, was hardly universal. In 1984, the Public Service Alliance of Canada (PSAC) challenged the federal government's "6 and 5" anti-inflation plan in federal court. Rec-ognizing the importance to society of fighting inflation (as the judges had in the 1976 Anti-Inflation Reference), the court held that Par-liament was within its rights to address financial emergencies at the expense of collective bargaining *(PSAC v. Canada* 1984). The court reasoned that the federal government's "6 and 5" program was constitu-tional because section 2(d) only accounts for individuals entering into consensual arrangements but does not protect the "objects" of that as-sociation or the "means" of attaining those objects.

A more stinging defeat came out of a 1983 Alberta dispute that re-sulted from the government making several amendments to three acts – the *Public Service Employee Relations Act,* the *Labour Relations Act,* and the *Police Officers Collective Bargaining Act* – amendments that, in effect, withdrew the right to strike for firefighters, nurses, and public servants and replaced it with a system of compulsory arbitration. Faced with declining oil revenue and a weakening provincial economy, the Alberta government's controversial labour law reforms were drafted in response to a number of strikes by nurses and Alberta public ser-vants. When the unions argued that the reforms were unconstitution-al, Premier Lougheed agreed to ask the Alberta Court of Appeal for clarification on the constitutionality of the legislation (*Reference re Judicature Act, 1984*). Given the uncertainty surrounding the Charter and the right to strike, however, Lougheed warned that he would use the notwithstanding clause if the Supreme Court found that the Charter included a right to strike (Lougheed 1998, 9–10).

The court's decision outlined what would become a familiar rationale for judges addressing the constitutional rights of unions: freedom of association is an individual rather than a collective right. Writing for the majority, Justice Kearns maintained that while individuals were free to form groups, the group itself does not have additional constitutional freedom of action. In his concurring decision, Justice Belzil argued that unions and employers bargained as equals and it was not for the court to choose sides. He also determined that the ability to strike in the modern era "is a right conferred by legislation, and ... what legislation has conferred, legislation may modify or abrogate" (*Reference re Judicature Act*, 1984, para. 117). Belzil went so far as to compare strikes to "coercion" and stated that it would be "unthinkable that a charter for the equal protection of the rights and freedoms of all citizens should guarantee to one citizen an inviolable right to harm another, or enlarge the freedom of one citizen to the detriment of the freedom of the other" (para. 112).

Given the ambiguity in the lower courts, it was left to the Supreme Court to examine how the associational rights outlined in the Charter worked with or against Canada's regime of labour relations. For the unions, elevating the Wagner/PC 1003 model of industrial relations to constitutional status was certainly an uphill battle. Not only did the unions have to defend their interests before a series of hostile lower court decisions; they were also opposed by nine intervening governments and a Supreme Court that had already ruled that strikes did not enjoy constitutional protection on the basis of expression. Unions were further limited by the restrictive policies at the Supreme Court, which limited legal intervention by labour movement allies. In fact, for reasons unknown, the CLC and several other unions were denied intervener status before the Supreme Court, notwithstanding the fact that the questions posed clearly had national implications (Carr 1987). In the end, only the NDP government in Manitoba sided with the unions in their constitutional struggle.

In April 1987, the Supreme Court of Canada rendered its decision on the unions' freedom of association in a series of simultaneous judgments arguing that the Charter did not protect the ability of unionized workers to strike. These cases, which collectively became known as the Charter's "labour trilogy," included *Reference re Public Service Employee Relations Act (Alta.) 1987*; *PSAC v. Canada 1987*; and *Retail, Wholesale and Department Store Union v. Saskatchewan 1987*.

Similar to the RWDSU's arguments in *Dolphin Delivery* and relying on the Supreme Court's previous jurisprudence, in *Reference re Public Service Employee Relations Act (Alta) 1987* (hereafter *Alberta Reference*) the unions and the Government of Manitoba called for a broad and liberal interpretation of the new constitution (*Alberta Reference* 1987, Government of Manitoba Intervener Factum, 6–7, citing *Hunter et al. v. Southam Inc*). CUPE argued that a broad and liberal interpretation of the Charter would avoid "the austerity of tabulated legalism" that had characterized judicial interpretation of labour disputes in the past (as quoted in CUPE Appellant Factum, 6). CUPE also argued that the only way to give freedom of association real constitutional meaning was to interpret it in an "absolute sense" with no inherent legal limitations on collective actions (CUPE Appellant Factum, 5; see also arguments in Alberta Union of Provincial Employees [AUPE] Apellant Factum, 6). In a similar fashion, the Alberta Union of Provincial Employees argued that "freedom" under section 2(d) guaranteed that persons may associate without any constraint from the state (AUPE Appellant Factum, 8). Since labour relations statutes and international treaties had long guaranteed the right for individuals to organize and to strike, it was problematic not to recognize these long-established legal activities as constitutional (7-8). In essence, the unions believed that freedom of association included the action of combining for a common purpose and acting on such purpose. In the words of the AUPE:

> Combining the definition of "freedom" with that of "association" leads to this: Persons are not to be restrained from engaging in common

purposes or actions. At a *minimum*, anything which may be done by one person may be done by a combination of persons. The purpose of the guarantee of "freedom of association" is to provide a constitutional protection allowing persons to do together what they are permitted to do alone. Any act which may be lawfully done by one person may not be prohibited merely because it is to be done by a group of persons – unless the prohibition of the group activity can be justified by s. 1. (9–10; emphasis added)

The AUPE further argued that workers combining to form a union did so recognizing that the union's core function was to bargain and possibly strike in order "to advance a common cause" (*Alberta Reference* 1987, AUPE Appellant Factum, 12). Therefore, to somehow separate the act of combining from the actions of the collectivity would be to render associational rights virtually meaningless.

By contrast, almost every government in Canada took the position that freedom of association should be interpreted in a cautious and narrow manner. The Government of Alberta argued that to interpret "section 2 fundamental freedoms ... in an absolute fashion without limit to their theoretical scope" would frustrate good and accountable government (*Alberta Reference* 1987, Government of Alberta Respondent Factum, 4). The governments of Saskatchewan and Ontario furthered this argument by stating that freedom of association was not a freedom to influence the rights of others but only to "facilitate a free market of ideas, interchange of views and unfettered debate on topics of public interest in order to ensure that our society is truly free and democratic" (Government of Ontario Intervener Factum, 7–8; see also similar arguments in Government of Saskatchewan Intervener Factum). The Government of Newfoundland (Intervener Factum, 6–7) reaffirmed its belief that associational rights were essential in a liberal democracy but maintained that the collective "right to strike was essentially an economic right ... that the Charter was not intended to protect." The Government of Prince Edward Island (Intervener Factum, 6) argued that interpretation of section 2(d) must balance competing interests, and thus judges were required to give "consideration" for "the impact which a particular activity will have on the employer."

Meanwhile, the Government of Canada (Intervener Factum, 10–11) took a far more antagonistic approach, warning that reading a right to strike into the Charter would "arm collectivities with constitutional weaponry for compelling others to take notice of and to respond to them." The Government of Alberta (Respondent Factum, 21) further cautioned that constitutionalizing the right to strike would "be perverse" in that "it would stunt the evolutionary process of improvement of labour management relations procedures by freezing the dispute solving mechanisms in the strike-lockout state." Notwithstanding the fact that the government seemingly restricted the "evolutionary process of the improvement of labour management relations" by legislating away the right to strike, this argument regarding the balance of power between unions and management carried significant weight with the Supreme Court in its final decision.

The Supreme Court gave its authoritative decision on the right to strike in the *Alberta Reference* (1987). In determining the extent to which the Charter's guarantee of freedom of association protected the activities of labour unions, the majority of justices approached the question of union rights narrowly, reducing freedom of association to an individual right with little collective substance. In fact, the majority of justices approached the question of freedom of association in a similar manner to that of the Liberal and Progressive Conservative members of the Special Joint Committee that had developed the Charter. Justices Beetz, Le Dain, and La Forest (writing together), in a short brusque opinion, suggested that freedom of association could not be reduced simply to protecting unions (*Alberta Reference* 1987, paras. 141–44). Consistent with the rationale presented by various governments in Canada, these justices reasoned that constitutionalizing the right to strike undermined the purposes and meaning of association. They further reasoned that the judiciary was ill suited to enter into debates over the delicate balancing act of creating labour relations legislation. Finally, the three justices concluded that labour freedoms were, in fact, "modern" rights and not fundamental freedoms in the constitution (paras. 141–44).

Writing with the majority in a concurring decision, Justice McIntyre outlined a more thorough yet equally narrow definition of freedom of association. In his view, freedom of association was not a collective right at all, but one that could only be possessed by individuals (*Alberta Reference* 1987, para. 151). McIntyre reasoned that because freedom of association could only be interpreted through the lens of individual rights, it would not be prudent to grant additional rights to the institutions that people create to perform collective activities, such as bargaining collectively or striking. Building on this theory, McIntyre outlined several possible interpretations of freedom of association: (1) the right is limited to a right to associate with others in common pursuits or for certain purposes, (2) the right guarantees the freedom to engage collectively in those activities that are protected for each individual, and (3) the right stands for the principle that an individual is entitled to do collectively that which is possible to lawfully do alone and, "conversely, that individuals and organizations have no right to do in concert what is unlawful when done individually" (para. 163). McIntyre outlined three final variations, all of which he rejected because they were explicitly collective in nature and thus ran counter to his ideological position that rights of association were inherently based on the sovereign individual (paras. 164–66).[2]

Following this logic, McIntyre adopted a hybrid of the second and third approaches outlined above to determine that freedom of association included the ability to establish and maintain an organization and that the Charter only protected collective acts that individuals could perform lawfully (*Alberta Reference* 1987, para. 175). He reasoned that the constitutional right of association was only triggered when the individual was free to engage in an activity and yet was forbidden to engage in that same activity as a group. Given this narrow interpretation, McIntyre concluded that association did not offer a positive right to strike because there was no legal right for an individual to strike. According to McIntyre, modern contract law required that an individual who refused to fulfill the terms of his or her contract "has, by reason of the cessation of work, either breached or terminated his [or her] contract of employment" (para. 177). While this is not necessarily true in all employment relations (see Mandel 1994, 265), McIntyre suggested that freedom of association could not be used to elevate a collective right to strike when such actions were not available to most individuals. Finally, relying on the argument presented by the Government of Canada, McIntyre concluded that the right to strike was really an economic right (which the Charter does not protect) that would inevitably tip the scales of the postwar industrial relations system in favour of the unions. At the root of this argument was McIntyre's assumption that modern labour law is

> based upon a political and economic compromise between organized labour – a very powerful socio-economic force – on one hand, and employers of labour – an equally powerful socio-economic force – on the other. The balance between the two forces is delicate and the public-at-large depends for its security and welfare on the maintenance of that balance. (*Alberta Reference* 1987, para. 182)

In concluding that unions and employers are economic equals, McIntyre was driven more by political ideology than by fact (Mandel 1994, 266). Clearly, the government had used its sovereign powers to legislatively end collective bargaining and to deny the rights of workers to strike. In the private sector, employers routinely use their rights of property to hire and fire workers, bring in replacement workers, or close a business (see discussion of *Plourde v. Wal-Mart* 2009 in Chapter 5). No such powers have ever been available to workers or unions.

McIntyre's logic concerning the individual right of association fit well into the logic that employers, state officials, and lawyers used to limit workers' collective rights in the nineteenth and early twentieth centuries (Fudge 1988; Mandel 1994, 266–67; Panitch and Swartz 2003). Picking up on these themes in his dissenting opinion, Chief Justice Dickson (writing for himself and Justice Wilson) highlighted that the majority's rationale seemed drastically out of step with the postwar model of labour relations and the international legal norms that are at the centre of modern labour law. In what was Dickson's first minority decision in a Charter case, he adopted the principles of existing labour law and international human rights protection in coming to the conclusion, after much deliberation with his own law clerks, that the right to strike was included in the Charter protection of association. Dickson thus accepted the call from the unions that the Charter should be interpreted more broadly (Sharpe and Roach 2003, 358).

In Dickson's view, freedom of association only had meaning if it protected individuals from the "vulnerability of isolation and ensur[ed] the potential of effective participation in society" (*Alberta Reference* 1987, para. 22). Dickson thus rejected the argument that freedom of association was a narrow right protecting individual combinations but not the actions of the group itself. Using what his biographers claim was "unusually strong language" (Sharpe and Roach 2003, 361), Dickson chastised the "constitutive" approach to associational freedoms adopted by his colleagues (*Alberta Reference* 1987, paras. 79–80), stating that such a narrow interpretation of freedom of association was "legalistic, ungenerous, indeed vapid" (para. 81). In his view, democracy could only grow and prosper when collective freedoms had meaning attached to them.

Having rejected a purely individualistic reading of freedom of association, Dickson sought to breath new life into the collective nature of section 2(d) by championing a "purposive" or more meaningful approach to interpreting the fundamental freedoms in section 2 (citing his reasonings in *R. v. Big M Drug Mart Ltd* 1985, para. 117). Dickson argued that freedom of association is recognized in section 2(d) as "fundamental" because it acknowledges "the profoundly social nature of human endeavors and protect[s] the individual from state-enforced isolation in the pursuit of his or her ends" (*Alberta Reference* 1987, para. 86). Because the pursuit of social betterment often occurs through the exertion of human labour, Dickson recognized that it would be inappropriate to not include associational protection for economic activities. He further reasoned that in the pursuit of economic fairness, labour unions were created to overcome the inherent vulnerability of individuals in a competitive labour market. Therefore, Dickson argued, Canadian constitutional law should reflect the collective activities of labour unions and freedom of association should include a collective right to strike subject to important limitations relating to the preservation of public safety (para. 106). Citing the International Labour Organization's definition of freedom of association, Dickson concluded that police and fire services were clearly essential, but other government services that merely "inconvenienced ... the public" fell outside of "the ambit of the essential services justification for abrogating the freedom to strike" (para. 106). Ultimately, he reasoned that the Alberta government's legislation was too sweeping and thus did not meet the "reasonable limits" threshold outlined in section 1 of the Charter.

The same judicial rationale used in the *Alberta Reference* was used to dismiss the Charter claims of PSAC and the RWDSU. Dickson's deference to legislative discretion with regard to essential services led him to side with the majority in *RWDSU v. Saskatchewan* (1987). In *PSAC v. Canada* (1987), the chief justice's commanding defence of labour union rights was pushed aside, since he was willing to defer to Parliament's command over regulating the national economy (Sharpe and Roach 2003, 362). The overall conclusions from these cases suggested that the Charter offered little protection to working people seeking redress from government and employer coercion. What is more, even if Dickson's arguments in the *Alberta Reference* had reflected the majority judicial opinion, workers' collective rights had to be weighed according to the court's deference to government-defined essential services or the broad health of the capitalist economy through its section 1 arguments. In short, both the majority and minority decisions took the position that collective rights did not trump the political or legal constraints demanded by the postwar labour law regime's requirement of "responsible unionism."

The court's rationale in the labour trilogy cases was the subject of intense academic criticism (Arthurs 1988; Fudge 1988; Mandel 1994; Panitch and Swartz 2003). At the centre of this criticism was the notion that the judiciary "individualized" rights that worked against the collective interests of the working class. Summarizing this position, Harry Arthurs (1988, 28–29) lamented that "if protection for the liberty of individual action is seen as a presumptive good under the Charter, labour law will fall into disrepute since it deliberately subordinates individual interests to group interests."

Union leadership across the country made similar observations, universally condemning the labour trilogy. Daryl Bean, president of PSAC, complained, "It's a bad day for workers" (quoted in Bindman 1987), while the Confédération des syndicats nationaux's Gérald LaRose dismissed the perceived class biases of the Supreme Court justices, stating, "It appears for the Supreme Court, a union is no different than a bowling league or a bingo club" (quoted in Kumar and Ryan 1988, 78.) Alberta Federation of Labour president Dave Werlin defiantly condemned the ruling: "You can pass all the laws you want [but] the ruling means forced labour. You can't withdraw the right to strike. You can make strikes illegal but you can't deny the right to strike [because] we've always taken the position that the right to bargain collectively and to strike are inherent rights of the people" (quoted in Hardisty 1987). Margaret Ethier, president of the United Nurses of Alberta, confirmed Werlin's view, maintaining, "We do believe that nurses have the fundamental right to strike and that right cannot be taken away by law. Regardless of the legislation, the members of this union will decide when to go on strike and when not. That is basically the only strength that unions have" (quoted in Hardisty 1987).

The RWDSU's Len Wallace cried for twenty minutes after hearing the ruling, and CLC president Shirley Carr hyperbolically predicted that the court's anti-union biases would plunge Canada's system of labour relations into "utter chaos" (quoted in Bula 1987). Wayne Rogers, PSAC's Atlantic regional director, declared, "It's a setback for labour ... I don't think this was ever the intention when labour laws were being laid out for Canada" (quoted in Napier 1987). Ontario Federation of Labour president Gordon Wilson was perhaps the most defiant, bluntly criticizing the judges and stating, "The courts have seldom been the worker's friend. Nobody ever gave us the right to strike. We took it. We'll do it again if governments pass unjust laws" (quoted in Deverall 1987).

Labour Strategy after the Labour Trilogy
Less than a month after the labour trilogy rulings, the CLC's director of policy and planning, Ron Lang, produced a discussion paper on the Charter of Rights that attempted to put the loss in the best light possible. He began by arguing "that the impact of the Court's decision is neutral. We are no worse off now than we were before the Charter came into force" (CLC 1987, 2). Lang's bold argument reflected the view of many private sector union leaders who, the Quebec issue notwithstanding,

reasoned that because the Charter only applied to government actions, it was of little consequence for private sector labour relations. While public sector union leaders were clearly more interested in the Charter than their private sector counterparts, who outnumbered them on the CLC Executive Council, the CLC's cynical perspective on the Charter was bolstered by the general sense that, if anything, the labour trilogy rulings seemed to confirm that the Charter would not be interpreted by the Supreme Court in a manner that would enhance, let alone protect, rights and freedoms for labour unions. The report continued:

> The Congress needs to make a decision on the fundamental issue of whether, in light of this judgment, it wants to have the right to bargain collectively and the right to strike put in the Charter. Do we as a Congress want to give the Courts power to determine our future, or do we want this to remain a matter for the legislatures? (3)

Hinting at his own answer to this question, Lang asked: "In light of these decisions by the Supreme Court, is it not better for labour to re-affirm its support for electing NDP governments which will be good employers and which will also protect labour rights through sound labour legislation?" (CLC 1987, 4). In his conclusion, Lang argued, "If we want good employers and good governments which will give labour the legislative protection it needs, we need to stay the course and fight it out in the political arena. We know how to fight for our rights with the politicians, but the Courts have never been an area on which we could rely" (3).

Lang's report was no doubt influenced by a fairly steady surge in support for the federal NDP in the first half of 1987, which culminated in July with the party topping a federal public opinion poll for the first time in its history, sitting at 37 percent of the popular vote (CBC 1987). With the NDP riding high in the polls and union density at an all-time high (34.2 percent, according to Akyeampong 2004, 6) the Charter, and the expensive lawyers and unsympathetic judges that accompanied it, did not have much appeal for the leadership of the labour movement. Rather than work to entrench labour rights in the constitution or craft a concerted legal strategy to have labour rights read into the Charter by Supreme Court justices, CLC leaders redoubled their efforts to elect labour-friendly NDP governments.

This strategic decision did not go uncontested. Public sector unions, especially those who had never shared close ties with the NDP, continued to press for constitutionalized labour rights. This is hardly surprising given that public sector unions during this period were witnessing the passage of laws that undermined workers' rights and freedoms in their sector (Panitch and Swartz 2003). PSAC, in particular, was interested in pursuing Charter guarantees that would protect the right to organize, bargain collectively, and strike. This tension became apparent when CLC representatives presenting the Congress's position on the proposed Meech Lake Accord seemed unable to agree on whether the Charter should be amended to protect the collective rights of workers. When asked by Liberal committee member André Ouellet to comment on the recent "labour trilogy" decision and to explain what could be done to better protect the association right of workers, CLC vice-president Dick Martin responded that the Congress "wanted to comment directly on what was in the Meech Lake Accord rather than be here proposing substantial amounts of amendments." Martin added that the CLC would "be most happy to be back if the committee and the government sees fit to start the process over and consider our concerns about the right of association" (quoted in Special Joint Committee 1987, 10:12). Martin's answer obviously did not sit well with Ron Lang, the CLC's director of policy and planning who felt the need to clarify the Congress's position on labour rights in the Charter by suggesting that

> there is a fundamental point on the question of enshrining labour rights in the Charter of Rights. The question is whether they should be enshrined in a Charter of Rights, thereby handing the power to interpret our rights to a court, or whether those rights should remain silent in the Charter. We will fight it out with the politicians provincially and federally on election day. (10:12)

Executive Vice-President Nancy Riche, who confirmed the CLC's judicial phobia in a response to a question from NDP MP Pauline Jewett, later supported Lang. "As much as we are not crazy about a lot of the politicians who are in power across the country," Riche said, "we would still want to take our chances with the political leaders and the lobby effort and the pressure we could bring to bear on getting change as it affects the trade union movement, as opposed to leaving it to the courts" (quoted in Special Joint Committee 1987, 10:17).

Although the CLC leadership did not want to officially entrench labour rights in the constitution, some Congress affiliates continued to push for them. In their respective presentations to the Special Joint Committee, both PSAC and the United Electrical, Radio, and Machine Workers of Canada (UEW) argued explicitly for amendments to the Charter that would extend constitutional protection to collective bargaining, picketing, and strike activity (PSAC 1987, 48; UEW 1987). Comparing the decentralizing trends in the Meech Lake Accord with the recommendation by the Royal Commission on the Economic Union and Development Prospects for Canada (the Macdonald Commission) for a Canada–United States free trade agreement, the UEW called for a "labour bill of rights" to protect the interests of working people. The UEW believed that the Supreme Court's interpretation of the Charter had led the court to ignore "the collective rights of labour," and now that interpretation amounted to nothing more than a Charter "right of individuals not to participate" (UEW 1987, 111–12). Equally concerned with the decentralization trends in Meech, PSAC argued that a constitutional amendment to section 2(d) that "explicitly recognizes freedom to organize and bargain collectively" would protect working peoples' collective rights against intrusions by government and the courts (PSAC 1987, 48–49).

When asked to explain why some in the labour movement had demonstrated a newfound interest in constitutional reform, Fred Pomeroy, president of the Communication and Electrical Workers of Canada, confessed, "I think we goofed as a labour movement, we should probably have paid a lot more attention to the Charter than we did" (quoted in Kumar and Ryan 1988, 222).

In an effort to correct this perceived mistake, a number of union organizations sent resolutions to be debated at the 1988 CLC convention advocating a constitutionally entrenched bill of rights for labour. A resolution submitted by the St. Catharines and District Labour Council read as follows:

> Whereas the Canadian Constitution has no provision for a Bill of Rights for labour;
>
> Whereas there is an increased use by the state, of the courts and police to break strikes and thereby weaken the labour movement; and
>
> Whereas governments are increasingly introducing legislation which interferes with workers' rights to organize and bargain collectively;
>
> Therefore be it resolved that the Canadian Labour Congress initiate a coordinated program to secure a Bill of Rights for labour enshrined in the Constitution; and Be it further resolved that included in a Bill of Rights for labour is the guarantee of unfettered right to organize, to bargain collectively, to strike and to picket. (CLC 1989)

The fact that neither this resolution nor similar resolutions reached the convention floor did not deter other labour organizations from trying again in later years. PSAC president Daryl Bean, in particular, continued pursuing his union's 1987 demands for a workers' bill of rights. However, as the following passage from the minutes of the April 1990 CLC Executive Committee meeting demonstrates, his colleagues at the CLC did not share his enthusiasm:

> Brother Bean explained that the Legislative and Government Employees' Committee has some Resolutions dealing with Workers' Bill of Rights and wondered how the Executive Committee felt about any of these Resolutions reaching the floor. Several members of the committee felt that if possible, it should be avoided. (CLC 1990a, 4)

Most private sector union leaders could not bring themselves to make a reformed bill of rights a priority. They perceived such an instrument as having no benefit for private sector workers and only a marginal one for workers in the public sector – and even the latter was doubtful. Their suspicion with regard to a bill of rights for labour was very much influenced by the labour movement's well entrenched distrust of judges and the courts.

Professional Institute, *Lavigne,* and the Right Not to Associate

The labour trilogy rulings only confirmed organized labour's worst suspicions about the Supreme Court's bias against workers' collective rights. Subsequent Charter decisions added fuel to the fire. When the federal government transferred responsibility for health care services to the Government of the Northwest Territories in 1986, the Professional Institute of the Public Service of Canada (PIPSC) applied to represent its former members under the territory's *Public Service Act* (*Professional Institute of the Public Service of Canada v. Northwest Territories (Commissioner),* 1990 [*PIPSC v. NWT*]). Unlike similar legislation in other jurisdictions, section 42(1) of the *Public Service Act* allowed the government to effectively sanction which unions or "employees' associations" it would enter into negotiations with. The government defended the act on the basis that it was its legislative prerogative to create the conditions under which collective bargaining took place (*PIPSC v. NWT* 1990, Government of NWT Respondent Factum, paras. 32–39). In the NWT, bargaining fell to the NWT Public Service Association (NWTPSA), which, PIPSC argued, gave the association a "statutory monopoly in collective bargaining [that] infringes the guarantee of freedom of association [recognized] ... in the *Alberta Reference*" (PIPSC Appellant Factum, para. 44). PIPSC believed that section 42(1) restricted which unions could act as collective bargaining agents and thus violated the Charter's *individual* guarantee of freedom of association. The union initially won its case at the Superior Court, but that judgment was overturned on appeal.

In a 4–3 decision handed down in 1990, the Supreme Court rejected PIPSC's claim that the *Public Service Act* violated section 2(d) of the Charter. Writing for himself, LaForest, L'Heureux-Dubé, and Dickson, Justice Sopinka noted that because collective bargaining itself was not protected by the Charter's guarantee of freedom of association, a restriction on which unions were able to engage in collective bargaining could not be considered a violation of section 2(d). Sopinka further argued that the legislation in question "has no effect on the *existence* of the Institute; and it is equally plain that, as a result of the *Alberta Reference*, the activity for which constitutional protection is sought (collective bargaining for working conditions) satisfies neither of the tests for protected activity" (*PIPSC v. NWT* 1990, 405; emphasis in original). Sopinka was also unsympathetic to the "legislative monopoly" argument, suggesting that nothing in the act restricted the union from existing; rather, the act was simply "the means by which the territorial government has chosen to recognize the union or unions with which it will bargain collectively" (407).

If Sopinka's rationale seemed to dance around the fact that PIPSC had been denied the right to act as a collective bargaining agent by legislative fiat, Chief Justice Dickson's reasoning for rejecting a constitutional right to bargain was even more bizarre. In his *Alberta Reference* dissent, Dickson had mounted a fairly substantive defence of workers' collective right to strike but had managed to win over only Justice Wilson to his rationale. In the *PIPSC* appeal, however, Dickson represented the swing vote between those who saw no constitutional right to bargain and those, like Justice Cory (writing for himself, Wilson, and Gonthier), who recognized that "a union can only exist if it is allowed to bargain collectively. That is the *raison d'être* of a union" (382). Seemingly ignoring his own passionate defence of the collective right to strike in the *Alberta Reference*, Dickson "reluctantly" (374) sided with the majority in *PIPSC*, explaining that the labour trilogy decisions had rejected the notion of collective bargaining as a constitutional right. Similar to his decision in *Harrison v. Carswell* (1976), Dickson refused to step outside of precedent and ruled against the unions (Sharpe and Roach 2003, 364). The *PIPSC* decision seemingly represented yet another nail in the constitutional coffin for the labour movement.

Yet while organized labour was clearly losing the war in the judicial arena, the labour movement's efforts in the political arena were paying significant dividends. Between September 1990 and October 1991, the NDP formed majority provincial governments in Ontario, British Columbia, and Saskatchewan and appeared poised to compete in forming the next federal government. But even as the labour movement was retreating from the judicial arena, anti-union crusaders in the business community were determined to drag unions back into the courtroom, undoubtedly motivated by the Supreme Court's hostility towards constitutionally protecting the collective zones of legal toleration in Canada's system of labour relations.

The notorious *Lavigne v. Ontario Public Service Employees Union* (1991) case was a long time in the making. Business had made several attempts to use the Charter to limit union freedoms in both the public sector (*Baldwin v. B.C.G.E.U.* 1986) and the construction industry (*Pruden Building Ltd., v. Construction and General Workers' Union, Local 92* 1985; *Arlington Crane Service Ltd. v. Ontario (Minister of Labour)* 1988), as well as in the private sector more generally (*Bhindi v. BC Projectionists' Local* 1986; *Metropolitan Stores (MTS) Ltd. v. Manitoba Food and commercial Workers Local 832* 1990). A more promising case for business emerged in the early 1980s from a disgruntled college teacher named Mervin "Merv" Lavigne, who worked in the public sector at the School of Mines in Haileybury, Ontario. Lavigne believed that the Rand-like formula in sections 51, 52, and 53 of Ontario's *Colleges Collective Bargaining Act* (CCBA) forced him to associate with the Ontario Public Service Employees Union (OPSEU). Under the *CCBA*, Lavigne was not required to join the union (which he refused to do), but he was legally required to pay union dues. Lavigne had been a Liberal candidate who had come into direct conflict with the union when he crossed a picket line during a legal strike in 1984 (Clancy et al. 1985, 6). Lavigne objected to the fact that a portion of "his" union dues were used to support causes not directly related to collective bargaining, causes that included support for the NDP, striking mine workers in Britain, nuclear disarmament campaigns, and abortion rights.

At the centre of Lavigne's legal challenge was his claim that the agency shop requirements (i.e., mandatory dues) in the *CCBA* violated his individual right to expression and his right not to associate.[3] Given that his grievances originated in the public sector and were tied directly to a union's political activities, Lavigne was recruited and then financed by anti-union crusaders in the National Citizens Coalition (NCC; Clancy et al. 1985, 7), a libertarian lobby group committed to the "defence and promotion of free enterprise [and] free speech" (national citizens.ca). The NCC's vice president, David Somerville, publicly argued that the coalition's support of Mr. Lavigne was to set "a strict precedent that would restrict unions to what they were originally envisaged as – collective bargaining organizations" (quoted in Slotnick 1985a). In its fundraising letters to supporters, however, the NCC divulged that the Lavigne challenge's political goal was to "hit at the heart of the left wing, not only in Ontario but across Canada as well" (Kershaw 1985).

The NCC's determined attempt to strike a blow against organized labour and the political Left was not lost on interested observers. The *Globe and Mail*'s labour reporter explained that "a favorable decision by the courts on Mr. Lavigne's application would send shudders throughout the entire union movement because of the fetters it would place on union activities" (List 1985, B3). So nervous was the labour movement about Lavigne that CLC president Dennis McDermott called on labour as early as 1985 to start thinking proactively about how to engage with the Charter:

> If there are two or three cases that could set a precedent, we have to make sure we pursue the best one, instead of having everybody running off to court on the advice of their own lawyer. We could have a proliferation of cases right across the country. Let's face it, the next 10 or 15 years are going to be a lawyer's banquet. The Charter was put together by lawyers. It will be interpreted by lawyers. So it's important that we control, or try to, how we react to this sort of thing. ("CLC Decides" 1985, 11)

Reflecting McDermott's concerns, the Canadian Union of Public Employees (CUPE) warned its members that the individualizing influences of the Charter might undermine the collective strength of their union. Pointing indirectly to the *Lavigne* challenge and its attack on the Rand formula, CUPE warned that it was conceivable that "some people will seek to make the case that individuals now have the right ... to opt out from collective decisions and collective actions" (CUPE 1985, 8–9). Meanwhile, Ontario Federation of Labour (OFL) president Cliff Pilkey chastised the "right-wing band of ideologues" in the NCC, stating that the Charter might become a weapon for business to limit labour unions from engaging in political activity (quoted in Slotnick 1985b).

The Ontario High Court of Justice's decision in July 1986 gave added momentum to the NCC (*Re Lavigne and Ontario Public Service Employees Union et al.* 1986). In deciding in favour of Lavigne, Justice White concluded that mandatory dues requirements in public sector (and perhaps private sector) collective bargaining agreements represented a violation of individual rights of association. In coming to this conclusion, White had to jump two legal hurdles that had, somewhat ironically, hindered labour unions from acquiring constitutional rights in the past. The first hurdle concerned the application of section 32, the "governmental action" clause that triggered Charter review. In *Dolphin Delivery*, the Supreme Court had taken a rather narrow view of section 32 of the Charter in ruling that state institutions like courts or the common law (as created by government and judges) did not constitute government action. In this case, White had to extend the rationale for "government action" not just to the college's bargaining agent (the Ontario Council of Regents for Colleges of Applied Arts and Technology) but also to the decisions of the union, which were clearly made by a private entity. White determined that the independent bargaining agent constituted government action because the mandatory dues clause in the act (s. 53) was created and enforced by government (*Re Lavigne and OPSEU* 1986, 74). Since union finances were tied to government action, White reasoned, the union's political actions were also subject to Charter review.

White then had to tackle the thorny legal question regarding rights of association and labour union activity. For White, freedom of association included both the right to combine together for a common cause and the liberty to freely choose (or not to choose) to associate with like-minded individuals. White argued that one's freedom of association could be infringed even if one was not closely identified "with a group or cause." In other words, freedom of association also included the right not to associate (*Re Lavigne and OPSEU* 1986, 100). Reading into the Charter a clause that did not exist, White then proceeded to dismiss Justice Rand's long-standing legal principle protecting unions against "free riders" reaping the benefits of unionization without financially supporting the union's collective interests. Contrary to four decades of common law and legislative reform, White then stepped back to nineteenth-century legal reasoning to conclude that any form of compelled or "forced" financial support to a union represented a violation of individual freedoms (Etherington 1987, 3). White argued that it was not "necessary for the collective agreement to require Mr. Lavigne to join the union for there to be a forced association; it is the compelled combining of financial resources that has the effect of forcing Mr. Lavigne to associate with the Union" (*Re Lavigne and OPSEU* 1986, 102). White therefore ruled in favour of Lavigne and deferred to legal council to submit recommendations for appropriate remedies. A full year later, he constructed a convoluted formula that attempted to separate union dues into two categories: dues that supported collective bargaining (which included support for striking workers) and dues used for political purposes (which included support for the NDP or pro-choice organizations). All funds not directly tied to collective bargaining, White concluded, could only be collected on a voluntary, "opt-in" basis (*Re Lavigne and Ontario Public Service Employees Union et al.*, 1987).

Reaction to Lavigne's victory at the High Court was swift. For labour leaders, their worst fears of the Charter and the courts' pro-business leanings had been realized. CLC president Shirley Carr said she was "shocked by this decision, which runs counter to all the principles Canadian society and the Canadian labor movement have pursued over the past 100 years and more. We cannot and will not accept this decision as final" (quoted in "Political Use" 1986). Carr felt that White's decision challenged not only the structures of postwar labour law but also the very foundation of modern unionism. Some legal commentators agreed, suggesting that White's reasoning would inevitably impose "judicial values and assumptions" in determining legitimate and illegitimate union activities (Etherington 1987, 3–4). However much truth there might have been in these views, there was certainly concern that White had handed employers and anti-union crusaders a significant legal tool to dismantle labour unions. In fact, Colin Brown, president and founder of the NCC, believed that White's decision represented a victory for all workers, proving "that in our system the little guy can still get justice even when he's up against the power of big unionism" (quoted in "Labour to Fight" 1986).

The unions found a more sympathetic interpretation of industrial legality and the constitution in the Ontario Court of Appeal (*Lavigne v. OPSEU* 1989), which was strongly critical of White's interpretations of sections 32 and 2(d) of the Charter. While the justices were willing to extend the section 32 "government action" clause to the Council of Regents, it did not follow that the actions of the union fell under the same section. In fact, the court criticized White's reasoning that the Rand formula somehow extended "government action" to private parties. Here, the Court of Appeal concluded, "The mere making of the funds available to the union by the Council without direction of any kind as to use does not convert the union's expenditures into governmental action. The use of the dues by OPSEU was a private activity by a private organization and hence beyond the reach of the Charter" (14). Having dismissed Lavigne's appeal on section 32 grounds, the Court of Appeal briefly commented on section 2(d) and Lavigne's argument regarding the right not to associate. Using the labour trilogy as their guide, the justices concluded that freedom of association was a right that pertained to individuals but could only be exercised by a plurality seeking a common interest. As a result, the Rand formula could not be interpreted as limiting Lavigne's right not to associate. He was free, for instance, to oppose vocally any or all of the political causes supported by the union (24). The justices therefore concluded that a mandatory dues requirement was simply a financial agreement among union members regarding services rendered.

Having breathed a sigh of relief, the unions braced themselves for the inevitable appeal. When the Supreme Court agreed to hear the case, union lawyers laid out a fairly consistent narrative on the importance of the Rand formula to contemporary structures of industrial legality. Perhaps not surprisingly, all of the unions maintained that the use of dues by a union is a private matter and therefore beyond the reach of the Charter (*Lavigne v. OPSEU* 1991, CLC/OFL Intervener Factum, para 3–7). The unions acknowledged that were the Charter to apply, the majoritarian and exclusivity principles at the centre of Canada's system of labour relations recognized that unions were not "'purely' voluntary organizations" (OPSEU Respondent Factum, para. 17). To be sure, an employee who opposed a unionization drive but came out on the losing side of the certification vote still had to abide by the decision of the majority. Yet OPSEU submitted that "unions are not "purely" involuntary organizations either" (para. 17). By their nature, unions are democratic associations that are organized and governed by union members themselves. This system of internal union democracy suggests that individual members are not "coerced" into association with the union. If an individual chooses to oppose the decisions of the union, they are entirely free to do so. That form of democratic protection is at the very centre of Canada's system of industrial legality, which balances the need for individual dissent with the "need to empower workers" collectively in negotiations with their employer (NUPGE Respondent Factum, para 24). The Canadian Civil Liberties Association (CCLA) built on this argument, critiquing Justice White's decision that union dues should be separated into collective bargaining and political funds (CCLA Intervener Factum, para 9-10). Not only would a remedy of this nature undermine the association rights of the majority of union members, but it would also force judges to act as *de facto* stewards of a union's finances. Such a scheme would pose a "significant risk" to the independence of judges, because they would be forced to police an arbitrary dividing line between dues used for purely "collective bargaining," on the one hand, and political or social action, on the other (para 14).

For the first time in a Charter case, the governments of Canada, Ontario, and Quebec sided with the unions in defending the long-established regime of industrial legality (*Lavigne v. OPSEU* 1991, Government of Canada Intervener Factum, para 9-25; Government of Ontario Intervener Factum; Government of Quebec Intervener Factum). While this alliance was purely self-serving (they were simply defending their own legislation), the governments argued that section 32 did not apply to the affairs of private entities, including labour unions or organizations like the College of Regents. The governments argued that in the event that the Charter did apply, financial contributions to an organization could not be equated with forced or coercive association. If this were the case, the Government of Canada worried, "the payment of taxes could be seen as 'associating' with government objectives" (Government of Canada Intervener Factum, para 38). All the legislation did, the Government of Ontario claimed, was compel a certain bargaining relationship once certain conditions had been met (Government of Ontario Intervener Factum, para 10-11). Indeed, nothing in the legislation required Lavigne to join or support the union. Such actions were purely voluntary.

Lavigne's arguments sought to defend Justice White's reasoning in the trial court. Relying heavily on American jurisprudence and the anti-union sentiments in the *Alberta Reference* (*Lavigne v. OPSEU* 1991, Lavigne Appellant Factum, para 48-52), Lavigne argued strongly for a freedom "from" compelled association. His lawyers argued that freedom "to" associate only had legitimacy in the absence of coercion or constraint. If one is forced to join or financially support an organization with which one does not want to associate, then there is no real individual freedom. That being the case, embedded in section 2(d) of the Charter "are complimentary components of the broader concept of association and it would be illogical to give effect to one but not the other" (para 49). Since government compelled association through sections 51–53 of the *CCBA*, Lavigne asserted that his individual rights had been violated.

The Supreme Court reached its conclusion in *Lavigne* in early 1991. Recognizing the complexity of the decision, the court was split on the questions pertaining to section 32 – on the right not to associate and, ultimately, on whether Canada's regime of industrial legality withstood Charter scrutiny. Writing for the majority, Justice LaForest (writing for himself, Sopinka, and Gonthier, with McLachlin concurring) ruled that the *CCBA* actually violated Lavigne's right not to associate but upheld the collective bargaining scheme based on their interpretation of section 1, the reasonable limits clause. Justice Wilson, writing for the minority (herself and L'Heureux-Dubé, with Cory concurring) ruled that the *CCBA* did not violate Lavigne's right to not associate and thus ruled against Lavigne (*Lavigne v. OPSEU* 1991, 223).

Having reinforced the individual nature of association within Canada's labour relations framework while reading in the right to not associate, LaForest nevertheless upheld the *CCBA* on grounds that it contributed to industrial peace and stability. In fact, Laforest was in agreement with Justice Wilson and L'Heureux-Dube, who concluded that the Rand formula in the *CCBA*, is

to promote industrial peace through the encouragement of collective bargaining. It does not purport to align those subject to its
operation with the union or any of its activities, since it specifically provides for dissent by stipulating that no member of the bargaining unit is required to become a member of the union. (*Lavigne
v. OPSEU* 1991, 216)

Implicit in Laforest's reasoning is the idea that the boundaries of constraint imposed by the Rand formula equally benefit labour and business and therefore must be weighed against the individual's right not to
associate. The court also ruled that the union was free to spend its dues
without government restriction. Justice LaForest explained:

The integrity and status of unions as democracies would be jeopardized if the government's policy was, in effect, that unions can spend
their funds as they choose according to majority vote provided the
majority chooses to make expenditures the government thinks are
in the interest of the union's membership. It is, therefore, for the
union itself to decide, by majority vote, which causes or organizations it will support in the interests of favourably influencing the
political, social, and economic environment in which particular
instances of collective bargaining and labour-management dispute
resolution will take place. (335)

With that conclusion, LaForest dismissed Lavigne's challenge and
upheld the Ontario government's legislation. As part of the remedy, the
court ordered Lavigne – and by extension, the NCC – to pay the union's
legal costs, which, by several estimates, totalled $1 million (Vienneau
1991).

OFL president Gordon Wilson "heaved a great sigh of relief" after
the decision was released (Lajoie 1991). In recognizing the importance
of the Rand formula to modern labour relations, the Supreme Court
refused to be drawn into what was an internal union fight. But since
the court sided with the government (as well as the unions), *Lavigne*
was, at best, a pyrrhic victory for the union movement in that judicial
acceptance of existing legal rights was weighed against the question of

economic and political stability in the form of labour peace. This situation overwhelmingly benefitted business and the state. Furthermore, the decision in *Lavigne* did nothing to advance the interests of organized labour; it merely upheld the status quo.

Notwithstanding the narrow union victory in *Lavigne*, right-wing commentators interpreted it as a substantial victory for the Left. The NCC portrayed the ruling as a fundamental "blow against freedom" and stated that the coalition was committed to creating a new fund to fight for the protection of "the victims of forced unionization" (York 1991). Ian Brodie (2002, 70–71) later grumbled that the Supreme Court's decision to impose costs on Lavigne (and by extension, the NCC) was designed to punish conservative business interveners.

While organized labour unquestionably dodged a bullet with the *Lavigne* decision, overall, the first era of Charter challenges only confirmed the union movement's enduring fears about the judiciary's perceived anti-union bias. The Supreme Court's narrow interpretation of freedom of association meant that workers' collective rights would not be recognized in the constitution. In fact, the labour movement was so distrustful of the judiciary that in the wake of the *Alberta Reference* decision, the leadership of the CLC told a parliamentary committee on constitutional reform that it was not interested in constitutionalizing labour rights for fear of how the courts would interpret them.

Admittedly, some labour organizations began openly questioning the wisdom of the CLC's approach to the Charter, leading them to propose amendments to the constitution that would include explicit rights for labour or a separate workers' bill of rights. These efforts proved unsuccessful, however. The dominant view within the labour movement continued to be that a constitutional, rights-based approach to defending and enhancing workers' rights was naïve at best and dangerous at worst, especially given the Supreme Court's track record in the first era of Charter challenges. The terrain, however, was clearly beginning to shift.

A Legal Response to Neoliberalism   **4**

At the beginning of the 1990s, workers and their unions were facing multiple economic and political crises that were compounded by a decade of losses in court. The intensification of neoliberalism through international capital mobility and the passage of the Canada–United States Free Trade Agreement (later extended to Mexico through the North American Free Trade Agreement) placed downward pressure on unionized industrial workers, leading to tensions between private sector employers and unions. In Ontario and Quebec, the recession of the early 1990s intensified the process of deindustrialization in auto, steel, and chemical manufacturing, leading to increased job losses. Meanwhile, from coast to coast, workers in resource extraction industries faced greater levels of unemployment due to an intensification of the work process through automation, and public sector workers faced growing threats of privatization and contracting out. All of these changes led to increased pressure on public finances, which in turn led to rigid austerity programs and a dramatic scaling back of the welfare state at both the federal and provincial levels by the end of the decade (Evans and Smith 2015; McBride 2001; Teeple 2000).

Though acute, the economic context of the early 1990s was, in many ways, overshadowed by the interrelated political context, particularly multiple efforts by federal and provincial governments to amend the constitution in an effort to preserve national unity. While labour organizations had strategically sidestepped opportunities to participate in processes of constitutional reform in the 1980s, the early 1990s offered unions yet another opportunity to push for constitutionally protected labour rights. Such a course of action, however, was highly divisive, pitting different segments of the labour movement against one another based on competing visions of Canada's constitutional future and different interpretations and understandings of the role and utility of the courts and rights-based documents.

In order to provide greater context for the debates that were emerging within the labour movement, it is useful at the outset of this chapter to review how labour lawyers and labour scholars interpreted the first decade of Charter decisions in the realm of labour law. After the judicial defeats in the 1980s, Brian Etherington (1992, 685) usefully classified mainstream legal observers of the Supreme Court's constitutional labour jurisprudence into three categories: liberal romantics, realist skeptics, and pragmatic pluralists. While romantics such as David Beatty seemed thoroughly discredited by the courts' labour decisions in the 1980s and early 1990s, committed pragmatic pluralists such as Paul Weiler were happy to see the courts defer labour relations issues to the legislatures and labour boards, where he felt they belonged (Weiler 1990, 117). For more hardened critics (or realist skeptics), however, the prospect of further constitutional engagement was not only a waste of resources; it was based on a fundamental misunderstanding of the structural place of judges and the courts within the capitalist state. For the skeptics, while courts remained institutionally independent from government, the labour trilogy, discussed in the previous chapter, validated the view that the vast majority of Supreme Court justices viewed workers' collective rights as antagonistic to the private rights of individuals and businesses (Panitch and Swartz 2003). Moreover, skeptics argued that the Supreme Court's labour cases had simply demonstrated that the Charter was a document grounded in nineteenth-century liberal thinking, one that focused on negative liberties at the expense of positive freedoms (Hutchinson and Petter 1988). For some, it was taken as a given that judicial training in common law traditions created a structural predilection for individual property rights that were antagonistic towards collective rights for workers (Arthurs 1988; Fudge 1988; Fudge and Glasbeek 1992b, 45–70; Drache and Glasbeek 1992, 104–5; McIntosh 1989). Summarizing the failures of the labour movement in court throughout the 1980s, Harry Glasbeek (1990, 18) went so far as to suggest that the courts' Charter rulings demonstrated nothing more than long-standing "anti–working class biases."

If the courts did indeed suffer from an anti-union bias, some elements of the labour movement reasoned that the solution lay in amending the constitution to explicitly recognize labour rights. They argued that this option had the potential to at least strengthen the institutions of the Wagner/PC 1003 model of industrial relations in order to help labour to withstand the crisis. For others, however, the most viable response was to throw labour's resources behind its traditional social democratic ally, the NDP. The unprecedented election of NDP provincial governments in three provinces and one territory in the early 1990s (together representing a majority of Canadians at the provincial level) initially offered the labour movement hope that the neoliberal tide would subside, but it did not take long for New Democrats to jettison key social democratic policies and adopt austerity programs of their own, thus alienating labour and throwing into question the logic of the party-union relationship (Carroll and Ratner 2005; Savage 2010). As we demonstrate in this chapter, both the electoral route and the constitutional reform route failed to advance the cause of workers in any significant way.

We begin by describing the failed effort to enshrine a social charter in the constitution as part of the Charlottetown Accord. In the wake of that constitutional defeat, organized labour's strategic approach to Charter litigation was transformed by a shifting political landscape, which saw the ascendancy of neoliberalism and the decline of social democratic electoralism. We argue that this political dynamic is key to understanding the rapprochement between the labour movement and the Supreme Court. Indeed, by the end of the 1990s, some segments of the labour movement, facing an increasingly hostile political and economic climate, gravitated back to the Supreme Court in search of an ally. A number of minor Charter victories for labour in the late 1990s and early 2000s seemingly validated the decision of unions to give the

Charter a second chance. We review those cases with a view to demonstrating how the expanded zone of legal toleration gave organized labour renewed hope that the Charter could not only protect but also expand workers' rights and freedoms.

A Social Charter for Labour

The narrow victory in the *Lavigne* case renewed calls within the labour movement for increased constitutional protection for workers' rights, and the Mulroney government's new round of constitutional reform in the early 1990s provided organized labour with several opportunities to advance proposals to entrench new forms of labour rights in Canada's constitution.

After the death of the Meech Lake Accord in 1990, the Mulroney government, determined to overcome the constitutional impasse, committed itself to developing a new constitutional proposal through a more open and participatory process. While Quebec's Bélanger-Campeau Commission deliberated, the federal government's Citizens' Forum on the Future of Canada was being launched in the rest of Canada. The Forum held a series of unstructured public consultations across the country in an attempt to involve ordinary Canadians in the process of constitutional reform. At the same time, a Special Joint Committee of the House and Senate reviewed the process for amending the constitution. Several provinces in English Canada launched their own initiatives. The Nova Scotia Working Committee on the Constitution, the New Brunswick Commission on Canadian Federalism, the Select Committee on Ontario in Confederation, the Manitoba Constitutional Task Force, and the Constitutional Reform Task Force of Alberta collected the views of thousands of organizations and individuals interested in constitutional reform.

At the behest of the Quebec Federation of Labour (QFL), the Canadian Labour Congress (CLC) initially resisted participating in the Citizens' Forum on the Future of Canada, opting instead to take a wait-and-see approach (CLC 1990b). Some CLC affiliates, however, could not help but be drawn into the unfolding constitutional debate. As part of a joint presentation to the 1991–92 Renewed Canada Committee, the National Union of Public and General Employees (NUPGE) and the Public Service Alliance of Canada (PSAC) criticized the labour movement for its non-involvement in previous rounds of constitutional reform. NUPGE president James Clancy admitted to committee members that he was "bitter" that organized labour "did not involve itself in the debate in those early years" (PSAC/NUPGE presentation to the 1991–1992 Renewed Canada Committee, 47). Similarly, PSAC president Daryl Bean told the committee that the CLC's non-involvement in the patriation process in 1981 "was a mistake then and I still believe it was a mistake" (49). Contrary to the CLC's position in 1987, these unions argued in favour of constitutionalized labour rights.

Amid the contradictory messages about the labour movement's vision for constitutional reform, the CLC felt forced into entering the constitutional debate, despite protests from the QFL. The political dynamic that had allowed the QFL to prevent the CLC from wading into the debate in the early 1980s no longer held sway. The determination of affiliates like PSAC and NUPGE to break ranks with the Congress and the presence of three NDP provincial governments at the constitutional table fundamentally changed the political equation for most labour leaders in English Canada. In April 1991, in an effort to influence the content of the new constitutional package, the Congress decided to establish "points of discussion in cooperation with the NDP" (CLC 1991a). The CLC established a sub-committee consisting of NUPGE president James Clancy, Canadian Auto Workers (CAW) president Bob White, Canadian Brotherhood of Railway, Transport, and General Workers (CBRT) president Jim Hunter, and Canadian Union of Public Employees (CUPE) national president Jeff Rose to develop a consensus position on the constitutional question (Vallée 1991). The sub-committee established a number of guiding principles for the labour movement to consider based on a report drafted by Shirley Carr's assistant, Émile Vallée. The guiding principles included reaffirmation of Quebec's right to self-determination; support for asymmetrical federalism; support for Aboriginal self-government and self-determination; redistribution of constitutional powers that "would build toward a social democratic society"; and the provision for the constitutional recognition of social, economic, and environmental rights (CLC 1991b). The latter demand, which would take the form of a social charter, became the CLC's main constitutional focus as the process of reform took shape. The social charter, as proposed by the Ontario NDP government, was designed to constitutionalize a statement of political and social objectives that would protect workers' rights, universal health care, access to education and housing, and other social programs. Unlike the Charter of Rights and Freedoms, the social charter would promote the notion of positive economic and social rights for workers.

Almost a year passed before the CLC made its 4 February 1992 presentation to the Special Joint Committee on a Renewed Canada. By then, it was clear that the Congress's ringing endorsement of a social charter was more symbolic than substantive. Neither the CLC nor its affiliates who promoted the concept of a social charter were very specific about how it would work or how it might be enforced. Matt James (2006, 108) correctly argues that

> while other activists promoted the social charter as a tool for confronting neoliberal governments in the courts, trade union representatives viewed the idea in a more symbolic light. When asked by a sceptical committee member how a social charter would "create more jobs, provide better housing, or do all the good things you see forthcoming from it," [NUPGE president James] Clancy shrugged that it would "not solve all the ills of the world tomorrow," and that there were "difficulties [with] the whole question of enforceability and so forth."

Union leaders, it seemed, were content to see the social charter serve an emblematic rather than a legal function, arguing that it would play an important role in Canadian political life because it would act as the social conscience of future federal and provincial governments. In addition to providing the labour movement with a platform to highlight why basic principles regarding union organizing and free collective bargaining were worthy of constitutional recognition, crafting the CLC's submission to the committee around the social charter also helped to bridge the gap between private and public sector union leaders and brought the Ontario-centric CLC in line with the main constitutional policy objective of the Ontario NDP government. It is worth noting, however, that the CLC's support for the social charter placed it at odds with the Harcourt NDP government in British Columbia, which rejected the Rae government's proposal for a justiciable social charter on the basis that it would shift too much power to the judiciary (Walkom 1994, 230). Finally, a focus on the social charter was also one of the few useful rhetorical tools available to the labour movement in the face of anti-Mulroney working-class opposition to the Charlottetown Accord (CLC 1992c).

After months of public consultation and intergovernmental negotiations, former prime minister Joe Clark, now minister of constitutional affairs, presented the final draft of the Charlottetown Accord on 28 August 1992. The Accord enjoyed the support of the prime minister, every provincial premier, both territorial leaders, and the Assembly of First Nations. It included several controversial proposals: distinct society status for Quebec; an elected Senate; a guarantee that Quebec would retain at least 25 percent of the seats in the House of Commons; an ambiguous reference to Aboriginal self-government; exclusive provincial jurisdiction over culture, forestry, mining, and natural resources; shared jurisdiction over telecommunications, training, regional development, and immigration; stricter control over federal spending authority; reduced barriers to interprovincial trade; and the CLC's much lauded social charter, albeit in a non-justiciable form.

Because the right to organize and bargain collectively were included in the social charter but excluded from the proposed "Canada clause," which would legally codify a set of values to direct the Supreme Court of Canada in its decision making, there would be no formal mechanism in place to force governments to comply with the labour rights contained in the social charter. In effect, the social charter was largely symbolic, falling far short of what some segments of the labour movement had been calling for in terms of a workers' bill of rights or an amendment to the Charter to include explicit protection for labour rights.

Nevertheless, on 30 August 1992, the NDP federal council voted unanimously in favour of endorsing the Charlottetown Accord. The next day, the CLC's Executive Council met and "cautiously" endorsed the constitutional package, despite the fact that both the party and the

Congress had failed to convince the federal government to include the right to bargain collectively in the "Canada clause" (CLC 1992a). This outcome, however, was hardly surprising. The CLC's support for constitutional reform in 1992 was not driven primarily by a desire to see workers' rights enshrined in the constitution. Rather, the Congress's cautious endorsement of the Charlottetown Accord was more a product of pressure from the provincial NDP administrations in Ontario, British Columbia, and Saskatchewan, which had played a central role in developing the content of the Accord. The social charter aside, the Congress understood that failed constitutional negotiations would hurt its provincial NDP allies. This view is supported by comments made by labour leaders at a CLC Executive Council meeting in Regina in September 1992. The CLC's task at that meeting was to decide if and how to participate in the upcoming referendum on the constitutional package. Newly elected CLC president Bob White – a former president of the CAW who, a year earlier, had sat on a Congress committee to develop the framework for labour's position on constitutional issues – opened the discussion with a brief overview, summarized in the meeting minutes:

> With the new Constitution we should remember where we are, what we have gained, i.e., equal senate, social clause, sharing of powers, recommendation of distinct society, aboriginal rights, free collective bargaining, right of workers to join a union, etc. He continued by stating we had a role to play in forming this package, now we have to decide what role to play in the referendum. (CLC 1992b)

Executive Vice-President Nancy Riche, who was serving simultaneously as president of the federal NDP, suggested that the CLC officially join the pro-Charlottetown Canada Committee. However, "discussion followed where it was felt that the Congress should not participate in the Canada Committee" (CLC 1992b). The majority of labour leaders felt that associating themselves with a national campaign spearheaded by key figures in the decidedly anti-labour Mulroney government "would complicate the problems, confuse the membership and put the

Congress in conflict with various organizations" (CLC 1992b). Notably, "it was agreed that support must be given to the provinces, especially those with NDP governments. The national and provincial/territorial campaigns are different" (CLC 1992b).

However, neither the importance of presenting a unified front with provincial NDP governments nor the inclusion of the social charter within the constitutional package was enough to sway a number of unions who continued to oppose the Accord on the basis that it would promote decentralization, threaten equality rights, and render it nearly impossible to build new national social programs. Echoing the concerns of a number of social movement organizations like the National Action Committee on the Status of Women, various union locals adopted a neutral stand on the Accord, as did the Alberta Federation of Labour (AFL). A general membership meeting of the Labour Council of Metropolitan Toronto and York Region endorsed a resolution from its Political Education Committee that appealed to the CLC "not to actively campaign in support of Mulroney's Unity package" (Toronto and District Labour Council, Correspondence from President Linda Torney to Bob White dated 8 September 1992). Members of the Canadian Union of Postal Workers (CUPW) and PSAC went one step further, actively organizing against the Charlottetown Accord.

The Canadian labour movement's endorsement of the yes position was "strategically critical," according to political scientist Richard Johnston, because the union movement was traditionally viewed as a clear opponent of the Mulroney government. If labour were able to accept the government's economic union proposals and the Accord's decentralizing features, it would indicate that "the compromise was honourable, as the crisis was grave" (Johnston 1996, 64). However, the CLC's intervention had the opposite impact. Although the yes side built an impressive left-right coalition that included support from both business and labour, "the union movement was utterly ineffectual in overcoming its allies natural aversion to the Accord. Indeed, there is a hint that awareness of the union movement's position increased resistance to it" (139). The contradictory messages about the Accord being sent out by labour organizations no doubt contributed to this dynamic. In the end, the Accord was defeated soundly on 26 October 1992 in a national referendum.

Given the growing level of constitutional fatigue across Canada, those segments of the labour movement that remained committed to fighting for constitutionalized rights for workers faced a number of important obstacles. First and foremost, the Supreme Court's decisions in the realm of labour law offered an extremely narrow interpretation of freedom of association. More enduring and difficult questions also simmered below the surface. For instance, to what degree were unions willing to accept judicial meddling with labour boards or collective bargaining? Did the Charter decisions of the 1980s simply represent an affirmation of the status quo, or had labour indeed lost ground in the legal arena? In the short term, labour unions did not have to answer these questions, precisely because their losses had been so complete in the 1980s. After the near miss in *Lavigne*, unions could concentrate on the same political project they had been building since the early 1960s: electing labour-sympathetic governments like the NDP in English Canada and the Parti Québécois (PQ) in Quebec. Yet what became more tenuous for the labour movement was how to respond when the strategy of electing the NDP and PQ failed and unions, desperate for a political fight-back strategy, turned once again to the courts in the late 1990s. It is to those tensions that we now turn.

Political Gains and Political Setbacks

Despite the economic and constitutional woes of the early 1990s, the Canadian labour movement had reason to be cautiously optimistic. As discussed in the previous chapter, the attempts by right-wing business interests to eliminate mandatory dues requirements through the courts went down to defeat. More importantly, in British Columbia, Saskatchewan, and Ontario, the NDP rode to power on a wave of optimism that promised an alternative to the neoliberal policies of the 1980s. However, it did not take long for organized labour to recognize the limits of social democratic electoral politics as NDP provincial governments failed to reverse a trend of declining union density and instead, to varying degrees, adopted coercive neoliberal measures of their own, including public sector austerity programs, restrictions on the right to strike, and wage rollbacks in the public sector (Panitch and Swartz 2003, 163–222).

Whereas NDP provincial governments in the 1970s pursued what could reasonably be described as social democratic policy agendas, the provincial governments of the 1990s demonstrated just how dramatically the political terrain had shifted. In Saskatchewan, the cradle of Canadian social democracy, the Romanow government, elected in 1991, embraced a neoliberal policy orientation that prioritized deficit reduction through dramatic reductions in social programs and hospital closures (Stanford 2001, 95). Cuts to social programs freed up revenue for the Saskatchewan NDP to pay for corporate income tax cuts as part of a business-friendly agenda that included support for free trade, resistance to the Kyoto Protocol on climate change, and "piecemeal privatization" of public assets (Warnock 2005, 89–91).

In terms of workers' rights, the Saskatchewan NDP government dampened the hopes of the labour movement throughout the 1990s, bringing only piecemeal reforms to the province's *Trade Union Act* after three years of searching for a labour-business "consensus" (Smith 2011). The union movement's disappointment turned to outrage in 1999, when the Romanow government ordered an end to strikes by nurses and power utility workers through the use of back-to-work legislation (Warnock 2005, 95). In private, the province's union leadership was livid, but in public, most union leaders were careful not to criticize the party (Byers 2002, 75). Warnock (2005, 95) explained labour's paralysis by arguing that union leaders felt "trapped, choosing always to support the NDP as the lesser of the evils. With labour in its back pocket, the NDP leadership has concluded that it has to do very little to retain labour's support."

In Ontario, the party-union dynamic played out somewhat differently. Despite modest pro-union policy innovations, which included the adoption of an anti-scab law, the NDP government's 1993 decision to roll back wages and suspend collective bargaining rights in the public sector was met with fierce opposition and resistance by public sector unions and had repercussions for union-party relations across the country (Morton 2007, 120; Panitch and Swartz 2003, 172–81). In the eyes of many unionists, the NDP's infamous "social contract" austerity program basically negated any good the party had done in the field of labour relations and led to a fundamental re-evaluation of the traditional link between organized labour and the NDP.

In British Columbia, the NDP provincial government did not undermine the party-union relationship to the same extent (Stanford 2001, 97). The context, however, was very different. Rather than run on traditional class-based themes like the Ontario NDP had, the BC NDP had deliberately run a campaign in the 1991 provincial election based on "appeasing the business sector, avoiding radical departures from the status quo and, above all, appearing moderate" (Cohen 1994, 151). The party also made a concerted effort to recruit candidates with business rather than labour or social movement backgrounds (Sigurdson 1997, 325). This strategy served to lower the expectations of the party's base of union supporters once it took office. In this context, the Harcourt government's new *Labour Code* – which included mandatory first contract arbitration, an anti-scab law, and provisions for regulating secondary picketing – won praise from the province's labour movement.

However, in its second term of office, the NDP government shed "any pretence of using the power of the provincial state toward redistributive objectives" (Evans 2012, 88), embarking on a neoliberal campaign of public sector austerity, deficit reduction, income tax cuts, and deregulation. A hostile corporate media and an unreceptive bureaucracy seriously hampered the party's ability to pursue broader social democratic objectives in government, especially given the broader neoliberal political economic context of the mid-1990s. The party's unwillingness to seriously challenge the logic of neoliberalism by looking outside the market for alternatives to austerity meant that the NDP would eventually alienate its traditional supporters, leading to the government's colossal electoral defeat in 2001 (Carroll and Ratner 2005, 190–91).

Overall, the experience of the BC, Saskatchewan, and Ontario NDP governments of the 1990s cast serious doubt on the wisdom of the labour movement's traditional political strategy. Serving as an electoral machine for the NDP was not paying dividends and, in some cases, was actually undermining labour's core political values. Seemingly facing dead ends in every political direction, some unions, in search of new allies, drifted back towards the judicial arena in hopes of shielding themselves from further political attacks on the collective rights of workers.

The Labour Movement Goes Back to Court

The imperative to go back to court did not come easily. Although the *Lavigne* case represented a victory, albeit a hollow one, the Supreme Court ruled in 1992 that union "societies" could be prosecuted under criminal contempt provisions for defying a labour board order deeming a strike illegal (*United Nurses of Alberta v. Alberta [Attorney General]* 1992; see also Fudge and Glasbeek 1992a). In a separate case, the court reaffirmed the government's constitutional ability to use back-to-work legislation against legally striking workers (*International Longshoremen's and Warehousemen's Union – Canada Area Local 500 v. Canada* 1994). In a ruling on a public sector labour dispute in 1997, the Supreme Court further narrowed workers' collective freedoms in determining that "the health and safety of the greater populace will thus always take priority over the workers' and/or employers' interests in achieving a fair and equitable settling of the terms of employment" (*Canadian Union of Public Employees, Local 301 v. Montreal [City]* 1997, para. 34). Given the court's hostility to labour unions, the fact that workers were willing to go back to court speaks to the extent to which the union movement's relationship with the NDP had deteriorated.

The friction between labour and the NDP, however, was not the only factor that pushed labour back to court. The hyperpatriotic political and cultural climate that emerged after the events of 9/11 dampened militancy and seriously undermined attempts by social movements, including the labour movement, to push for change through direct action, street protests, or demonstrations (Ross et al. 2015, 67). Forced to reconsider organized labour's strategic options given the declining economic and political clout of unions, labour organizations, on the defensive, gave the judicial system a second look.

Matt James (2006, 107) convincingly argues that the labour movement's "sense of declining economic clout was aggravated by awareness that workers were losing their political voice at precisely the moment that Charter recognition was helping amplify feminist and minority struggles." James notes that that the labour movement spent the 1980s watching "from the sidelines while Charter-recognized movements became high-profile defenders of their constitutionally sanctioned symbolic capital" (100). While the courts had not been a hospitable forum for labour's concerns in the 1980s, the Canadian labour movement was "impressed by the gains made by enumerated movements" throughout the 1990s (108). The court's liberal interpretations on gay and lesbian rights, women's issues, and Aboriginal claims, to name just a few, made the prospect of constitutional challenges more attractive as a powerful "tool of recognition with which to amplify working-class concerns" (108). The influence of other social movements' successful Charter litigation on the attitudes, ideas, and strategies of the labour movement should not be understated. Working-class concerns are, to varying degrees, intertwined with identity-based struggles for recognition. After all, workers do not simply identify with their own class interests. They also identify as citizens made up of different sexes, races, ethnicities, languages, regions, and sexual orientations. The formal relationship between the Canadian labour movement and identity-based social movements was clearly solidified in the late 1980s in the fight against the US–Canada Free Trade Agreement. These ties were further strengthened through successful efforts by unions to achieve human rights gains for their members, particularly women, via employment arbitration. These important developments unquestionably helped many union activists overcome their deep suspicion or distrust of the judicial system (Savage 2007, 196–97).

Freedom of Expression and Secondary Picketing

After the defeat of the Retail, Wholesale, and Department Store Union (RWDSU) in *Dolphin Delivery* in 1986, few unions thought much of the Charter's protection of freedom of expression as it pertained to union struggles. Yet thirteen years later, in *U.F.C.W., Local 1518 v. KMart Canada Ltd.* (1999) and a companion case, *Allsco Building Products Ltd. v. UFCW, Local 1288P* 1999, the Supreme Court showed signs of greater openness. The *KMart* case emerged out of a series of secondary picketing actions by Kmart workers in British Columbia in the early 1990s.

While the court did not reverse its decision in *Dolphin, UFCW v. KMart* was significant insofar as it represented a clear expansion of the court's interpretation of freedom of expression with regard to picketing, signalling the court's willingness to interpret the Charter in ways that could further strengthen certain collective rights for workers. The *KMart* case arose out of a labour dispute between the big box retailer and the UFCW. During the strike, UFCW Local 1518 members in Campbell River and Port Alberni, British Columbia, attempted to extend a consumer boycott to several Kmart stores in Victoria and Vancouver. The secondary Kmart locations were not organized by the union and thus were not directly involved in the dispute. In a bid to pressure the employer, union members peacefully engaged in consumer leafleting urging Kmart customers to support the workers by shopping elsewhere. Kmart challenged the workers' action before the BC Industrial Relations Council (which became the Labour Relations Board after the NDP came to power) stating that the leafleting was in fact picketing and thus a violation of the *Industrial Relations Act* (*IRA*). In 1993, the NDP government repealed the *IRA* and replaced it with the *Labour Relations Code*. Notwithstanding the ideological differences between the NDP and previous right-wing Social Credit governments, however, the new code did not differ on the rules surrounding secondary picketing. As a result, the board ruled that the union's action was not a peaceful protest but was picketing in an industrial relations context and was therefore illegal.

The union argued before the board (and later in court) that the code's ban on secondary picketing was too broad and therefore unconstitutional. According to its submission, the union had not engaged in typical picketing actions such as setting up a human line, stopping customers from entering the premises, or encouraging workers at secondary locations to walk off the job. There was also no evidence of violence or illegal behaviour on the part of the workers.

In order to make its legal case under the rules of the *Labour Relations Code*, the union had to prove that its dispute was not with the secondary employer, was peaceful, and did not interfere with employees of secondary locations – even if those locations were separate divisions of the same employer (*UFCW v. KMart* 1995, para. 24). To pass constitutional scrutiny, the union had to further demonstrate that the legislation limited workers' freedom of expression rights by equating strike activity with consumer leafleting. This argument narrowed the union's constitutional position, since it was seeking not Charter protection for strikes, but rather clarification that the act of leafleting was not the same as picketing. While the board and the lower courts accepted that the *Labour Relations Code* did limit secondary acts of expression during labour disputes (and therefore violated the Charter), they maintained that such limitations were justified under section 1 of the Charter.

Based on the lower court decisions, the union had few options before the Supreme Court. It could not credibly argue for a constitutional right to strike, because union lawyers had insisted all along that leafleting did not constitute a strike and represented separate and therefore distinct forms of expression (*UFCW v. KMart* 1999, UFCW Local 1518 Appellant Factum, para. 31). The UFCW maintained that it was unreasonable to limit the rights of workers simply because speech occurs during a labour dispute. The union further argued that consumer leafleting by employees is a core value of free expression because it transmits information about important social and political issues (para. 27–29; 33–36). The union's position was supported by the CLC, which argued that the the court must "review the reasons why" the *Labour Relations Code* specifically "singles out speech in the labour context" (CLC Intervener Factum, para. 11). Both the UFCW and the CLC based their arguments on past Supreme Court decisions that were unwilling to uphold legislative restrictions that limited the rights of "vulnerable groups" (*Ramsden v. Peterborough (City)* 1993; *Rocket v. Royal College of Dental Surgeons of Ontario* 1990), including retail workers (*Slaight Communications Inc. v. Davidson* 1989, 1051; *R. v. Edwards Books and Art Ltd.* 1986, 773). According to the unions, Kmart workers (most of whom were women) were an extremely vulnerable group whose rights could not be trumped by the code's alternative goals of balance, labour peace, and the protection of so-called innocent third parties (UFCW Local 1518 Appellant Factum, para. 45–47).

Employers showed little sympathy for union arguments concerning the applicability of freedom of expression. For employers, there was no meaningful distinction between leafleting secondary locations and traditional picketing. According to Kmart, the union was primarily seeking to impose "economic harm" on an a third party rather than disseminate public information (*UFCW v. KMart* 1999, KMart Respondent Factum, para. 56). The Coalition of BC Businesses (Intervener Factum, para. 21–23) further argued that restrictions on picketing needed universal application regardless of employment criteria (or vulnerability) because union representation neutralized any preconceived imbalance of power between workers and employers. Given the NDP's traditional alliance with labour, it was surprising that the Clark government echoed these arguments by suggesting that the *Labour Relations Code* is a "complex, interlocking network of provisions" that seeks to balance the interst of labour and management (Government of BC Intervener Factum, para. 22). Therefore, the BC government urged the court to exercise "judicial restraint" (para 23).

In a surprise decision, the Supreme Court sided with the union. In writing for the majority, Justice Cory agreed that the legislative definition of picketing was too broad and therefore violated the Charter. Yet, given that the BC legislation attempted to craft a delicate peace between labour and business, the real question was whether the Charter violation could withstand section 1 scrutiny. For Cory, the question of legislative balance had to take into account the pressing and substantial objective of labour peace. Did the legislation intend to "insulate" third parties from labour disruption or merely to protect them from "unreasonable" harm? Cory answered this question by concluding that it would be impossible to completely insulate third parties from the consequences of a strike. This fact was a small but vital distinction between *KMart* and *Dolphin Delivery*, as the court in *KMart* recognized the economic, political, and social aspects of strikes (*UFCW v. KMart* 1999, para. 35). Recognizing that the law should (or even could) completely insulate third parties from a strike or social protest was unrealistic, according to Cory. In essence, businesses could not reasonably be insulated from economic harm if that protection trampled on the right of workers to "peaceful persuasion" (para. 43).

Given the importance the court had given to employment in fulfilling an individual's self-worth, it was no small matter to limit that same person's right to inform the public about harmful or unfair workplace conditions (see Dickson's comments in *Alberta Reference* 1987, para. 91; *McKinney v. University of Guelph* 1990, 300; *Wallace v. United*

Grain Growers Ltd. 1997, para. 94; and *Delisle v. Canada (Deputy Attorney General)* 1999, para. 66). In *KMart*, the court ruled that it was through the act of free expression "that vulnerable workers" were able to challenge their employers and thus "enlist the support of the public in their quest for better conditions at work" (*UFCW v. KMart* 1999, para. 25; see also *Slaight Communications Inc. v. Davidson* 1989, 1051; and *R. v. Edwards Books and Art Ltd.* 1986, 773). As long as the union's activity (and messaging) was accurate and not defamatory and did not entice people to commit unlawful or tortious acts, the act of expression needed to be constitutionally protected (*UFCW v. KMart* 1999, para. 58).

In coming to this conclusion, however, Cory reverted to traditional judicial antagonism towards picketing. Indeed, it was the very fact that the workers had *not* engaged in traditional strike activities that provided constitutional protection for their expression (*UFCW v. KMart* 1999, para. 38). Cory argued that picketing brought with it a "signal effect" that attracted an "automatic reflex response from workers, suppliers and consumers" (para. 38), which in turn led to societal harm. Specifically, Cory argued that the coercive messaging in a strike had the effect of limiting public access to goods and to workplaces and (here Cory accepted the arguments from businesses) inevitably harmed "innocent" third parties. Further demonstrating a disdain for the collective action and solidarity of workers, Cory then cited former BC Labour Relations Board chair Paul Weiler's unsympathetic definition of a picket line as contributing to a "Pavlovian" response from fellow workers to not cross (para. 40, citing Weiler 1980, 79). With that observation, Cory concluded that the act of secondary picketing ought not be extended Charter protection. By contrast, secondary leafleting, especially for vulnerable workers, was the very form of expression the Charter was designed to protect.

The decision in *UFCW v. KMart* (1999) opened the door to further questions pertaining to freedom of expression and picketing. To what extent could union picketing during an actual strike equate with constitutionally protected speech? That question was at the centre of *Retail, Wholesale and Department Store Union, Local 558 v. Pepsi-Cola Canada Beverages (West) Ltd.* (*RWDSU v. Pepsi* 2002). This case arose out of a particularly tumultuous strike in Saskatoon, Saskatchewan. After bargaining broke down between the union and the company, Pepsi locked out its bottling plant workers. In protest, these same workers occupied the Pepsi plant and used pallets of Pepsi product to block management access to the warehouse. When the company filed an injunction against the occupiers, these same workers slipped out the back door and resumed picketing outside the plant. These actions raised the ire of Pepsi management, who sought to weaken the union through the use of replacement workers, which, in turn, led to heated confrontations on the picket line (for more detail, see C. Smith 2014).

The union's counteroffensive to the use of replacement workers was both creative and effective. Through the use of "scab-mobiles," the union created a fairly sophisticated communications network to inform striking members of replacement worker activity. This tactic expanded the conflict to secondary locations and led to picketing outside the homes of Pepsi management, at hotels where out-of-town management and replacement workers were staying, and at secondary business locations throughout Saskatoon. Because there was no statutory regulation on picketing in Saskatchewan, Pepsi sought to prohibit the union's actions through a court injunction. That injunction contained several restrictions on the union's activity but specifically restrained the union from picketing anywhere but at the Pepsi plant and prevented the union from impeding the work of replacement workers (*RWDSU v. Pepsi* 2002, para. 7). The union challenged the injunction as a violation of its Charter right to free expression.

Pepsi was well prepared for the union's legal argument. Having appeared as an intervener in both the *KMart* and *Allsco* cases, the company had consistently maintained that there was no constitutional right to secondary picketing. Thus, Pepsi's position was a familiar one. Following *Hersees*, the company maintained that secondary picketing was simply illegal *per se* (*UFCW v. KMart* 1999, Pepsi Intervener Factum). Noting that no court had overturned *Hersees*, the company suggested that where there was legislative silence, common law rules and principles became *de facto* law (*RWDSU v. Pepsi* 2002, Pepsi Appellant Factum, para 27). Because secondary businesses were not part of the collective agreement to which the dispute was related, Pepsi argued, the traditional economic tort framework continued to apply. Relying on Justice Cory's comments in *KMart* that the "signal" of a picket line may be "based on its coercive effect rather than persuasive force of the picket-ers," Pepsi maintained that the prohibition of secondary picketing was legally justified (*RWDSU v. Pepsi* 2002, Pepsi Appellant Factum, para 30, citing *UFCW v. KMart* 1999, para. 42). The Government of Alberta (Intervener Factum, paras. 26–27) supported Pepsi's position, arguing that secondary picketing was a private matter that caused damage to neutral businesses. Since it created irreparable damage to neutral third parties, secondary picketing could not be justified or made legal. More-over, in the dispute with RWDSU, Pepsi maintained that the union's secondary picketing activities involved "intimidating, threatening and often dangerous conduct" that should not be elevated to constitution-ally protected speech (Pepsi Appellant Factum, para. 18).

The union's legal arguments challenged the employer's belief that the common law torts justifiably limited workers' free expression. The union submitted that picketing was a universally recognized form of expression that positively contributed information to the public, further arguing that because workers have the individual right to express their opinion in public, there cannot be legal restrictions on the collective ability to exert those same freedoms. RWDSU also took issue with the employer's primary argument regarding "innocent third parties." Stat-ing that *Hersees'* long restriction of all secondary picketing activity was now "dead," the union attempted to broaden the ally doctrine that grew out of the modified *Hersees* rule (see Chapter 1) (*RWDSU v. Pepsi* 2002, RWDSU Respondent Factum, para. 53). In so doing, the union believed that any business that had an "interest" in the outcome of the strike was an *ally* and thus the legitimate target of social protest (para 93). The union argued that a business could not be neutral if it contributed to an organization that was publicly opposing the strike, lobbied government to change laws in the interest of the struck employer, supported laws that made it illegal to strike, or continued to do business with a struck employer (paras. 96–98). In any of the above situations, the idea of a "neutral" or "innocent" third party was simply indefensible.

Once again, in a surprise decision, the Supreme Court sided with the union and effectively expanded Charter rights to include secondary picketing. In coming to this conclusion, Justices McLachlin and LeBel walked a fine line between Pepsi's argument regarding "balance" in labour relations and the union's constitutional position regarding freedom of expression (Adell 2003, 135–59). In writing for the majority, McLachlin and LeBel declared that the *Hersees* "illegal *per se*" doctrine could not be sustained in an era of evolving Charter values. For the Supreme Court, there was little debate that expression was one of the most important rights in a free society.

Moreover, the court recognized that policy-makers had long accepted the right to picket but had refused (except in British Columbia) to define it legally. According to the justices, this legal ambiguity suggested that most governments accepted that the right to strike could take many forms (*RWDSU v. Pepsi* 2002, paras. 23–29). In taking this position, the court extended Justice Cory's reasoning in *KMart* by declaring the act of picketing, including secondary picketing, an important exercise of free expression. The court reasoned that it was inconsistent with the Charter to suggest that labour groups could be denied the right to disseminate information outside a place of business when the constitution guaranteed those same rights to individuals and other groups (paras. 32–37). In coming to this conclusion, the court dismantled Pepsi's primary argument regarding the union's secondary actions.

To be sure, the court was careful not to suggest that evolving Charter rights could not also protect business interests. Rather, following the issues in *KMart*, the question was how to balance the constitutional rights of workers while limiting third parties from "undue" harm. The Supreme Court argued that in its current form, the "illegal *per se*" doctrine from *Hersees* was a relic of the nineteenth century that reflected "a deep distrust of unions and collective action in a labour dispute" (*RWDSU v. Pepsi* 2002, para. 55). The court also reasoned that the "modified" *Hersees* rules, as well as the ally doctrine, suffered from inconsistent application and were thus entirely unhelpful in balancing the right to strike with the rights of third parties. These observations were certainly important victories for the union. Although *Hersees* had largely fallen into disuse, it remained a stubborn thorn in the side of any union attempting to place economic pressure on an employer.

Having dismissed the *Hersees* precedent, the court then endorsed the "wrongful action" model as an appropriate legal tool to "treat labour and non-labour expression in a consistent manner" (*RWDSU v. Pepsi*

2002, para. 80). In essence, the wrongful action model begins with the assumption that all picketing is permitted unless that picketing is tortious (a civil wrong) or criminal in nature. By maintaining that all picketing is legal, the court downplayed Cory's concern in *KMart* regarding the "signal effect" and picket line coercion, suggesting that such an argument undermines the peaceful nature of most picketing (para. 95). As most picketing in the contemporary era is largely peaceful, the Supreme Court's endorsement of the wrongful action model suggested to many observers that the court handed unions a significant legal tool to challenge employers. The potential for workers to strike more freely certainly raised the anxiety of management-side lawyers concerned that the law would no longer "provide adequate protection to the economic and property rights of neutral third parties" (Dinsdale and Awrey 2003–4, 806).

The Supreme Court was confident that existing common law torts provided adequate legal protection to third- party property interests during a legal strike (C. Smith 2014, 115–19). By highlighting the wrongful action model to restrain workers' collective freedoms, the court drew a distinct and somewhat arbitrary line between the constitutional rights of workers to free expression, on the one hand, and the economic and common law interests of business, on the other (*RWDSU v. Pepsi* 2002, para. 67). Although McLachlin and LeBel hinted that it may be time to re-examine existing tort doctrines, the justices, in the absence of such reform, argued that existing civil torts such as trespass, intimidation, and inducing breach of contract would "protect property interests and ensure free access to private premises" (para. 73) and would control the "most coercive picketing" (para. 103). By constructing these boundaries, the court recognized that torts were an effective deterrent to unions stepping on the rights of property. That was certainly the position of Harry Arthurs, who recognized that most picket line activity brushed up against the established torts, thus restricting workers' ability to act collectively during strikes (Arthurs 2007, 49).

Notwithstanding the inherent limitations in *KMart* and *Pepsi,* there was a noticeable difference in both tone and substance in the Supreme Court's interpretation of picketing as a constitutional right of expression in these cases. In the 1980s, the court was willing to recognize that picketing was free expression but was more concerned with the economic disruption that exercising such expression might generate. By the early 2000s, the Supreme Court recognized that picketing under Canada's Wagner/PC 1003 model of labour relations, while potentially economically harmful, caused no serious threat to property. While certainly a step forward for judicial reasoning with regard to workers' collective freedoms to picket, there remained a series of unanswered constitutional questions regarding freedom of association and the ability of workers to freely organize. It is to these questions that we now turn.

Freedom of Association and the Right to Bargain Collectively

Given the evolving jurisprudence in *KMart* and *Pepsi,* unions began to demonstrate optimism that associational rights to organize and bargain would eventually fall under the ambit of the Charter. However, the road to workers' collective rights through the freedom of association provisions in the Charter continued to be a rocky one, as evidenced by the decision in *Delisle v. Canada* (1999), a case that challenged federal restrictions in the *Public Service Staff Relations Act* (*PSSRA*) and the *Canada Labour Code* that prevented members of the Royal Canadian Mounted Police (RCMP) from forming a union. Delisle himself was a long-serving member of the RCMP and head of a quasi-independent and informal labour association. He argued before the court that limiting the rights of RCMP members to form their own independent union, "or even the right to vote on the issue," violated the Charter guarantee of association (*Delisle v. Canada* 1999, Delisle Appellant Factum, para 9). Delisle also argued that RCMP members were discriminated against based on their employment status, which he claimed violated their equality rights. Quite simply, he argued, to deny rights at work violated the equality rights of all workers. The CLC, PSAC, and Ontario Teachers' Federation (OTF) supported Delisle in their mutual belief that legislative exclusions denying public sector unions the right to independent unionization was discriminatory. As the unions emphasized, "Where the state has enacted a comprehensive code to protect and facilitate the freedom of association of employees, the state cannot then impose obstacles to the exercise of such rights" (OTF Intervener Factum, para. 11). According to the unions, when this occurs, there is a positive obligation on the state to protect the associational and equality rights of all workers to access a collective bargaining regime.

All of these arguments failed before the Supreme Court. Like previous freedom of association cases, the court continued to interpret section 2(d) narrowly, determining that it only protected individual workers. The majority confirmed that since the Charter only protected an individual right, freedom of association did not include a collective right to bargain. In coming to this conclusion, the court determined that the Charter did not guarantee access to any one particular statutory scheme. Thus, exclusion from the *PSSRA* or the federal *Labour Code* was not a violation of the Charter. Rather, the court reasoned, workers are free to establish independent employee associations and to exercise their lawful rights (*Delisle v. Canada* 1999, para. 12). Although Delisle had argued that such organizations could not perform the duties of *bona fide* labour unions and were unduly influenced by management – a position accepted by the dissenters – the majority refused to gauge the substance of such organizations. Quite simply, the court concluded that there was no positive obligation for the government to bring workers into a particular legislative framework. Since RCMP members had already taken steps to form an association, there was no intimidation on the part of the employer or government for workers to individually associate (paras. 28–31).

The court continued to be dismissive of union arguments concerning equality rights. Writing for the majority, Justice Bastarache refused to recognize employment status as analogous for the purpose of Charter equality. He argued that it would be inappropriate to read employment characteristics into equality protection because it "is not a matter of functionally immutable characteristics in a context of labour market flexibility" (*Delisle v. Canada* 1999, para. 44). This was especially true, he maintained, in view of the status that RCMP workers hold in Canadian society. In essence, exclusion from Canada's regime of industrial legality did nothing to change the overall power and status of police officers. Somewhat ironically, Bastarache's reasoning in denying Charter protection for police officers was based on a recognition of the police's unique role "in maintaining order during conflicts that may arise in society" (para. 45). It could not have been lost on the court that one of the

Charter's fundamental purposes remained the protection of individual rights from the egregious power that police have "in maintaining order." Yet because the police have this special power, the court reasoned that Parliament was justified in setting "them apart from other public service employees" (para. 45). Since these workers were neither vulnerable nor discriminated against in the eyes of the court, Delisle's section 15 arguments failed.

Similar questions over vulnerability, workplace status, and access to a particular statutory regime were at the centre of the dispute in *Dunmore v. Ontario (Attorney General)* (2001). In this case, however, unions were defending the rights of agricultural workers who enjoyed little of the privilege or status of RCMP officers. To the surprise of many, the court opted to expand its interpretation of freedom of association in the Charter, recognizing for the first time that there were collective dimensions to this right. In *Dunmore*, the court took the surprising step of recognizing that section 2(d) included a positive obligation on the part of government to provide legislative support for vulnerable workers to exercise their Charter rights. Although the court did not overturn the labour trilogy (nor constitutionalize the right to bargain or organize), it did begin the process of elevating Dickson's dissent in the *Alberta Reference* (1987) to that of established constitutional law, a process that was completed in the decision in *BC Health Services* (2007; see Chapter 5).

Dunmore had its origins in the last days of Ontario's NDP government: in 1994, the government passed the *Agricultural Labour Relations Act (ALRA)*, which extended collective bargaining rights to agricultural workers in Ontario. The *ALRA* was a significant reform to the province's labour relations framework. Since the creation of the *Ontario Labour Relations Act (OLRA)* in 1943, agricultural workers had been excluded from forming unions or engaging in collective bargaining of any form (Smith 2009; Tucker 2006, 256; Walchuk 2009, 150–63). Liberal and Conservative governments maintained that the agricultural exclusion was justified on the basis that the business of farming was too tenuous to be burdened by unions or collective bargaining. Specifically, governments did their best to portray a romantic image of the "family farm," claiming that collective bargaining, which brought with it the threat of a strike or lockout, could erode the sustainability of small independent commodity producers (*Dunmore v. Ontario* 2001, Dunmore Appellant Factum, para. 24). The romantic image of the small family farmer remained strong enough in the minds of rural politicians that no Ontario government was willing to include agricultural workers in the act.

After four years of study, the NDP finally brought agricultural workers into a collective bargaining regime but continued to deny protection under the *OLRA*. When the NDP was routed in 1995, the Conservative government wasted little time repealing the *ALRA*. Noble Villeneuve, Conservative minister of agriculture, food and rural affairs, defended this decision, stating, "Agriculture, in its uniqueness, cannot and should not come under any sort of labour legislation ... Farmers told [the government], almost to the last one, that ... in order for them to be competitive, that due to its uniqueness, agriculture must be exempt from industrial-style collective bargaining" (Villeneuve 1995). During debate, Villeneuve singled out Highline Produce Ltd. and Mushroom Farms Inc. – producers of factory-farmed mushrooms – as two companies that had written to him personally to lobby for the repeal of the *ALRA*. In his statements before the legislature, the minister referred to the threatened union "challenge" to these firms as one of the reasons for the government's actions.[1] That threat emerged out of a certification dispute between the UFCW and Highline that had only concluded on 26 June 1995, shortly after the election of the new Progressive Conservative government (*United Food and Commercial Workers International Union v. Highline Produce Ltd.* 1995). In that drive, the UFCW was successful in organizing two hundred workers at Mushroom Farms Inc. in Leamington, Ontario. Notwithstanding the UFCW's successful certification, the minister's candour regarding who actually benefited from the repeal of the *ALRA* was important, because the firms and the government were soon to be at the centre of a constitutional battle regarding the rights of agricultural workers to form unions.

The UFCW's legal challenge to the government's repeal of the *ALRA* and the legislative exclusion of agriculture workers from the *OLRA* was unsuccessful before Ontario's lower courts. In the Ontario Superior Court of Justice, Robert Sharpe leaned heavily on *Dolphin Delivery* and the labour trilogy decisions to rule against the union (*Dunmore v. Ontario [Attorney General]* 1997). In Sharpe's view, freedom of association was a negative liberty that did not confer a positive obligation on the state "to curb the exercise of the private economic power of employers and to constrain the exercise of common law rights of property and contract" (para. 28). Despite the obvious economic and power imbalance between agricultural workers and farm employers, Sharpe's reasoning was entirely consistent with the Supreme Court's position in the labour trilogy. Yet his decision actually went further in narrowing the right of association in that he interpreted the statutory exclusion of a group of workers from Ontario's existing collective bargaining framework as entirely consistent with the Charter. Sharpe evidently saw no correlation between the precarious nature of agricultural workers and the legal restrictions placed upon them to form an association for the purposes of collective bargaining. Upon appeal, the question presented concerned the judges' comfort level with a further narrowing of the freedom of association guarantees in the Charter.

Before the Supreme Court, the Ontario government defended its legislation on the grounds that the Charter did not impose positive obligations on the state to protect new rights. Relying on *Delisle*, the Conservatives maintained that the repeal of the *ALRA* did not necessarily prevent farm workers from forming an independent union or employee association, even though none ever had (*Dunmore v. Ontario* 2001, Government of Ontario Respondent Factum, para. 6). Moreover, the Conservatives maintained that the repeal of the *ALRA* was a complex policy decision regarding the sustainability of a family farm and large agro-companies handling perishable goods. To introduce the traditional system of industrial legality into such unique workplaces was ill suited to the sector (paras. 24–28). The government was particularly concerned that extending the right to strike to workers, especially "during crucial periods of the year, dictated by season and climate, could result in the loss of an entire crop, the neglect and potential loss of livestock, and consequent economic loss so great as to threaten the economic survival of an employer" (para. 45). The bottom line for the Ontario government was that the economic interests of the employer had to take precedent over the perceived rights of workers to collectively bargain or strike.

Although the Ontario government based its policy decision on the preservation of the family farm, no independent farmers appeared as interveners at the Supreme Court. Rather, the Ontario Federation of Agriculture's Labour Issues Coordinating Committee (LICC) and Fleming Chicks Ltd., a chicken operation with sixty-five employees, intervened to support the provincial government.[2] Although the LICC had stated publicly that there was a need for increased protection for farm workers, the committee continuously cautioned delay because of the fragility of the farm economy (Tucker 2006, 272). In fact, the LICC emphasized that Ontario farmers could not meet the increased costs of enhanced regulation or collective bargaining because "Ontario farmers are price-takers, so they cannot pass along any increase in their costs to consumers" (*Dunmore v. Ontario* 2001, LICC Intervener Factum, para 2 [d]). In other words, the realities of the agricultural economy prevented them from paying benefits or living wages.

The UFCW and the CLC built their arguments around the vulnerable and precarious nature of agricultural workers within the broader labour market. Advancing section 2(d) and section 15 equality arguments, the UFCW suggested that workers in the agricultural sector were overwhelmingly racialized minorities – recent immigrants or temporary migrants – who laboured in poor working conditions for little pay (*Dunmore v. Ontario* 2001, Dunmore Appellant Factum, paras. 6–17). These realities were further exacerbated by the fact that work on farms is seasonal and thus offers little job security. In large agribusiness, such as at Highline Farms and Fleming Chicks, workers complained of "horrendous" working conditions that did not meet basic workplace health and safety standards (para. 34). In this regard, the exclusion of workers from the modern labour protections – in an industry where over half of all wages were paid by 10 percent of farms – could not be justified (para. 29). Citing the government's own economic experts, the UFCW maintained that the economic conditions in the agricultural sector were not the idyllic image of a small independent rural farmer but a "sophisticated business unit with a minimum capital value of

$500,000 to $1,000,0000, depending on the commodity and type of operation" (para. 29). In effect, the union convincingly demonstrated that Ontario's agricultural economy was more reflective of modern industry than a small family business.

The Supreme Court ultimately sided with the union, ruling that agricultural workers could not be denied collective rights to associate under section 2(d) of the Charter. In coming to this conclusion, Justice Bastarache, writing for the majority, made a surprising departure from previous jurisprudence. While relying on Sopinka's four-point interpretation of 2(d) from *PIPSC* (1990), Bastarache departed from the position that associational rights were simple individual freedoms (see Chapter 3). Rather, he argued that the "purpose of 2(d) commanded a single inquiry: has the state precluded activity because of its associational nature, thereby discouraging the collective pursuit of common goals" (*Dunmore v. Ontario* 2001, para. 16)? If the answer is yes, then it is logical to conclude that the government was attempting to violate the rights of workers to act collectively. By posing the question in this manner, the court indicated that there was a substantive shift in judicial thinking with regard to its interpretation of 2(d). For the first time, the Supreme Court was willing to recognize "qualitative differences between individuals and collectivities" (para. 17). In the context of unionization, Bastarache acknowledged that a host of labour union activities – including collective representation to employers – was simply beyond the purview of individuals.

Having concluded that associational rights applied to collective interests, Bastarache reasoned that it was not a "quantum leap" to then suggest that "under-inclusive state action falls into suspicion not simply to the extent that it discriminates against an unprotected class, but to the extent it substantially orchestrates, encourages or sustains the violation of fundamental freedoms" (*Dunmore v. Ontario* 2001, para. 26). While Bastarache maintained that there was not a positive obligation for the workers to join a specific legislative scheme, it was clear that the government's actions placed a "chilling effect" on "non-statutory union activity" (para. 45). While the court reasoned that the government's objective to protect family farms might be "rationally" connected to the infringement of section 2(d) rights, the Harris government's actions went too far in denying "vulnerable agricultural workers" the right to associate (para. 55). Quite simply, the government's objectives to protect the economic privileges of agricultural employers did not outweigh the Charter rights of society's most vulnerable workers.

In expanding its interpretation of associational rights, the Supreme Court ruled that the Conservative government's actions were unconstitutional. The court also declared that the *OLRA*'s exclusion of agricultural workers was unconstitutional. Moreover, the court concluded that in circumstances where vulnerable individuals had proven incapable of exercising a Charter freedom, there was a positive obligation on the state to provide some form of protection. In arriving at this conclusion, Bastarache emphasized the vulnerability of agricultural workers in terms of independently exercising their Charter rights. Unlike RCMP workers, he argued, "the evidence is that the ability of agricultural workers to associate is only as great as their access to legal protection" (*Dunmore v. Ontario* 2001, para. 45). In the court's view, there was no general right to collective bargaining per se, and workers' rights had to be balanced against their general occupational status. This was a position emphasized by Justice L'Heureux-Dubé, who, in a concurring opinion, stressed that vulnerability could trigger an equality rights claim based on occupational status. Thus, while the court refused to prioritize a particular form of industrial legality, its emphasis on vulnerability elevated the state's responsibility to protect the associational rights of farm workers to organize.

It is important to note that in taking this position, the justices stopped short of declaring a Charter right to collective bargaining. In fact, Bastarache emphasized that it was essential for the court to "distinguish between the associational aspect of the activity and the activity itself" (*Dunmore v. Ontario* 2001, para. 18). As a result, *Dunmore*, albeit a victory, was relatively limited in its ability to assist all workers to achieve union representation or to actually bargain. Because the court was willing neither to examine the substance of collective representation, nor to endorse an institutional regime of collective bargaining, it was not entirely clear how the *Dunmore* decision would actually change conditions on the ground (Fudge 2004, 433; Panitch and Swartz 2003, 210–12). Moreover, *Dunmore* only handed a small group of workers a constitutional right to organize, while seemingly denying that same right to the vast majority of non-organized workers. It was this ambiguity that led several critics, including management lawyers, to suggest that the court's interpretation of section 2(d) created a confusing body of jurisprudence (Craig and Dinsdale 2003; Doorey 2012; Langille 2009).

Notwithstanding the limits of *Dunmore*, the case certainly elevated the hopes of union leaders like UFCW national director Michael Fraser who believed that government could no longer "run roughshod over workers' rights" (MacCharles 2001). Labour lawyers for the CLC took a similarly positive, albeit cautious, view of the ruling by suggesting that it "breathes new life into the possibility of a meaningful role for s. 2 (d) in protecting worker and trade union activity" (Barrett 2003, 84; see also Hughes 2003). By far the most sanguine interpretation of *Dunmore* came from Industrial Relations professor Roy Adams. In Adams's view, *Dunmore* signalled "revolutionary potential" for labour law reform in Canada (Adams 2003). Adams was particularly impressed that the Supreme Court chose not to constitutionalize the Wagner model of labour relations, thus reinforcing his contention that freedom of association rights should not be dependent on state certification. Rather, Adams endorsed Bastarache's defence of "non-statutory unionism," which, he argued, would bring Canada into closer alignment with international human rights norms, specifically elevating unionization (or other forms of employee representation) to the level of human rights protection.

Post-*Dunmore* Setbacks

The Supreme Court's recognition that Charter rights for unions had collective implications was almost universally recognized by anyone in the labour movement as a positive step for workers. Yet not everyone agreed that the decision in *Dunmore* contained what Adams referred to as "revolutionary potential." This point hit home with the Supreme Court decisions in *R. v. Advance Cutting and Coring Ltd.* (2001) and *Newfoundland (Treasury Board) v. N.A.P.E.* (2004). In *Advance Cutting,* the Supreme Court ruled on the constitutionality of Quebec's *Construction Act.* The act required workers to join one of five union federations in order to obtain a certificate granting permission to work in Quebec's construction industry. In essence, the act legislated a form of union security, because workers had to join one of the five federations (workers were able to choose which federation) in order to work. Similar to Lavigne's argument a decade earlier, André Gareau, owner of Advance Cutting and Coring Ltd., argued that this legislative requirement imposed a form of ideological conformity on his employees and therefore violated the Charter's right not to associate. In a narrow 5–4 decision, the Supreme Court ruled that section 2(d) included a right not to associate, but, for similar reasons laid out in *Lavigne*, upheld the act based on section 1 arguments that it preserved labour peace in Quebec.

To be sure, *Advance Cutting* represented a razor-thin victory for the five labour unions in Quebec's construction industry. Yet the victory was limited and spoke to the divided nature of the Supreme Court with regard to unions and collective labour rights. *Advance Cutting* was, in fact, four separate decisions, with Justice LeBel writing for himself, Arbour, and Gonthier in the majority and with justices L'Heureux-Dubé and Iacobucci concurring.[3] Led by Justice Bastarache the four dissenting judges (which included Chief Justice McLachlin), took a much harsher view of unionization and freedom of association rights, stating that unions are "participatory bodies holding political and economic roles in society which, in turn, translates into the existence of ideological positions. To mandate that an individual adhere to such a union is ideological conformity (*R. v. Advance Cutting and Coring* 2001, para. 3). Somewhat interestingly, the minority expanded on Justice McLachlin's arguments in *Lavigne* surrounding "ideological conformity." Using Bastarache's logic surrounding unionization and conformity, the minority found that the Quebec legislation represented an affront to individual rights not to associate and thus imposed an unnecessary burden on individuals to conform to the values of the unions in the Quebec construction industry.

The arguments surrounding the right "not" to associate became a defining characteristic of the *Advance Cutting* case. As was demonstrated in the 1991 *Lavigne* case, the right not to associate is particularly troubling for labour unions. Reinterpreting section 2(d) to include a negative right for individuals to be free from association would seem to undermine the very nature of union security provisions in Canada. In writing for the majority, the newly appointed Quebec justice, Louis LeBel, recognized the individualized nature of section 2(d) but was prepared to accept internal limits on it. At the heart of LeBel's reasoning were strong undertones of judicial deference in the area of labour law, a consistent theme throughout the 1980s, 1990s, and 2000s. LeBel lauded the Quebec government for creating a working labour peace in the construction industry. After outlining the tumultuous history of the industry, he argued that preservation of peace and "democracy undergirds the particular form of union security provided for by the *Construction Act*" (*R. v. Advance Cutting and Coring* 2001, para. 228). Like the Court's defence of the Rand formula in *Lavigne*, LeBel believed that paying union dues or joining one of five construction unions was more reflective of "payment for service" and thus did not equate to forced "ideological conformity" (paras. 229–31).

The most immediate consequence of *Advance Cutting* was the preservation of Quebec's mandatory unionization regime in the construction industry. Yet the court's conclusion that 2(d) included a negative right not to associate led lawyers for the company to claim victory for employers (Thompson 2001). Moreover, the Supreme Court's ongoing concern with unionization and "ideological conformity" suggested that judicial recognition of labour rights was closely tied to a contractual obligation rather than to broader notions of class solidarity among workers. Ultimately, therefore, *Advance Cutting* spoke as much to the limits of labour rights as it did to their defence.

Judicial hostility towards labour rights was also on display in *Newfoundland v. N.A.P.E.* In June 1988, the Newfoundland Association of Public Employees (NAPE)[4] and the Conservative government of Brian Peckford concluded negotiations on a pay equity agreement that provided women in six different health care units substantial remuneration for past sex-based wage discrimination. Under the terms of the settlement, the government agreed to compensate the women through five pay equity adjustments, which were to occur over a four-year period (ending in 1992). Negotiations over the amount of compensation, however, delayed the payment until 20 March 1991, and the sex-based wage discrimination continued throughout that period (*Newfoundland v. N.A.P.E.* 2004, "Women's Legal Action Fund" [WLAF] Intervener

Factum, para. 4). Under the final agreement, the women were to receive four pay-equity adjustments in 1991 and a final payment in 1992, totalling roughly $24 million.

However, on 18 April 1991, the new Liberal government of Clyde Wells enacted Bill 16, the *Public Sector Restraint Act* (*PSRA*), a severe austerity program that, in addition to delaying the pay equity agreements, resulted in a drastically downsized public sector (Cox 1991). The Liberals argued that the provincial government had to take this drastic step because of "macroeconomic factors completely beyond its control" that would have resulted in a mounting deficit (*Newfoundland v. N.A.P.E.* 2004, Government of Newfoundland and Labrador Respondent Factum, para. 5). Not surprisingly, NAPE and several other public and private sector unions challenged the government's action, launching a "Clyde Lied" campaign that resulted in a series of protests throughout the province (Cadigan 2015). Given the contractual terms agreed to by the government, the unions also launched a general grievance on behalf of the women affected by Bill 16. The arbitration board ruled that the government's actions had violated the equality rights of the employees and ordered the government to live up to its contractual obligations. The lower court and the Newfoundland Court of Appeal overturned that decision, arguing that section 15 had been violated, but maintained that "a severe fiscal crisis" took precedent over women's equality rights (*Newfoundland v. N.A.P.E.* 2004, Government of Newfoundland and Labrador Respondent Factum, para. 5; see also para 6-11).

When the decision finally made its way to the Supreme Court, there was considerable optimism that the court's new interpretation of workers' rights and the importance of work towards securing individual dignity and self-respect would be expanded to include equality provisions in the Charter. Given the social, political, and economic circumstances surrounding the case, NAPE maintained that the government could not ignore decades of human rights abuses, arguing that they were "created by the Government who as the employer was responsible for the payment of discriminatory wages ... since the 1960's" (*Newfoundland v. N.A.P.E.* 2004, NAPE Appellant Factum, paras. 30–31). By enacting the *PSRA*, the government was "reinforcing the undervaluation of women's work ... [by] perpetuat[ing] recognized stereotypes and assumptions about the value of women's work which has been the historical cause of systemic discrimination in compensation against women" (para. 47). The union further claimed that the government's discriminatory policies could not be saved by the Charter's section 1, the reasonable limits clause. To limit the equality rights of women in order to finance the public debt, the union argued, would reinforce "the very stereotypes and prejudices that are the historical cause of sex-based discrimination" and that undermine "the equality principles in the Charter" (para. 80).

The Government of Newfoundland was joined in its appeal by Liberal and Conservative governments in British Columbia, Alberta, and New Brunswick. The Newfoundland government's position was straightforward. The recession of the early 1990s and the federal cutbacks in transfer payments left the province with a significant fiscal gap. It was incorrect to conclude that the passage of pay equity obligations limited future governments to end those agreements if the fiscal situation deteriorated. The Liberals did not believe that cancelling these agreements triggered the enumerated provisions in section 15 (since a pay equity agreement did not constitute admission that discrimination occurred), and even if discrimination had occurred, it was justifiable to terminate these agreements in order to respond to the province's fiscal emergency (*Newfoundland v. N.A.P.E.* 2004, para. 31). The intervening governments took similar positions, arguing that the executive had no capacity to bind future parliaments or legislatures and that courts had no ability to sit in judgment over how public money is distributed (*Newfoundland v. N.A.P.E.* 2004, Government of British Columbia Intervener Factum, para. 5).

The Supreme Court's ruling in *NAPE* roughly followed the reasoning from the lower courts and was consistent with the court's traditional reluctance to advise governments as to how to spend public money (as in *Reference re Canada Assistance Plan [B.C.]* 1991). While the court found the government's actions in violation of section 15, it also concluded that such actions were justified given the economic crisis in the province. In its section 1 analysis, the court loosened its normal evidentiary standard by accepting at face value statements made by government in the legislature concerning the scale and impact of the province's fiscal woes (Fudge 2007b). In an effort to carefully sidestep what it called the "dollars versus rights" debate (para 65), the court concluded that it could not turn a blind eye to the periodic financial emergencies that sometimes overwhelm governments. When such emergencies surface, governments must make difficult decisions in order to prioritize spending and survive the crisis. Those decisions, while difficult, reflect broad social values rather than simple dollars (*Newfoundland v. N.A.P.E.* 2004, para. 72). In recognizing these broad social values, the court was fairly consistent with its past ruling that had long prioritized government fiscal priorities over workers' rights. In fact, the decisions in the *Reference re Anti-Inflation Act* (1976), *PSAC* (1987), and the *Alberta Reference* (1987) all reflected deference to government fiscal priorities.

Activists, academics, and unions universally criticized the court's stunning omission that Charter rights could be pushed aside by a financial crisis. Judy Fudge, for instance, argued that substantive equality issues such as pay equity were taking "a back seat to the issues of fiscal crisis and institutional competence" (Fudge 2007b, 246). The National Association of Women and the Law (NAWL), the Feminist Alliance for International Action, and Newfoundland and Labrador's Provincial Advisory Council on the Status of Women organized a protest against the Supreme Court decision. The organizations all called on the federal and provincial governments to meet their obligations to defend women's equality in Canada and compensate the health care workers for past discrimination. NAWL spokesperson André Cole chastised the court, stating that if it "stops upholding rights when money is at stake, it will always be women, and others who are unequal, whose equality rights will be overridden" (quoted in Moorcroft 2005).

The Supreme Court's mixed decisions in *R. v. Advanced Cutting and Coring* and *Newfoundland v. N.A.P.E.* did little to dissuade unions from pursuing legal strategies. Labour's judicial victories in *Pepsi* and *Dunmore* clearly set in motion a broader and more concerted effort to advance Charter-based strategies for enhancing workers' rights. The union movement's traditional political strategy of bolstering electoral support for the NDP in English Canada and the embrace, within some organized labour sectors, of strategic voting schemes to prevent the election of Conservative governments yielded very little in terms of positive public policy outcomes for workers in the latter half of the 1990s or early 2000s. Unions in Canada had grown accustomed to finding imaginary silver linings in political defeats at the ballot box, but in the judicial arena, the Charter decisions at the turn of the century offered interesting possibilities, if not important victories, for unions. In other words, labour's legal response to neoliberalism seemed to offer much more hope than its electoral efforts, thus convincing an increasingly growing number of unions to embrace judicial strategies for advancing workers' rights.

The Possibilities and Limitations of Constitutional Labour Rights **5**

The small victories in cases like *KMart, Dunmore,* and *Pepsi* elevated the hopes of many labour activists that constitutional labour rights might finally act as a shield against aggressive neoliberal attacks by governments and employers (D. Fudge 2012, 239). No doubt this optimism fuelled union advancement of constitutional cases, especially as federal and provincial governments continued to pursue anti-union austerity programs throughout the 2000s. Many unions responded to state-led attacks on bargaining rights or the right to strike through organized public protests or electoral political action, but neither approach seemed to have much of an impact. Decades of broadsides against the labour movement and neoliberal restructuring of the economy had severely weakened unions' ability to effectively mount a successful strike, leading to a precipitous decline in the number of work stoppages by the turn of the century (Akyeampong 2001). Given the alternatives, the courts represented an increasingly reasonable and pragmatic strategic route for unions to defend the postwar labour relations framework against further erosion by governments.

At the centre of this pragmatic Charter-based legal strategy was the National Union of Public and General Employees (NUPGE). Throughout the 2000s, NUPGE launched a fairly prominent campaign to constitutionally protect "labour rights as human rights." The union had taken its cue from a group of labour lawyers and labour scholars who were arguing that a more sympathetic interpretation of labour's constitutional freedoms had the potential to advance labour's political and economic power (on these debates, see Fudge 2007a; MacNeil 2011). This effort was designed to sway public opinion and perception of workers' rights – conventionally treated as statutory rights – towards a human rights understanding of work and labour based on Canada's international obligations, in general, and on Article 23 of the United Nations' Universal Declaration of Human Rights, specifically.[1]

The labour movement's growing embrace of a "labour rights as human rights" strategy was fuelled in part by a need for public sector unions to protect the sanctity of their contracts against government austerity. While these struggles occurred everywhere (see the essays in Evans and Smith 2015), it was in British Columbia's education and health care sectors where the actions of Gordon Campbell's Liberal government opened the door for the Supreme Court to revisit the question of constitutional bargaining rights. Out of that dispute came the first case to substantially advance the constitutional rights of labour: *Health Services and Support – Facilities Subsector Bargaining Assn. v. British Columbia* (2007 [*BC Health Services*]). In *BC Health Services*, the Supreme Court took the historic step of recognizing, for the first time, that the Charter of Rights and Freedoms protected a right to collective bargaining. While that victory provided a moment of euphoria for labour lawyers, and for the labour movement more generally, the Supreme Court followed up with two decisions, *Plourde v. Wal-Mart* (2009) and *Ontario v. Fraser* (2011), that severely tempered the labour movement's expectations by shrinking the zone of legal toleration for labour rights that many believed had been established in *BC Health Services*.

BC Health Services and the Right to Bargain Collectively

BC Health Services originated with the election of Gordon Campbell and the BC Liberal Party in 2001. Within the context of BC's class-divided political landscape, the Liberals represented the 1990s incarnation of a centre-right coalition designed to defeat the labour-backed NDP and the broader Left (Pilon 2015a). Campaigning against an incredibly unpopular NDP government, the Liberals promised a "New

Era" for British Columbia through a series of dramatic policy proposals, which included the now familiar neoliberal promises to "dramatically" reduce personal and business taxation, along with reigning in costs in the heavily unionized public sector (BC Liberal Party 2001; Thompson and Bemmels 2003). With regard to labour relations, Campbell promised to honour existing contracts but committed to stripping teachers of the right to strike while outlawing sectoral bargaining, eliminating the union "hiring hall" in the construction industry and "restor[ing] workers' democratic right to a secret ballot vote on certification under the Labour Code" (BC Liberal Party 2001, 4).

The 2001 lopsided election victory (77 of 79 seats) provided the Liberals with the parliamentary latitude to restructure the province's labour laws in favour of employers. Within its first week of governing, the provincial government restricted nurses' ability to strike and then imposed an agreement on nurses that had been previously rejected by the union membership (Panitch and Swartz 2003, 207). An essential component of Campbell's austerity plan was to privatize many of the non-medical services in BC hospitals. Most of the workers in non-medical servicers were (and still are) members of the largest health care union in the province, the Hospital Employees' Union (HEU).[2] The HEU represents a diverse assortment of workers, including care aides, trades people, kitchen staff, housekeepers, and licensed practical nurses, or LPNs (Camfield 2006, 14–17; Cohen 2006, 629; Walchuk 2011, 106–24). HEU's membership also reflects the unequal gendered divisions of labour within the health care field. In 2002, the HEU consisted of over 85 percent women, 27 percent of whom identified as visible minorities with another 57 percent over the age of 45 (*BC Health Services* 2007, Heath Services and Support-Facilities Subsector Bargaining Association, Public Factum, para. 7). The vulnerability of these workers within the health field led to the HEU organizing militant campaigns in the 1980s and 1990s demanding pay equity for its membership. It speaks to the strength of the union that many of these campaigns were successful, with the wage gap between men and women being significantly reduced by the early 2000s (Camfield 2006, 15).

The vulnerability of the province's hospital workers made them an easy target for the BC Liberals' agenda of privatization and contracting out. The government's plan was both swiftly executed and extreme. In a special weekend sitting of the legislature, the Liberals introduced Bill 29, the *Health and Social Services Delivery Improvement Act.*[3] Bill 29 unilaterally overrode existing contracts between health employers and the unions, limited the time period for layoff notices, and restricted severance packages, all while virtually eliminating union "bumping" rights (i.e., replacing a less senior employee with a more senior employee whose position has been eliminated). The government also extended the ability of government to contract out what it defined as "non-clinical" work to the private sector (*Health and Social Services Delivery Improvement Act*, S.B.C. 2002). These actions were a blunt way for the government to downsize the workforce: Labour Minister Colin Hansen recognized that Bill 29 would encourage "a significant number of layoffs," estimated to exceed fifty thousand jobs in the sector (Beatty and Craig 2002). To add a layer of insult to the HEU (and the other public sector unions in the health field), the government only informed the unions of the contractual rollback twenty minutes before the bill was introduced (*BC Health Services* 2007, para. 7).

Bill 29 was internally devastating for the HEU. The first private contracts signed by the government after Bill 29 was passed were with the British firm Compass. In their first contract with Compass, former HEU members were paid 49.5 percent less than in their previous jobs in the public sector (*BC Health Services* 2007, Heath Services and Support-Facilities Subsector Bargaining Association, Public Factum, para. 12). Those who remained in the HEU were determined to fight the open assault on their workplaces. Many local activists and some union leadership attempted to rally support internally, while also reaching out to the province's labour movement in the hope of escalating theirs and the teachers' dispute towards a general strike. In the end, the general strike idea was rejected. As David Camfield (2007, 23) explains,

> Despite the resolutions demanding a general strike passed by many union locals and labour councils, the mass demonstrations in BC's two largest cities in 2002 were not followed by an escalation of resistance by BC's official labour leadership. Instead, the BCFL executive pursued a strategy centred around preparing to reelect the NDP in

the provincial election fixed by law for 2005. Within this strategy, direct action was to be eschewed and working-class anger at the cuts toned down lest they damage voter support for the NDP.

Notwithstanding the electoralist response from the broader labour movement, the HEU continued to ratchet up its workplace-based militancy, resulting in a rejected contract, an illegal strike, and even more draconian back-to-work legislation in 2004 (Camfield 2007, 18; Walchuk 2011, 113–14). In addition, the health care unions simultaneously pursued a two-pronged legal strategy: joining with the Canadian Labour Congress (CLC) and NUPGE in filing a complaint with the International Labour Organization's (ILO's) Committee on Freedom of Association and then launching its own constitutional challenge to Bill 29 on the grounds that the law violated the Charter's guarantee of freedom of association (s. 2[d]) and the equality provisions (s. 15).[4]

In March 2003, the ILO's Committee on Freedom of Association ruled that the government's actions violated international freedom of association conventions, finding that "recourse to legislative restrictions on collective bargaining can only, in the long term, prejudice and destabilize the labour relations climate" (ILO, Freedom of Association Committee 2003, Case 2180 and 2173). Notwithstanding the strong rebuke by the ILO, the BC government essentially ignored the ruling. In keeping with tradition (Norman 2004, 604–7), Premier Campbell simply stated that his government would not be swayed by the ILO's findings, affirming further, "I feel no pressure whatsoever. I was not participating in any discussion with the UN" (Steffenhagen 2003). Despite the government's decision to ignore the ILO's findings, the HEU continued to pursue its legal challenge in domestic courts.

Before the lower court, the unions argued that the 2001 *Dunmore* decision substantially moved the jurisprudence on freedom of association to include a collective right to bargain for vulnerable workers (*Health Services and Support-Facilities Subsector Bargaining Association et al. v. Her Majesty The Queen et al.* 2003, paras. 7, 60–65). The court was not convinced that *Dunmore* represented such a departure; rather, it maintained that the government's actions were fully consistent with the Charter. The HEU appealed the ruling, but the BC Court of

Appeals upheld the trial judge's ruling. Similar to their colleagues in *Newfoundland v. N.A.P.E.* (2004), the judges at the Court of Appeals maintained that notwithstanding the *Dunmore* precedent, legislative intervention in the health sector was about controlling costs in times of crisis (*Health Services and Support – Facilities Subsector Bargaining Assn. v. British Columbia* 2004). Undeterred, the union appealed its case to the Supreme Court of Canada.

Before the Supreme Court, the unions took issue with the government's position that Bill 29 was about protecting patients' rights and preserving public health care in British Columbia. The unions took the position that Bill 29 was deliberately aimed "at increasing the rights of management" through legislative decree (*BC Health Services* 2007, Heath Services and Support-Facilities Subsector Bargaining Association, Reply Factum, para. 15). In allowing management to break existing collective agreements, Bill 29 represented a legal attempt to impose concessions on vulnerable workers at the margins of the health care sector. Moreover, the unions argued that Bill 29 breached section 2(d) of the Charter because it deliberately voided existing collective agreements that had been negotiated in good faith while also precluding future negotiations on workplace conditions, benefits, and wages (*BC Health Services* 2007, Appellants' Factum, Public Copy, para. 27). The unions also argued that Bill 29 targeted "associational activity by singling out *collective* bargaining and *collective* agreements for restriction and prohibition, without imposing the same restrictions and prohibitions on *individual* bargaining and *individual* agreements" (*BC Health Services* 2007, CLC Intervener Factum, para. 5; emphasis in original).

The unions grounded their constitutional argument on the evolving jurisprudence regarding the collective dimensions of freedom of association in the Charter. All of the unions that intervened in the case argued that Dickson's "purposive approach" to freedom of association in the labour trilogy was recognized and elevated by the *Dunmore* decision (*BC Health Services* 2007, Appellants' Factum, Public Copy, paras. 47–54; CLC Intervener Factum, paras. 3–5; CSN Intervener Factum, 8). According to Judy Fudge (2008b, 29–30), relying on *Dunmore* was "a risky strategy" because the court clearly stated that the collective dimension of 2(d) excluded both the right to strike and collective bargaining.

Nevertheless, the unions believed that *Dunmore* did not "foreclose the possibility" that collective bargaining should be protected under 2(d) of the Charter (CLC Intervener Factum, para. 17). In fact, all of the unions argued that *Dunmore* recognized collective organizations as being "qualitatively distinct" from the individual "because communities can embody objectives that individuals cannot" (*Dunmore v. Ontario* 2001, para. 16).

In putting their case forward, the unions expressed the belief that human rights jurisprudence in Canada had been enriched by *Dunmore's* acknowledgment that collective activity contributed to the Charter values of democracy and human dignity. Collective action, they contended, took on added meaning in the workplace because such endeavours contribute to the dignity of human labour; in essence, the freedom to improve human dignity through association is most valuable and thus transformative in the workplace (*BC Health Services* 2007, Appellants' Factum, Public Copy paras. 69–70). Finally, the appellants were not seeking to constitutionalize their bargaining unit or specific aspects of the *Labour Relations Code* but rather to protect a process "to negotiate terms and conditions of a collective which allow them to maintain a collective" (para. 105). Once that process was completed and an agreement was reached, those terms could not be unilaterally eliminated by government acting as the employer (para. 109).

The union factums identified two crucial hurdles that had to be overcome in order for *BC Health Services* to be successful. The first was to demonstrate that collective bargaining was an internationally recognized right that has been endorsed by the Government of Canada (*BC Health Services* 2007, Appellants' Factum, Public Copy, paras. 82–83). Citing reports from Human Resources Development Canada, the CLC made the bold claim that international law represents "a global consensus" that collective bargaining is a "fundamental human right and an integral component of freedom of association in the labour context" (CLC Intervener Factum, para. 24).

The second hurdle was to prove that the collective bargaining process itself predates the Wagner/PC 1003 model of labour relations. The unions believed it was important to counter the statements made by the majority in the *Alberta Reference* (1987, paras. 141–44) that collective bargaining was a "modern" right and therefore not a fundamental free-dom in the constitution. This position, however, was more challenging because there was no consensus on the origins or historical definition of "collective bargaining." For some radical unions, for instance, collect-ive bargaining and strikes were political ways to challenge both em-ployers and the state, while other more pragmatic unions interpreted collective bargaining as a meaningful dialogue with employers. Union lawyers, however, were not interested in the nuances of labour history. Instead, union counsel employed what Eric Tucker (2008, 160) refers to as "law office" history designed solely "to generate data and interpreta-tions that are of use in resolving modern legal controversies." In so do-ing, the BC Teachers' Federation (BCTF) maintained that the modern framework of industrial relations

> did not grant to working people any basic or core rights to trade unionism or collective bargaining that had not been achieved, exer-cised and recognized previously. Historically, trade unionism, col-lective bargaining with employers, and the right to strike had been fought for, developed, practiced, and recognized in Canada for many decades prior to PC 1003. The fundamental effect of PC 1003 and subsequent provincial legislation was not to create a basic right to collective bargaining. Rather, the legislation was passed to regulate and provide an institutional framework for the exercise of the pre-existing rights to bargain collectively and to strike. (*BC Health Services* 2007, BCTF Intervener Factum, para. 9)

However much truth there was in such a statement, what the BCTF wanted to cement in the collective mind of the court was the percep-tion that collective bargaining was organic and not tied to a specific statutory regime.

As has been true of almost all Charter cases relating to the rights of labour, the governments argued against the constitutionalization of collective bargaining. Perhaps not surprisingly, the BC government de-fended its legislation on the basis that government has a constitution-ally mandated duty to act in order to provide necessary health care services (*BC Health Services* 2007, Government of British Columbia

Respondent Factum, paras 23–24; citing *Chaoulli v. Quebec (Attorney General)* 2005, paras. 96–97). The government interpreted its responsibility as managing the public purse so as to control public health care costs. The government defended this position as creating the conditions for "effective management of complex health care policy issues," to which Bill 29 was a "nuanced and innovative response" (*BC Health Services* 2007, Government of British Columbia Respondent Factum, para. 25).

Having defended the political necessity of Bill 29, the government then took a truculent position on collective bargaining, arguing that it "does not fit comfortably within the public sector" given its political nature (*BC Health Services* 2007, Government of British Columbia Respondent Factum, para. 27). Recognizing that the court's decision in the labour trilogy had long affirmed that the Charter did not apply to labour relations, the BC government also asserted that labour policy is best left to government. Stating that healthcare unions already had "monopoly power in the collective bargaining process," the BC government asserted that the only way it could control costs in the public health field was through a legislative decree (para 36). It adamantly argued that constitutionalizing collective bargaining would unfairly impose a "positive obligation" (para 54–55; 58) on public authorities to conclude agreements that it otherwise would have rejected. Finally, the government argued that since the 1990s, a dynamic combination of fiscal pressures and "new philosophies about the appropriate role of government" (para 31) had shifted the terrain about controlling costs within the public service. Of course, these "new philosophies" referred to the politics of neoliberalism and its accompanying demand for austerity and lean public service delivery. It is noteworthy that the provincial government based its position on the idea that the ascendency of neoliberalism was an adequate legal defence for eliminating the collective bargaining rights of health care workers.

Similar to the BC government, all of the other intervening governments maintained that labour rights had no place in the constitution. The Government of Ontario argued that the framers of the Charter consciously omitted economic rights – including contractual rights – from the constitution (*BC Health Services* 2007, Government of Ontario

Intervener Factum, para. 23–25–27). The governments also argued that the unions had misinterpreted the transformative nature of *Dunmore*'s interpretation of freedom of association. These same governments leaned on the Supreme Court's assertion in the labour trilogy that collective bargaining was a modern statutorily derived right that should not be protected by the constitution. The Government of Alberta, for instance, made an important distinction between collective bargaining as a tool of voluntary association of employees, on the one hand, and the modern notion of collective bargaining as a statutory creation by governments, on the other (*BC Health Services* 2007, Government of Alberta Intervener Factum, para. 5). Building on this point, the Government of New Brunswick argued that modern labour relations law fundamentally altered the employment relationship between unionized workers and employers. Non-unionized workers, for example, had no legal right to withdraw their labour and maintain their employment, whereas unionized workers did have that ability (*BC Health Services* 2007, Government of New Brunswick Intervener Factum, para 10).

The Progressive Conservative governments in both Alberta and New Brunswick argued that collective bargaining schemes were designed to elevate and, indeed, promote collective employee power (*BC Health Services* 2007, Government of New Brunswick Intervener Factum, para. 11; Government of Alberta Intervener Factum, paras. 15–17). The governments contended that if the court were to constitutionalize such provisions, the balance of power in the workplace would be permanently altered and the union would be given additional power to effectively "achieve its purpose" (Government of New Brunswick Intervener Factum, para. 18). Elevating labour union power in this way, argued the Government of Ontario (Intervener Factum, para. 52–53), would impose on government a constitutional "duty to negotiate," which could spill over into the private sector by forcing government to create a new "prescriptive" labour code. The Government of New Brunswick (Intervener Factum, paras. 17–18) also argued that since the Supreme Court had consistently refused to recognize the constitutional status of commercial associations (e.g., in *R. v. Skinner* 1990; *Canadian Egg Marketing Agency v. Richardson* 1998), it would be patently unreasonable to elevate the activities of labour unions to the status of constitutionally protected rights.

The Supreme Court finally decided *BC Health Services* in 2007. The court struck down several sections of British Columbia's *Health and Social Services Delivery Improvement Act* and, for the first time, ruled that the Charter "protects the capacity of members of labour unions to engage, in association, in collective bargaining on fundamental workplace issues" (*BC Health Services* 2007, para. 19). Writing for the majority, Chief Justice McLachlin and Justice LeBel came to their conclusion through four observations regarding the importance of collective bargaining. First, the jurisprudence since *Dunmore* demonstrated that there was a collective nature to freedom of association that now included a Charter right to collective bargaining. Second, collective bargaining was not the product of a single statutory regime; rather, it predated a single legal model and was deeply rooted in historical relations between workers, employers, and the state. Third, international legal recognition of collective bargaining carried important weight in interpreting the Charter. Finally, the court suggested that the "right to collective bargaining is consistent with, and indeed, promotes, other Charter rights, freedoms and values" (para. 20).

In order to arrive at this decision, the Supreme Court had to revisit the cases that had previously denied constitutional protection for collective bargaining: the labour trilogy and *PIPSC*. For McLachlin and LeBel, the majority's rationale for denying a collective dimension to labour rights in these earlier cases (see Chapter 3) rested on a "narrow focus on individual activities," which, in agreement with the labour unions, "has been overtaken by *Dunmore*" (*BC Health Services* 2007, para. 28). For the majority, *Dunmore* seemed to clarify three developing aspects of constitutional law: the meaning of association under the Charter and what constitutes "substantial interference" with the "associational aspect" of collective activity; the need to interpret violations of association within the context in which those damages took place; and the idea that Charter rights of association could impose a positive obligation on government (paras. 31–35). Having highlighted the conclusions from *Dunmore*, the majority in *BC Health Services* argued that previous jurisprudence erred in concluding that collective bargaining was a "modern" right. Rather, the court was now convinced that these rights were deeply rooted in Canadian (and British) history and were therefore not tied to a specific statutory framework (para. 25). Previous jurisprudence had also suggested that labour relations questions should be deferred to the expertise of the legislature. McLachlin and LeBel brushed that conclusion aside, stating that in the age of evolving "Charter values," it was no longer defensible to declare a "judicial 'no go' zone for an entire right on the ground that it may involve the courts in policy matters" (para. 26).

Having put aside the previous court's reluctance to intervene in the field of labour relations, the court now had to address the issue of collective bargaining directly. In *PIPSC v. NWT* (1990, 392), L'Heureux-Dubé had argued that section 2(d) was never meant to protect the "object of an association whose fulfilment is fundamental to the existence of the association" (referenced in *BC Health Services* 2007, para. 29). In *BC Health Services*, the majority maintained that it was entirely realistic to separate the procedure of collective bargaining "without mandating constitutional protection for the fruits of that bargaining process" (para. 29). In other words, the actual process of collective bargaining could be constitutionally divorced from the gains or concessions made at the bargaining table. Finally, the court dismissed the decontextualized interpretation of freedom of association in the labour trilogy. Using unusually strong language to critique their predecessors, McLachlin and LeBel dismissed Justice McIntyre's comparison of labour unions with golf or gun clubs (*Alberta Reference* 1987, paras. 171, 175) as a "generic approach" ignoring fundamental "differences between organizations" (*BC Health Services* 2007, para. 30).

The Supreme Court's conclusions on these issues came through a truncated summary of British and Canadian labour history. For historians, the court's historiography was certainly suspect; it was designed to tell an uncomplicated and easy-to-understand chronology of events that led to ever increasing collective freedoms for workers under the current Wagner/PC 1003 model (*BC Health Services* 2007, paras. 40–63; for more detail, see Langille 2009, 188–93; Tucker 2008, 151–80). For the court, however, that story was important to the conclusion that collective bargaining had no connection to a specific legal institution. Having determined that collective bargaining predated the current industrial relations model, the court then made several incandescent observations about the democratizing influences of collective bargaining in the workplace. Examining international and national labour relations frameworks, the court determined that an international consensus existed around the importance of collective bargaining. Perhaps the most obvious example of this argument was the borrowed language from the 1968 Task Force on Labour Relations (the Woods Commission), in which the court stated that collective bargaining imposed legal responsibilities on its participants and therefore deserved government support. Generally, workers accepted the Wagner/PC 1003 model of industrial democracy but, in so doing, also had to consent to "the rule of law in the workplace" (*BC Health Services* 2007, para. 85). In this case, the court believed that collective bargaining itself was integral to peaceful relationships in the workplace and therefore was deserving of constitutional protection.

Finally, the court concluded that constitutionalizing collective bargaining fit well with its own understanding of "Charter values." For the court, Charter values were those legal and policy instruments that promote human dignity, equality, liberty, respect for the autonomy of the person, and democracy (*BC Health Services* 2007, para. 81). In language that almost all union activists would find agreeable, the court determined that "the right to bargain collectively with an employer enhances the human dignity, liberty and autonomy of workers by giving them the opportunity to influence the establishment of workplace rules and thereby gain some control over a major aspect of their lives, namely their work" (para. 82). So important was collective bargaining to this new era of Charter values that the Supreme Court concluded this section of its analysis by recognizing that collective bargaining was the primary tool to "palliate the historical inequality between employers and employees," thus recognizing the power imbalance that exists in modern workplaces (para. 84).[5]

Having arrived at the conclusion that the Charter now protected collective bargaining, the court then turned to the substance of this new right. Given the glowing attributes that the court ascribed to collective bargaining to enshrining values such as democracy, equality, and liberty, it was somewhat surprising to learn that in fact "the right to collective bargaining ... is a limited right" (*BC Health Services* 2007, para. 91). In effect, this newfound freedom was nothing more than a procedural right with inherent limitations:

> This protection does not cover all aspects of "collective bargaining," as that term is understood in the statutory labour relations regimes that are in place across the country. Nor does it ensure a particular outcome in a labour dispute, or guarantee access to any particular statutory regime. What is protected is simply the right of employees to associate *in a process of collective action to achieve workplace goals.* (para. 19; emphasis added)

This caveat suggested that the right to collective bargaining was not fundamental at all but rather simply a procedural right that protected only against "substantial interference" with associational activity (para. 90). By this standard, substantial interference in the collective bargaining process was measured by two things: the importance of the matter altered or eliminated by government and the "impacts on the collective right to *good faith* negotiation and consultation" (para. 93, emphasis added).

The Supreme Court's two-pronged "substantial interference" test narrowed the constitutional scope of collective bargaining and also raised important questions: What aspects of government interference in the collective bargaining process would be considered essential? Moreover, for the purpose of the Charter, what constitutes good faith negotiations? The court's answers to both questions were ambiguous, stating that "substantial interference" would be "any law or state action that prevent or deny meaningful discussion and consultation about working conditions between employees and their employer ... [or] laws that unilaterally nullify significant negotiated terms in existing collective agreements" (*BC Health Services* 2007, para. 96). Lesser areas of bargaining such as employee uniforms or the availability of parking spaces would be considered not as significant and thus not protected by the Charter. Put simply, in order to meet a constitutional threshold, the parties would need to agree to meet and, in good faith, attempt to reach an agreement on substantial workplace issues (paras. 97–109). As had become clear in most Charter jurisprudence related to freedom of association, the answers to what would be considered "substantial interference" and "good faith bargaining" would be determined through future litigation.

The court then determined that the impugned sections (ss. 4, 5, 6[2], 6[4], and 9, in conjunction with s. 10) of Bill 29 were unconstitutional. However, in determining whether these sections amounted to *substantial* interference, the court determined that only those sections that addressed contracting out and bumping rights (ss. 6[2], 6[4], and 9) interfered with the process of collective bargaining; those sections that dealt with the government's ability to reorganize service delivery or reassign work (ss. 4 and 5) and to void a collective agreement if it violated the act (s. 10) did not contravene the Charter. For a Supreme Court that had just demanded a more contextual approach to Charter rights, this was quite the concession to the power of governments and employers to radically alter workers' lives (Etherington 2009, 732–34). Nevertheless, the conclusion that only sections 6(2), 6(4), and 9 were unconstitutional still required the court to determine if such violations were reasonably justified under section 1 of the Charter. The government had attempted to claim that the economic crisis in health care required a heavy-handed approach (which was accepted by the lone dissenter in this case, Justice Deschamps). The majority, however, determined that the government had provided no evidence that such extreme tactics were necessary and struck down the offending sections.

The Aftermath of *BC Health Services*

Despite its significant limitations, the ruling in *BC Health Services* took almost all labour relations stakeholders by surprise. Immediately upon hearing the verdict, lawyers conceded that labour's judicial victory was unexpected given the existing jurisprudence and the Supreme Court's tendency to defer to legislatures on issues of labour relations. BC labour lawyer Arvay Finlay, who represented the appellant unions, could barely temper his enthusiasm: "This is huge; this is unbelievable ... I'm too excited to talk like a normal human being. This is going to change the landscape for collective bargaining for every union across the country" (quoted in Makin 2007). Steven Barrett, a lawyer for the CLC, was more grounded but equally happy: "We have seen 20 years of governments running roughshod over collective bargaining rights. The Court has recognized that, without constitutional protection, governments are simply going to disrespect collective agreements" (quoted in Makin 2007). Paul Cavalluzzo, a leading labour relations lawyer and UFCW counsel in *Dunmore*, stated quite simply that the decision "is a magnificent victory for workers in Canada" (quoted in Tracey 2007).

Labour leaders were equally elated. Judy Darcy, former Canadian Union of Public Employees (CUPE) national president and HEU secretary-business manager, stated, "It is a tremendous victory ... I can tell you, my phone, my e-mail, people coming into the building. People are, they jump for joy, they cry, they shriek, I mean front-line health-care workers have been through absolute hell" (quoted in Brethour and Drake 2007). This opinion was echoed by CLC president Ken Georgetti, who triumphantly declared that the "ruling takes Canada in the right direction. Finally, workers' freedom of association includes the right to bargain a collective agreement that cannot be ripped apart at the government's convenience" (quoted in O'Neil 2007). Janice St. John, an active HEU member who lost her job as a result of Bill 29 was equally sanguine, admitting that she "was trying to prepare myself for the worst situation but I think today is going to be one of the most memorable days of my life ... It feels good to finally have justice on the side of all workers" (quoted in Anderson 2007).

Numerous legal scholars echoed the jovial response from unions and workers. For those committed to the institutions of postwar industrial relations, the elevation of collective bargaining to constitutional status was a positive legal change because it signalled that the court "would act as a guarantor of employee rights in the labour relations context" (Bilson 2009, 71). There was certainly some truth to such a claim. In 2008, the BC government was forced to amend Bill 29 by removing the offending sections and to renegotiate agreements with the health unions. Although the government was able to retain some control over future contracting out and privatization provisions, in a series of "grinding" negotiations, the unions successfully bargained $85 million in additional compensation and retraining benefits for its members (McEvoy 2009; Palmer 2008). In Nova Scotia, the Supreme Court's decision in *BC Health Services* reluctantly persuaded the Conservative government of John Hamm to grant bargaining rights to two thousand seasonal and casual workers (Canadian Press 2007). Recognizing these benefits, Sara Slinn concluded that the court's decision represented a "tremendous change" because governments would have "to rethink their dependence on legislative intervention" when dealing with the legitimate workplace demands of public sector workers (Slinn 2011). Slinn's point was recognized begrudgingly by conservative government labour lawyers who continued to cling to the labour trilogy's claims that associational rights had no place in protecting modern statutory rights and their corresponding duties.

Roy Adams argued that the decision in *BC Health Services* opened the door for a more pragmatic interpretation of freedom of association under the Charter. In his view, the Supreme Court's further embrace of international law to enhance the collective aspects of freedom of association was an important advancement for workers' rights (Adams 2009b). Following his earlier work (see Chapter 4), Adams continued to view the court's embrace of international law standards as opening the door for non-statutory or minority unions. In fact, Adams argued that the "Supreme Court must compel legislatures to rewrite the Canadian labour code" so as to allow for minority unions to exercise collective bargaining rights for all workers (94), an argument that raised more than a few eyebrows in a labour movement still very much wedded to the Wagner principles of majoritarianism and exclusivity. Nevertheless, some labour lawyers and scholars have found Adams's argument convincing and have suggested that *BC Health Services* has opened the door to expand the range of collective representation for non-unionized workers (Blackett 2009; Braley-Rattai 2013; Doorey 2010; 2013; Harcourt and Haynes 2001).

Charter critics were less optimistic about the judicial victory in *BC Health Services*. Perhaps the tone of that criticism was best echoed by Leo Panitch and Donald Swartz (2013, 38), who argue that labour leaders interpreted the landmark decision "rather incautiously," noting that "expectations that this ruling would halt or reverse the assault on union rights rested on a misunderstanding of the manner in which the court used the term 'collective bargaining.'" Indeed, Charter enthusiasts seemed to gloss over or ignore the court's distinction between collective bargaining as a familiar legal framework and collective bargaining as a mere abstract "consultative" process. The court's reliance on the latter definition meant that the constitutional right to collective bargaining did not include a dispute resolution mechanism that would normally include the ability to strike. In fact, a critical reading of the court's reasoning in *BC Health Services* suggests that the government's central constitutional mistake was not its heavy-handed approach to addressing the economic challenges in BC hospitals but rather its arrogant introduction of Bill 29 with no consultation with the unions (Fudge 2008b, 28).

A sober reading of *BC Health Services* reveals that there are few legal mechanisms to stop a determined anti-union government from rolling back labour union rights in existing collective agreements, provided such rollbacks come at the conclusion of a process of consultation with the union. Moreover, the decision did not address the substantive inequality of marginalized workers, especially in the private sector (Fudge 2008a, 224–26). This conclusion comes out of the Supreme Court's own reasoning that bargaining is a limited right that only guarantees some workers access to a process. What is not guaranteed is the outcome of bargaining; unions cannot expect the Charter to act as a counterbalance to employer power. An employer who simply goes through the motions of bargaining is afforded enough flexibility in this decision to ensure that bargaining outcomes are unlikely to be dramatically affected. As such, while the *BC Health Services* decision did force a dogmatic anti-union government to revisit its approach to labour relations, it did not prevent future governments from pursuing anti-union agendas, either overtly or by stealth (Savage 2009, 15).

In its long discussion about the historical roots of collective bargaining in Canada, the court was adamant that it was not constitutionalizing access to a specific statutory regime but to a bargaining process. The test to determine whether government interfered with that process was that of "substantial interference," by which the court would evaluate whether government intervention constituted "unfair interference" and contravened "good faith bargaining" (*BC Health Services* 2007, paras. 60, 133). Whether it was intentional or not, the constitutional recognition of "unfair interference" and "good faith bargaining" elevated two fundamental aspects of the Wagner/PC 1003 model of industrial relations (Fudge 2010, 42). To be sure, most labour lawyers will find it difficult to argue against that rationale since their profession is grounded on such an industrial relations framework. Yet the court's conclusion raised long-standing questions about the expertise of courts in regulating the day-to-day minutiae of contemporary labour relations (Langille 2010b). In defending the original labour trilogy, Peter Hogg, a long-time constitutional scholar and former union council for the Public Service Alliance of Canada (PSAC), critiqued the court's rationale that collective bargaining was a "modern right" supported by statutory protection. Hogg also believed that the court's recognition of collective bargaining as a constitutional right, paired with its chastisement of the BC government's unilateral altering of signed contracts, "elevated collective agreements above statutes in the hierarchy of laws, and granted them virtually the same status as the provisions of the Charter itself" (Hogg 2011, 44–9).

There is some irony that the court reached its conclusion on a constitutional right to collective bargaining at the same time that the postwar labour relations framework was proving incapable of reaching the vast majority of workers in the labour market. As of 2016, only 30 percent of workers in Canada were unionized and the proportion of workers in the private sector with access to collective bargaining was half of that.[6] In effect, the Charter's protection of collective bargaining reinforces the institutional limitations of the Wagner/PC 1003 model of industrial relations in that it tacitly recognizes that the vast majority of workers will rarely be able to access the freedom to bargain effectively (Langille 2009).

In a carefully nuanced analysis of the *BC Health Services* decision, labour lawyers Valerie Matthews Lemieux and Steven Barrett (who acted as co-counsel for the CLC in the *BC Health Services* case) argued that the future impact of the case would "depend on the extent to which future courts take an unduly narrow reading of the decision as simply imposing a mere consultation requirement on governments before overriding collective bargaining rights" rather than "view the decision as requiring governments to truly respect good faith bargaining by respecting negotiated collective agreements and avoiding legislation which limits the scope of bargaining" (Lemieux and Barrett 2007). This argument recognizes that the right of effective collective bargaining is not a top-down derivative of the Charter but rather a bottom-up process premised on workers' abilities to entrench the skills of collective solidarity. It was this reality that fed former Canadian Auto Worker president Buzz Hargrove's continuing mistrust of a constitutional approach to labour rights:

> I remain sceptical about the real value of constitutionalizing rights. Providing a minimal level of constitutional protection to a part of the collective bargaining process will not mean that there will be economic or social progress for workers. In my experience, such gains can only be made by exerting power at the bargaining table, by voicing workers' demands in the public forum, and by pressuring political actors to understand the importance of a worker's platform. (Hargrove 2009, 45)

In a broader political sense, by shifting the focus of collective bargaining towards a constitutional human rights understanding of labour management relations, unions risk undermining the class-based solidarity that created and sustained the institutions of collective bargaining in the first place (Savage 2009, 18). Notwithstanding these criticisms, the *BC Health Services* decision certainly opened the door for a beleaguered labour movement to further constitutionalize the existing system of labour relations. *BC Health Services* had effectively reversed the jurisprudence of the labour trilogy cases, but it also left the door open for a constitutional reinterpretation of a wider ambit of union rights, including who might access collective bargaining rights, what weight the "substantial interference" test might take, and, of course, the coveted constitutional right to strike (MacNeil 2011, 38–46). The open-ended nature of these questions emboldened organized labour to pursue an even more aggressive judicial strategy to challenge state-led attacks on collective bargaining, including legal challenges to back-to-work legislation, public sector austerity programs, and laws restricting union membership and collective bargaining rights. How far *BC Health Services* would take workers, however, was about to be revealed. The initial implications were far from encouraging.

Constitutional Litigation at the Crossroads: *Plourde* and *Fraser*

In 2009, the Supreme Court poured ice-cold water on the UFCW's decade-long North American campaign to unionize Walmart stores. After a 2004 organizing breakthrough in a store in Jonquière, Quebec, the union was unable to reach a first contract with Walmart. The union then filed for an arbitrated first contract, as was its right under Quebec's *Labour Code*. Walmart's response reflected both its power and stature in the retail sector: it decided to close the store and dismiss 190 employees rather than bargain with the union. Walmart worker Gaétan Plourde (supported by the union) challenged the store closure "based on the contention that Walmart is a union-busting employer with a long track record of anti-union activity" and "that the closing of the Jonquière store was intended not only as a reprisal against Jonquière employees ... but to send a 'chilling' signal to other Walmart employees" (*Plourde v. Wal-Mart* 2009, para. 25). The appellants argued that these actions were a clear violation of several sections of Quebec's *Labour Code* that forbid employers from arbitrarily punishing pro-union employees (para. 2; for more detail, see MacNeil 2010, 495–540). While Walmart's actions seemed to contravene broad interpretations of the *Labour Code* that had long been endorsed by the Quebec courts, Plourde's complaint later adopted a constitutional argument over the expansion of freedom of association rights that had progressed with the decision in *BC Health Services* (Bilson 2010, 283–97). Before the Supreme Court, Plourde argued that he and his colleagues were fired because of their union activities. For the union, the question at the centre of the dispute was this: How much did the associational rights of workers protect against a private business' decision to avoid unionization through a closure of the business (*Plourde v. Wal-Mart* 2009, Gaétan Plourde Appellant Factum, para. 24)? For Plourde, the answers seemed relatively simple: *BC Health Services* apparently confirmed that actions designed to break a union were a fundamental breach of the associational rights of workers (paras. 55, 62, 65).

Walmart and the intervening business organizations argued that the Charter did not apply to this case because businesses are private entities. In a capitalist enterprise, the choice to open or close a business is at the core of economic freedom; it is entirely the "prerogative of management and it is not subject to judicial review," argued the Canadian Chamber of Commerce (*Plourde v. Wal-Mart* 2009, CCC Intervener Factum, para. 24). Given that Walmart was a private entity, management was free to make a business decision regarding operational and labour costs, reasoned the Coalition of BC Businesses. Moreover, the coalition argued that workers could not expect the Charter to protect them from "the negative economic consequences" of those decisions (Intervener Factum, para. 23). Walmart argued that what Plourde and the UFCW were attempting to do was to "constitutionalize labour law in Quebec" and undermine the balance of power between business and unions in the province (Respondent Factum, para. 44). For Walmart, the constitutional question was frivolous since there was no government action to merit using the Charter at all. If the court were to read *BC Health Services* into this dispute, it would "impose new regulations in this area since it affects the very balancing of interests in labour laws which are the domain of the legislature" (para. 108). Such a conclusion would be a fundamental misinterpretation of *BC Health Services,* claimed the Coalition of BC Businesses (Intervener Factum, para. 16), since the Supreme Court had made clear that Parliament and legislatures were free to design collective bargaining processes that meet their unique jurisdictional circumstances.

In 2009, the Supreme Court ruled on Plourde's complaint and on a companion case dealing with reinstatement of employment after the Walmart closure (*Desbiens v. Wal-Mart Canada Corp.* 2009). Given Walmart's nefarious history of union avoidance, it would have been entirely plausible that the court's new "purposive" and "contextual" approach to associational freedoms would have led to a favourable decision for the workers (see Adams 2005; Gupta 2013; Lichtenstein 2006; 2008, 1462–1501; 2010, 156–96; Tucker 2005). In a 6–3 decision, however, the Supreme Court chose not to extend its newfound support for associational freedoms to vulnerable workers in the retail sector. Writing for the majority, Justice Binnie suggested that the issue in this case had "nothing to do with any general inquiry into Wal-Mart's business practices" but rather reflected a narrow procedural question about employees having to prove that an employer closed a store specifically to avoid unionization (*Plourde v. Wal-Mart* 2009, para. 4).

In ruling in favour of the company, the court both undermined the legislative remedies available to workers through Quebec's *Labour Code* and dismissed out of hand the constitutional argument that Wal-Mart was violating a procedural right to collective bargaining. Plourde and the intervening unions had argued that a generous and purposive reading of the *Labour Code* should reflect the Charter values that were highlighted in *BC Health Services*. The court, however, reprimanded the UFCW for making such a broad political argument, suggesting that it

> extends the reasoning in *Health Services* well beyond its natural limits. In that case the state was not only the legislator but the employer. Here the employer is a private corporation ... The legislature has crafted a balance between the rights of labour and the rights of management in a way that respects freedom of association ...
>
> Care must be taken not only to avoid upsetting the balance the legislature has struck in the Code taken as a whole, but not to hand to one side (labour) a lopsided advantage because employees bargain through their union (and can thereby invoke freedom of association) whereas employers, for the most part, bargain individually. (*Plourde v. Wal-Mart* 2009, paras. 56–57)

The court's reliance on the "balance of power" comparison between a union and Wal-Mart, the country's largest private sector employer, echoed some of the outdated judicial reasoning from the labour trilogy decisions and was certainly void of the contextual approach championed in *BC Health Services* (Smith 2012). What is more, the majority of the Supreme Court fell back on a traditional interpretation of individual rights in capitalist societies, placing the individual rights of corporations above the collective rights of workers and their unions.

The Supreme Court's unwillingness to expand labour rights in a manner that threatened the balance of power in the private sector was also demonstrated in *Ontario (Attorney General) v. Fraser* (2011). In *Fraser,* the Court was asked to rule on the constitutionality of Ontario's *Agricultural Employees Protection Act, 2002* (*AEPA*), which was the Ontario Progressive Conservative government's legislative response to *Dunmore* (see Chapter 4). The *AEPA* granted employees in the agricultural sector the ability to make a "reasonable opportunity to make representations" to employers regarding terms and conditions of employment (*AEPA*, s. 5[1]). The act also gave some protections for workers to be free from employer discrimination during a unionization drive and protection against employer interference (ss. 8–9). The act did not forbid employer-dominated associations, a fact that Rol-Land Farms Ltd. took advantage of during a 2003 unionization drive (*Ontario v. Fraser* 2011, Michael Fraser Respondent Factum, para. 59). While these provisions fell far short of the protections in the *Ontario Labour Relations Act* (*OLRA*), the government still felt the need to balance the *AEPA*'s protection for employee associations with employer demands. In particular, the act mandated that the "unique characteristics of agriculture, including, but not limited to, its seasonal nature, its sensitivity to time and climate, the perishability of agricultural products and the need to protect animal and plant life" were to be safeguarded during any union organizing drive (*AEPA*, s. 1[1]). In the event that the process of "representations" proved unworkable, employees were able to appeal their lack of access to a quasi-independent tribunal, the Agriculture, Food, and Rural Affairs Appeal Tribunal (*AEPA*, ss. 2, 11). The tribunal, however, had limited remedial powers such that it could only order farm workers' organizations access to private property under very limited circumstances (ss. 6–7).

Unlike the *OLRA*, the *AEPA* did not require farm employers to legally recognize or negotiate with *bona fide* labour unions. Employers had no legal obligation to reach an agreement with an employee association, and there was no guarantee that a collective agreement would result from negotiations. Workers were also denied a mechanism with which to resolve bargaining impasses, handing employers virtually all the power during any future negotiations. In effect, the *AEPA* denied farm workers the Wagner/PC 1003 model's statutory protection of good faith bargaining, majoritarian exclusivity, and a dispute resolution mechanism such as the right to strike or interest arbitration. The *AEPA* also denied financial protection for employee associations, which often took the form of the mandatory dues check off, or the Rand formula (Bartkiw 2009, 82; Walchuk 2009, 154). These limitations were not obscure or difficult to decipher. By the government's own admission, the *AEPA* was designed "to ensure that the freedom of association is meaningful" but that the legislation was "not intended to extend collective bargaining to agricultural workers" (*Ontario [Attorney General] v. Fraser* 2011, paras. 105–6). In response, three agricultural workers and the president of the UFCW went to court and questioned whether the *AEPA*'s vague protection of "representations" operated to substantially interfere with the ability of agriculture workers to create meaningful associations as determined in *Dunmore*.[7]

The lower courts were divided on the constitutionality of the *AEPA*. In the Ontario Superior Court of Justice, the court ruled that the legislation did not "substantially impede" vulnerable workers from exercising their freedom of association rights (*Fraser v. Ontario [Attorney General]* 2006, para. 19). Although Justice Farley lamented that it "may have been preferable" to simply apply the *OLRA* to the plight of agricultural workers' ability to organize, this was not the question he was asked (para. 18). Having come to the conclusion that the *AEPA* met the *Dunmore* threshold, he dismissed the case.

The union was much more successful before the Ontario Court of Appeal. Applying *BC Health Services* to the decision, a unanimous court ruled in favour of the union and overturned the *AEPA*. Writing for the court, Justice Winkler determined that the *AEPA* "substantially impairs" the ability of agricultural workers to participate in meaningful collective bargaining (*Fraser v. Ontario [Attorney General]* 2008, para. 79). In coming to this conclusion, Justice Winkler extended the logic of the Supreme Court's decision in *BC Health Services*. Winkler ruled that the evidence before the court suggested that collective bargaining was impossible for vulnerable agricultural workers if the regime did not include "(1) a statutory duty to bargain in good faith; (2) statutory recognition of the principles of exclusivity and majoritarianism; and (3) a statutory mechanism for resolving bargaining impasses and disputes regarding the interpretation or administration of collective agreements" (para. 80). In other words, Justice Winkler seemed to be highlighting the key components of Canada's Wagner/PC 1003 labour law regime.

Fearful that the Court of Appeal decision had indeed elevated the Wagner/PC 1003 model of labour relations to constitutional status, the province's new Liberal government quickly appealed the decision to the Supreme Court.

Before the Supreme Court, the unions argued that the *AEPA* was incapable of protecting farm workers' ability to establish "real or effective bargaining between agricultural employees and employers" (*Ontario v. Fraser* 2011, Michael Fraser Respondent Factum, para. 62). Recognizing that *Dunmore* required, in specific circumstances, that the state "enact legislation to ensure the meaningful exercise of freedom of association," the union argued that the *AEPA* was in fact "underinclusive" (paras. 68–69). According to the union, the *AEPA* failed to meet the Supreme Court's rationale for "meaningful collective bargaining" in *BC Health Services* because the associations permitted were highly vulnerable to employer intimidation. There was also no legal requirement for employers to "do anything other than passively listen to oral representations or read written representations"; this minimal requirement did not promote *bona fide* labour associations that could participate in collective bargaining (para. 62). In the post–*BC Health Services* world, the union argued that such associations were anything but "meaningful," pointing to the fact that no collective agreements had been signed in the Ontario farm industry since the *AEPA* had been introduced. Finally, the union was clear that it was not seeking to constitutionalize a specific statutory regime, but argued that "by excluding farm workers from statutory protection for collective bargaining, the impugned laws deny and foreclose the very process of collective bargaining that is protected under s. 2(d)" (para. 92).

According to the Government of Ontario and the four intervening governments, the Ontario Court of Appeal's decision that the *AEPA* was unconstitutional rested on the flawed assumption that "meaningful collective bargaining" was paramount to the Wagner/PC 1003 model of industrial relations. The Alberta government outlined the fundamental questions in this case to be about "common statutory elements of Canadian collective bargaining" (*Ontario v. Fraser* 2011, Government of Alberta Intervener Factum, para. 7). For all of the intervening governments, the Wagner/PC 1003 model was a bad fit for constitutional jurisprudence (Government of Canada Intervener Factum; Government of British Columbia Intervener Factum). These arguments were bizarre insofar as every single government was arguing against the principles embedded in their own labour relations acts. Nevertheless, the Ontario government put forward a constitutional argument suggesting that the Wagner/PC 1003 principles actually undermine the values enshrined in the Charter. For the system of union certification or mandatory dues requirements to be elevated to constitutional status, for instance, rested on "the notion that minority wishers *must* be subordinated to the majority view as an essential part of *freedom of association* under s. 2 (d)" and that this constituted "a marked departure from the conception of the Charter as a liberal constitutional instrument designed to protect minorities and dissenters in matters of expression, religion, conscience *and association*" (Government of Ontario Appellant Factum, para. 8; emphasis in the original).

The intervening governments also argued that they had to be free to design specialized policies that contributed to the economic viability of different sectors. According to the Ontario Liberal government, the *AEPA* was designed as a "sector specific labour policy balancing between employer and employee interests in relation to the farm sector." The government further argued for judicial deference in this area, arguing that judicial intervention ran the risk of destabilizing the "economic well-being and viability of the agricultural sector as a whole" (*Ontario v. Fraser* 2011, Government of Ontario Appellant Factum, para. 10).

The Supreme Court took almost a year and a half to reach a decision in *Fraser*, a delay that perhaps reflected the deep divisions among the justices on the meaning of collective bargaining in *BC Health Services*. As a result, the *Fraser* decision is widely interpreted to be much more than a decision over the right of agricultural workers to engage in collective bargaining. Rather, because the Ontario Court of Appeal seemingly opened the door to constitutionalizing the Wagner/PC 1003 model of labour relations, the Supreme Court had to decide whether to stay on or steer clear of that legal path. Therefore, the *Fraser* decision reads more like a debate over the legitimacy of *BC Health Services* rather than a judgment about constitutional protection for agricultural workers. *Fraser* was a split decision. Eight justices voted to uphold the *AEPA* while one (Justice Abella) argued that the *AEPA* was unconstitutional. Of the nine justices hearing the appeal, seven voted to uphold *BC Health Services* and two (Rothstein and Deschamps) argued that *BC Health Services* should be overturned. What the majority claimed to be doing in *Fraser* was clarifying that *BC Health Services* only required "the parties to meet and engage in meaningful dialogue" and that it thus "protects the right to a general process of collective bargaining" (*Ontario v. Fraser* 2011, para. 41). Writing for the majority, Chief Justice McLachlin and Justice LeBel argued that *BC Health Services* did not support the view of the Ontario Court of Appeal

> that legislatures are constitutionally required, in all cases and for all industries, to enact laws that set up a uniform model of labour relations imposing a statutory duty to bargain in good faith, statutory recognition of the principles of exclusive majority representation and a statutory mechanism for resolving bargaining impasses and disputes regarding the interpretation or administration of collective agreements. (para. 47)

Having concluded that freedom of association did not include a right to majority recognition or to a dispute resolution mechanism, the Supreme Court clarified that the test to determine the constitutionality of the *AEPA* was whether it "makes meaningful association to achieve workplace goals effectively impossible" (*Ontario v. Fraser* 2011, para. 98). This new, more stringent language certainly elevated the "substantial interference" threshold for violations of section 2(d) of the Charter that the court outlined in *BC Health Services*.

The court's narrower effective impossibility test allowed it to conclude that the *AEPA* did not make the associational freedoms in the act meaningless. That conclusion was certainly surprising given that the *AEPA* did not legally require the employer to recognize the union or to do anything more than "to listen to or read employee representations – to assure that the employer will in fact consider the employee representation" (*Ontario v. Fraser* 2011, para. 103). The majority reasoned that because the *AEPA*, "by implication," imposed a requirement on employers to "consider employee representations in good faith" and because the act "provides a tribunal for the resolution of disputes," the statute did not violate the freedom of association afforded to farm workers via section 2(d) of the Charter (paras. 101, 109). The court's decision suggested that the mere act of "listening to" a group of workers was meaningful enough to pass the *BC Health Services* threshold, despite the fact that the UFCW had been unable to sign a single collective agreement in the farm sector. The Supreme Court's refusal to recognize the power imbalance between farm workers and their employers reinforced the notion that labour rights in the Charter would not fundamentally challenge private sector employer power.

One of the oddities of the court's conclusion surrounding the constitutionality of the *AEPA* was how little time the majority spent actually discussing the contextual issues surrounding farm workers and their struggles. In fact, in reading the decision, farm workers themselves were almost completely absent (Cavalluzzo 2012; J. Fudge 2012). The great bulk of the majority decision involved a protracted debate with Justice Marshall Rothstein (and Justice Charron) over the legitimacy of *BC Health Services*. The debate arose out of Justice Rothstein's partial dissent (he also believed that the *AEPA* was constitutional), in which he called for the reversal of *BC Health Services*, declaring it "wrongly decided" (*Ontario v. Fraser* 2011, para. 130) because "a constitutionally imposed duty to bargain in good faith strengthens the position of organized labour *vis-à-vis* employers" (para. 126).

The only justice prepared to strike down the *AEPA* was Justice Rosalie Abella. While Abella agreed with the majority's defence of *BC Health Services*, she did not agree with the conclusion that the *AEPA* withstood Charter scrutiny. In applying a purposive and contextual analysis to *Fraser*, Abella concluded that there is "no point to having a right only in theory. Unless it is realizable, it is meaningless. There must therefore be an enforcement mechanism not only to resolve bargaining disputes, but to ensure compliance if and when a bargain is made" (*Ontario v. Fraser* 2011, para. 339). From Abella's perspective, the *AEPA* fell short of providing a mechanism guaranteeing that employers would consider submissions by farm worker associations in good faith. In other words, the *AEPA* "substantially interfered" with a meaningful process of collective bargaining and could not withstand the rationale from *BC Health Services*.

The Aftermath of *Fraser*

Plourde and *Fraser* certainly muddied the waters over constitutional labour rights for workers. In *Plourde,* questions over such rights for private sector workers seemed to be pushed off the table completely. In *Fraser,* while the court reaffirmed the idea that the Charter protects some form of collective bargaining, it seemed to close the door on the idea that the Wagner/PC 1003 model of labour relations represented a floor of rights.

The labour movement clearly interpreted the losses in court as a stumbling block. The bitterness of the setback was echoed in the comments from labour unions and their lawyers. UFCW national president Wayne Hanley stated that he was "shocked" by the ruling, adding that the Supreme Court had "abandoned Ontario's farm workers" (quoted in Hill 2011). Mendy Leng, a former worker at the Kingsville mushroom farm, stated that all the workers in the agricultural sector wanted was "to be heard by somebody," and now she was sure that "a lot of farm workers are very, very disappointed" (quoted in Hill 2011). Steven Barrett, the lawyer representing the CLC, argued that the Supreme Court majority had failed the agricultural workers: "It's naïve to think that agricultural workers or anyone else can engage in meaningful collective bargaining without many of the traditional protections that virtually all other workers have ... Collective bargaining works only if the employer and the employee have the right to engage in economic sanctions" (quoted in Melnitzer 2011).

For Judy Fudge, who acted as an expert witness for the farm workers, *Fraser* weakened the court's jurisprudence on freedom of association and suggested that constitutional protection for labour unions was ambiguous and offered little for workers. Part of this assessment arose from the ambiguity of the decision itself. Many believed that the movement from *Dunmore* to *BC Health Services* represented an incremental step towards broader protection for workers' collective rights. However, Judy Fudge (2012, 4) argues that *Fraser* represented a "shift both in tone of the judgement from consensus to conflict and the direction of the Court's freedom of association jurisprudence that began in *Dunmore.*" In this sense, as Alison Braley has argued, *Fraser* represents "a significant back-pedalling" on the broad question of constitutional labour rights and the meaning of the right to collectively bargain in particular (Braley 2011, 354).

Not all labour policy analysts interpreted *Fraser* as an outright defeat for labour. For Richard Chaykowski (2011), *Fraser*'s positive recognition that there was a duty on employers to hear representations from workers, while not as effective as the Wagner/PC 1003 model's principles of "exclusivity" or "majoritarianism," clearly limits the ability of governments to simply legislate away workers' collective freedoms. Chaykowski argues that *Fraser* "much more clearly identified the constraints on governments in terms of policy choices which impinge upon the existing framework, and on the rights which that framework provides and the outcomes it generates" (292). In effect, Chaykowski interprets *Fraser* as reflecting an ongoing constitutional dialogue that does not prioritize any one legal system (i.e., Wagner/PC 1003) but rather outlines the broad principles that balance workers' constitutional freedoms with those of employers. Similarly, David Doorey (2013) has argued that the court's acknowledgment of non-majority forms of worker representation as a potential alternative to the Wagner/PC 1003 model of labour relations represents a silver lining for non-union employees seeking greater workplace rights. For Doorey, the principles of the Wagner/PC 1003 model reflect an "all or nothing proposition" that does not necessarily reflect the collective aspirations of all workers (513). Non-majority forms of worker representation, Doorey argues, could offer stronger workplace rights for a much broader segment of the working class who, for all intents and purposes, are unable (or unwilling) to organize through the the traditional models of Canadian labour law.

By contrast, employer groups expressed understated appreciation for the court's decision in *Fraser*. John Craig, who represented the Ontario Federation of Agriculture, stated bluntly that "employers are breathing a sigh of relief that the protection afforded to collective bargaining is not as broad as the Court of Appeal suggested" (quoted in Melnitzer 2011). Peter Gall, who represented the Coalition of BC Businesses and the British Columbia Agriculture Council, was pleased that *Fraser* clarified the legal questions surrounding the right to collective bargaining in *BC Health Services*. In his view, *BC Health Services* represented nothing more than a procedural obligation of ... good faith consultation, but nothing else; and no obligation to reach a particular conclusion as a result of these good faith discussions/negotiations, and no entitlement to any other features of collective bargaining legislation that might be thought to complement or enforce that duty or obligation to negotiate/bargain in good faith, such as the right to strike. (quoted in Schmitz 2011)

Arguably, the only upside of the *Fraser* decision for the labour movement was that the court did not overturn its historic decision in *BC Health Services,* as was advocated by Justice Rothstein. Although *Fraser* certainly reined in the constitutional interpretation of collective bargaining in the aftermath of the *BC Health Services* decision, the majority believed that the constitution still protects a "meaningful pursuit of work place goals," which includes a "derivative" right to collective bargaining (*Ontario v. Fraser* 2011, paras. 43, 46). Yet there was no positive obligation on the part of government to create a statutory regime protecting vulnerable workers to access collective bargaining. This conclusion, however, left open a series of questions about the actual meaning of the constitutional freedom of association in the Charter of Rights and Freedoms (Barrett and Poskanzer 2012). Depending on whom you asked, *Fraser* represented a reversal of fortune, a brake, a caution, or even a silver lining for organized labour (see D. Fudge 2012). What did it mean to interpret collective bargaining as a derivative right? What did the right to collective bargaining now cover? Was government now able to limit collective bargaining rights for workers in the event of a fiscal emergency? And, because the court was not asked the direct question on the right to strike, might that freedom still exist in the constitution (Barrett and Oliphant 2013–14)? Given the ambiguous nature of the *Fraser* decision, it seemed almost inevitable that labour would quickly be back in court testing the meaning of labour rights in the constitution. These cases did not take long to emerge.

A New Era of Constitutional Labour Rights **6**

The decision in *Fraser* did somewhat deflate the optimism of labour activists who believed that a legal-based Charter strategy would continue to help expand labour's capacities to organize, bargain, and strike. The gloomy outlook from *Fraser*, however, did not stop labour unions from continuing to test the boundaries of freedom of association in the Charter. After all, since the turn of the twenty-first century, legal-based strategies had paid modest dividends on the whole, thus validating labour's overall strategic direction, despite its known limitations. Moreover, the broader political and economic environment was not very hospitable to the labour movement's aims and objectives during this period, as governments moved to strip away rights from unions in the wake of the economic crisis of 2008. With Stephen Harper's anti-union Conservative government winning majority status in the 2011 federal election and with the NDP holding power in just two provinces (Manitoba and Nova Scotia) when the *Fraser* decision was handed down, the prospects for unions achieving greater collective rights through traditional legislative channels were slim to nil. Political context aside, unions continued to aggressively pursue legal strategies for several practical reasons. First, numerous cases were launched immediately following the Supreme Court's landmark decision in *BC Health Services*. While many of them were successful in courts of first instance, they were unsuccessful in provincial and federal courts of appeal after the Supreme Court's decision in *Fraser*. It only made sense to test the ambiguity of the *Fraser* decision by further appealing to the Supreme Court. Second, *Fraser* demonstrated that the court was divided on the question of constitutional labour rights. Justice Rothstein's call for a repeal of *BC Health Services* and a return to the individualized associational rights in the labour trilogy contrasted sharply with Justice Abella's call for an expansion of the collective freedoms of workers to bargain. The rest of the court clearly fell somewhere in the middle, and that ambiguity opened the door for further constitutional challenges. Third, the decentralized nature of these constitutional challenges suggested that individual unions and associations would continue to test the judicial boundaries in court with or without approval from central labour bodies like the Canadian Labour Congress (CLC). Finally, the labour movement had invested a great deal of time and money in legal challenges after the breakthrough in *BC Health Services.* That investment of legal resources suggested that it was structurally difficult for unions to simply abandon the courts when so many questions pertaining to collective constitutional rights remained obscure.

At the centre of this chapter are the cases that have clarified the Charter's protection of collective bargaining since *Fraser* and have reversed jurisprudence on the right to strike. Organized labour's legal investment appeared to have paid off handsomely when, in January 2015, the Supreme Court both reaffirmed its constitutional commitment to collective bargaining in *Mounted Police Association of Ontario v. Canada (Attorney General)* (2015 [MPAO]) and constitutionalized the right to strike as part of its decision in *Saskatchewan Federation of Labour v. Saskatchewan* (2015).

MPAO arose out of a challenge from RCMP members who had long been denied the ability to unionize and thus to engage in meaningful collective bargaining. In siding with RCMP members, the Supreme Court ruled that the legislative exclusion of RCMP members from a *bona fide* collective bargaining regime violated the Charter. In making this decision, *MPAO* represented a real victory for workers and their ability to organize and bargain. Yet this case cannot be fully understood without comparing it to the conclusions in *Meredith v. Canada (Attorney General)* (2015), a companion case. In *Meredith*, the Supreme Court ruled that the *Expenditure Restraint Act, 2009*, which imposed a reduced wage structure on RCMP members, withstood constitutional scrutiny. The decision in *Meredith* represented an important caveat on the substantive rights of workers to benefit from the fruits of bargaining. While the court reaffirmed that workers were guaranteed access to a collective bargaining process, the government still had a wide range of legislative options to interfere temporarily with collective bargaining. On the surface, these two decisions simultaneously spoke to the significance and limitations of constitutional labour rights to further the substantive rights of workers through the constitution.

The contradictory conclusions from *MPAO* and *Meredith* were vastly overshadowed by the Supreme Court's decision a week later in *Saskatchewan Federation of Labour v. Saskatchewan* (2015). In *SFL v. Saskatchewan*, the Supreme Court overturned the final remnants of the labour trilogy, ruling that "the right to strike is not merely a derivative of collective bargaining, it is an indispensable component of that right." Justice Abella, writing for the majority, added, "It seems to me that it is time to give this conclusion constitutional benediction" (para. 3). For labour leaders like CLC president Hassan Yussuff, *SFL v. Saskatchewan* was a long time in the making and was truly transformative because it "recognizes once again that there is a fundamental power imbalance in the workplace that favours employers over employees, and that the right to strike restores balance and promotes equality in the bargaining process" (Yussuff 2015).

After decades of disappointment in the courts, do the recent decisions on bargaining and the right to strike represent, as Yussuff says, "an important win for all of us"? The answer to this question is complicated. It goes without saying that *MPAO*'s affirmation of a constitutional right to bargain and *SFL v. Saskatchewan*'s recognition of the freedom to strike are significant legal tools to challenge existing legal restrictions on workers' collective action. In fact, within a month of *SFL v. Saskatchewan*, decades-old restrictions on workers' freedoms began to be overturned in Alberta (*AUPE v. Alberta*, Alberta Court of Queen's Bench, 2015).[1] We recognize as well that there will be positive aspects for workers seeking to legitimize their collective activities in the eyes of the general public. That was certainly the position of the intervening unions in *SFL v. Saskatchewan* when they argued that the "collective withdrawal of labour must therefore be viewed as an intrinsically valuable exercise of democracy, self-governance and citizenship" (*SFL v. Saskatchewan* 2015, CUPW Intervener Factum, para. 8). It also goes without saying that the Supreme Court's recognition of these types of arguments represents a transformation of freedom of association jurisprudence.

Nevertheless, these legal victories need to be understood within a broader political and economic context. As we outlined in earlier chapters, working peoples' economic and political advancements have occurred through courageous and often illegal strikes (Abella 1974; Palmer 1992; Panitch and Swartz 2003). Rarely have working people been able to advance their collective freedoms through the law. Yet in *SFL v. Saskatchewan*, we have several paradoxes. For instance, not only did the court find a constitutional right to strike without an actual strike occurring, but at the very moment the court decided to extend constitutional protection to strike activity, the number of person days lost to work stoppages had fallen to their lowest levels in almost a century (Briskin 2007; Brym, Bauer, and McIvor 2013; Godard 2011). In fact, the central component of the postwar Wagner/PC 1003 model of labour relations was premised on limiting strikes. It is somewhat ironic, then, that some unions were demanding to constitutionalize aspects of the Wagner/PC 1003 model when that very system was proving incapable of furthering workers' interests, especially in the private sector (Fudge 2010; Tucker 2008, 2014). These paradoxes point to problems inherent within the constitutional legal rights strategy: while they certainly hold potential to expand the broader zones of toleration in which workers' collective activities occur, they also impose several legal constraints on workers' ability to challenge the law through broader social struggle. Therefore, the challenge for workers in the current instance is to build on their legal victories in order to transform them into broader political victories. That requires workers' struggles to escape the narrow confines of the courtroom.

MPAO and *Meredith*

The first post-*Fraser* cases came from two complainants in the RCMP. In these cases, RCMP officers challenged the federal legislative prohibition on unionization and collective bargaining in the police force and the wage restrictions in the Conservative government's *Expenditure Restraint Act, 2009*. Similar to the issues raised fifteen years earlier in *Delisle*, *MPAO* arose out of Ontario RCMP member grievances concerning their exclusion from the *bona fide* collective bargaining regime regulated by the *Public Service Labour Relations Act* (*PSLRA*; previously the *Public Service Staff Relations Act* [*PSSRA*]). As discussed in Chapter 4, *Delisle* was a constitutional challenge to the statutory exclusion of RCMP members from the *PSSRA*. While Delisle's Charter challenge was unsuccessful, it did engender a new system of labour management relations in the national police force. This new system was the Staff Relations Representative Program (SRRP), the only body that management and the federal government recognized for the purposes of discussing work-related issues "with the understanding that the final word always rests with management" (*MPAO* 2015, para. 12). The SRRP was rigidly hierarchal, representing the military-like chain of command structure within the RCMP. Although members of the SRRP were elected in regional divisions and raised non–wage-related issues to management, they did not engage in collective bargaining nor was the program institutionally or financially independent. For wage-related issues, RCMP members were only able to communicate pay and benefit demands through a management-created Pay Council – part of the complicated negotiation process "to advocate the views of RCMP members on issues that have been identified by the SRRP Caucus or by management" (para. 236).[2] Although members of the regional SRRPs had the ability to represent members in grievances, that right was limited by regulations if such representation "could impair the efficiency, administration or good government in the Force" (para. 24). In effect, management did not have a legal obligation to listen to SRRP representatives, nor could members challenge the authority of management once decisions were made. Some RCMP members argued that the system, as imposed by management, confined them "to a system without independent, employee selected representation or collective bargaining" (*MPAO* 2015, MPAO Appellant Factum, para. 3).

A number of RCMP members believed that the decisions in both *BC Health Services* and *Fraser* protected a meaningful process of collective bargaining. Any legislative or regulatory system that denied members an independent body to pursue collective demands, they reasoned, violated the principles of association in the Charter (*MPAO* 2015, MPAO Appellant Factum, paras. 5–6; CLC Intervener Factum, paras. 4–5). Notwithstanding the fact that RCMP members had formed associations to speak on behalf of members, such a fact ignored the qualitative difference between organizations in a labour relations context. In making this observation, the association was clearly arguing against the decision in *Delisle*, which some RCMP members believed was ripe for overturning in the wake of *BC Health Services*.

Relying on the *Fraser* precedent, the Government of Canada argued that the SRRP did not make freedom of association effectively impossible. Recognizing that collective bargaining was a "derivative" or secondary right, the government argued that the "Court's jurisprudence does not require an employer to 'collectively bargain' with every association chosen by employees" (*MPAO* 2015, Government of Canada Respondent Factum, paras. 5, 59; see similar observation made by Government of Alberta Intervener Factum, para. 10). For the federal government and intervening provincial governments, the SRRP met the "limited" procedural threshold of collective bargaining from *Fraser* because it was under no obligation to create a Wagner/PC 1003 model of labour relations (Government of Canada Respondent Factum, paras. 37, 40–41; Government of Ontario Intervener Factum, para. 10). In short, governments defended the legislative exclusion of RCMP members from the *PSLRA* on the basis that the SRRP was itself a limited process that corresponded with a more "restrained" interpretation of freedom of association in the Charter (Government of Saskatchewan Intervener Factum, para. 15). The federal government stated that even though it had chosen a "collaborative model of labour relations" for the RCMP, the SRRP still adequately represented employee interests free from "improper management interference" (Government of Canada Respondent

Factum, para. 43). While the government's definition of "improper inter-ference" was unclear, it did highlight the fact that RCMP members elected delegates to the SRRPs and that those delegates were required to represent the interests of their members in good faith.

Given the ambiguity surrounding the constitutional protection of collective bargaining in the arguments by various governments and unions, the Supreme Court chose to use *MPAO* as an opportunity to "explain" its decision in *Fraser* (*MPAO* 2015, cases cited). In so doing, the court ruled 6–1 in favour of the RCMP members and determined that freedom of association did indeed protect a meaningful process of collective bargaining. Writing for the majority, Chief Justice McLachlin and Justice LeBel overturned the court's previous decision in *Delisle* and ruled that the exclusion of RCMP members from a collective bargaining regime violated section 2(d) of the Charter. In coming to this conclusion, McLachlin and LeBel expanded their interpretation of freedom of association by connecting the "meaningfulness" of collective bargaining to a framework that "provides employees with a degree of choice and independence sufficient to enable them to determine and pursue their collective interests" (para. 5). In arriving at this conclusion, the members of the court undermined the *Fraser* precedent and weakened government and employer arguments that collective bargaining was a derivative or secondary right that could be easily circumvented by legislative decree. Justice Rothstein delivered the lone dissenting opinion in *MPAO*. In defending his position in *Fraser*, Rothstein argued that Charter rights to collective bargaining represented an unmerited judicial intervention into parliamentary jurisdiction that prejudiced labour relations outcomes in favour of unions.

The majority prefaced its conclusions in *MPAO* with the observation that there had been a seismic shift in judicial opinion with regard to constitutional labour rights. That shift was reflected in the two broad periods of jurisprudence that characterized freedom of association in the Charter: "the restrictive approach" associated with the labour trilogy and the "generous and purposive approach" of the current period (*MPAO* 2015, para. 30). Recognizing that *MPAO* fell firmly into the later period, the justices in the majority were critical of their former colleagues' "narrow view of freedom of association" as nothing more than the "collective exercise of individual freedoms" (para. 41). The majority agreed that since *Dunmore,* jurisprudence on labour rights had become centred on a more interpretative analysis with the "purpose of encouraging the individual's self-fulfillment and the collective realization of human goals, consistent with democratic values" (para. 46). In other words, the genuine collective dimensions of freedom of association are not secondary to other individual rights in the Charter but are rather substantive to the larger purposes and goals of the Charter itself.

The majority argued that a "contextual" analysis of freedom of association revealed that "it stands as an independent right with independent content, essential to the development and maintenance of the vibrant civil society upon which our democracy rests" (*MPAO* 2015, para. 49). This approach to understanding freedom of association elevated Dickson's purposive approach in the 1987 *Alberta Reference* (see Chapter 3). Under this interpretation, collective activity empowered "those who would otherwise be vulnerable and ineffective to meet on more equal terms the power and strength of those with whom their interests interact and, perhaps, conflict" (*MPAO* 2015, para. 54, citing *Alberta Reference* 1987, 365, 366).

Notwithstanding the Supreme Court's generous reading of associational rights, the majority continued to emphasize the limits of this right. Building on its conclusions in *BC Health Services,* the court reminded labour unions that collective bargaining only guaranteed a "meaningful process" and not an outcome or specific model of labour relations (*MPAO* 2015, paras. 67, 71). That said, the majority also rejected the ambiguous conclusions in *Fraser,* dismissing government efforts to defend legislative restrictions on *bona fide* collective bargaining for RCMP members on the basis that it was not "effectively impossible" to form an association. Rejecting the effective impossibility test from *Fraser,* the court also determined that collective bargaining was neither derivative nor a secondary right in the Charter. Rather, in keeping with the purposive approach to freedom of association, collective bargaining, the court reasoned, was itself a stand-alone right in the Charter (paras. 78–79). It therefore implied that government would be found in violation of 2(d) if it "substantially interferes" with a meaningful process in such a manner as to "disrupt the balance between employees and employer that s. 2 (d) seeks to achieve" (para. 72).

With the court having reinforced and defended collective bargaining as a "meaningful process," it was still unclear what that concept entailed for constitutional purposes. Here, the court concluded that a "meaningful process" must be effective enough to counter the power that management naturally possessed in the employment relationship. The court determined that in order to obtain a measure of equilibrium, such a process would also need to provide workers with a degree of choice and access to an independent (non–management dominated) structure to "determine their collective interests and meaningfully pursue them" (*MPAO* 2015, paras. 81, 88–90).[3] In order to pass constitutional scrutiny, therefore, the employees would be required to have effective input into choosing those who represent their collective goals while also having the freedom to form and join (or dissolve) new associations (paras. 85–86). Finally, the court determined that employee representatives would need to be accountable to the membership.

McLachlin and LeBel both determined that the SRRP was not independent from RCMP management and therefore was not capable of engaging in meaningful collective bargaining. While this conclusion did not leave the court to determine that the RCMP had to be included in the collective bargaining model used in the federal public service, it did mean that, in the court's view, the current system reflected management priorities rather than the priorities of RCMP officers themselves. Finally, the court concluded by determining that the government's arguments that unionization would compromise the neutrality of the national police force was not a reasonable limit under section 1 of the Charter. Based on all of the above, the SRRP was struck down.

While RCMP officers won an important legal victory in *MPAO*, they did not fare as well with the Supreme Court's decision in *Meredith v. Canada* (2015). In this case, two RCMP members on the national SRRP challenged the federal government's unilateral rollbacks of previously agreed-to wage increases through the *Expenditure Restraint Act, 2009* (*ERA*). In 2008, the SRRP and the RCMP Pay Council had successfully negotiated with the Federal Treasury Board to achieve pay increases for RCMP members. Although those institutions were deemed unconstitutional in *MPAO*, the Supreme Court maintained that the process by which they had negotiated the initial pay increases (which were then rolled back) did not violate the constitution. In upholding this legislation, the majority concluded that the *ERA* passed constitutional scrutiny because many of the wage rollbacks were "time limited in nature, were shared by all public servants, and did not permanently remove the subject of wages from collective bargaining" (*Meredith v. Canada* 2015, para. 27).[4] For the majority, the *ERA* was distinct from the BC government's *Health and Social Services Delivery Improvement Act*, which was at the centre of the *BC Health Services* decision. In that case, the BC Liberals had permanently removed the rights of workers, while the Conservative federal government's *ERA* did so only temporarily. The temporary nature of the *ERA* was enough to convince the majority that the "evidence of *outcomes* supports a conclusion that the enactment of the *ERA* had a minor impact on the appellants' associational activity" (para. 29; emphasis added).

When analyzed together, the decisions in *Meredith* and *MPAO* reveal an important limit in the Supreme Court's view of freedom of association. Although RCMP officers could now freely use their collective rights under the Charter to form a *bona fide* union and to bargain collectively, government still maintained the ability to weaken the substantive nature of those rights through measures like temporary wage rollbacks. It was therefore clear that workers required a more substantive dispute-resolution process to make the right to collective bargaining more meaningful.

A Constitutional Right to Strike

The constitutional right to collective bargaining having been reaffirmed, the great unanswered question regarding a constitutional right to strike took centre stage in *SFL v. Saskatchewan*. Since the court's decision in *BC Health Services*, labour lawyers had been pondering whether the Supreme Court's newfound rationale connecting Charter values with expansive freedom of association rights might now be extended to a right to strike (Etherington 2010, 315–32; Langille 2010a, 129–32). The initial responses were certainly not encouraging.

The BC government's decision in 2002 to severely curb the bargaining ability of workers in the health and education professions led to a series of court challenges that culminated in the 2007 decision in *BC Health Services*. In addition to those judicial challenges, however, the Hospital Employees' Union (HEU) and the BC Teachers' Federation staged separate one-day strikes to protest the government's policies. These protests occurred notwithstanding the fact that the BC Labour Relations Board had already determined that the unions' strike actions constituted a violation of the no-strike provisions in the provincial *Labour Relations Code*. The unions, unsatisfied with the ruling, asked the BC Court of Appeal to weigh in. In effect, the unions believed that the Wagner/PC 1003 long-time ban on mid-term, political, and other non-collective bargaining-related strikes violated the Charter's protection of expression and association. The BC Court of Appeal reasoned that such legislative bans did indeed violate a union's rights of expression but were justified under section 1 of the Charter. Writing for the majority, Justice Mackenzie reasoned that there is a qualitative difference between private and public sector strikes. Whereas private sector strikes represent an economic war between a single employer and a union, public sector strikes are directed against "the public sector employer to make concessions. In that sense a public sector strike is more a political than an economic weapon" (*British Columbia Teachers' Federation v. British Columbia Public School Employers' Assn*. 2009, para. 21). Having come to that conclusion, the court determined that

> the appellants' protest strikes were political in the sense that they were aimed at the government but the legislation they were protesting changed conditions of employment and overrode collective bargaining processes. The protests illustrate the symbiotic relationship between governments and public sector employers that blurs the line between bargaining and politics. (para. 22)

Furthermore, the Court of Appeal upheld the "general agreement that at some point legislative intervention to restrict political protest work stoppages is justified" (para. 64). In short, the Wagner/PC 1003 model's historical limit on the collective rights of workers to strike was rationally connected to protecting the broader public interest. Leave to appeal was later denied by the Supreme Court.

Notwithstanding this decision, the Supreme Court did appear to open the door on the right to strike in *Alberta (Information and Privacy Commissioner) v. United Food and Commercial Workers, Local 401* (2013 [*Alberta v. UFCW*]). Dubbed the "Palace Casino" dispute, the case addressed state-imposed limits on the picket line with regard to personal privacy (Elder 2013).

In 2003, the provincial government passed the *Personal Information Protection Act (PIPA)*, which was designed to protect Albertans' privacy by requiring private sector businesses to obtain individual consent to collect and disseminate personal information. *PIPA*'s definition of what constituted personal privacy became a focal point in *Alberta v. UFCW*. Ostensibly, the law was designed to protect Albertans from private organizations using personal information without individual consent. In this case, management – and later, the Alberta government – argued that a union collecting and disseminating images from a picket line violated individual privacy rights.

The dispute arose out of a year-long strike at an Edmonton casino during which the UFCW captured numerous images of replacement workers, managers, and others who crossed the picket line. The union used those images on a public website and in union pamphlets. Management complained that the union's actions violated *PIPA*. Alberta's privacy commissioner later agreed with the complainants and ordered the images and personal information destroyed. The UFCW sought relief in the courts, asking that the decision of the privacy commissioner be overturned on the basis that the decision violated the Charter's guarantee of freedom of expression.

Upon judicial review, the Supreme Court overturned the decision of Alberta's privacy commissioner and ruled that *PIPA* could not be used to limit the expression of the union. Building on its reasoning in *RWDSU v. Pepsi* and *UFCW v. KMart* (see Chapter 4), the court concluded that the right to picket during a strike was inextricably linked to free expression. The court reasoned that picketing during a strike was an "invaluable tool in the economic arsenal of workers in the collective bargaining process" (*Alberta v. UFCW* 2013, para. 35). Given the centrality of strikes to collective bargaining, the court determined that the use of images taken from the picket line to dissuade the public from crossing the line, to build public support for their cause, to gather evidence for future litigation, to build the morale of strikers, and to shame possible replacement workers was certainly a legitimate act of expression (para. 6). Moreover, the union captured these images in a public place and during public demonstrations (para. 26). The Supreme Court ultimately argued that the sweeping nature of *PIPA* was disproportionate to the goals of protecting individual privacy and could therefore not be saved by section 1. In effect, the legislation's goal of protecting personal privacy did not outweigh the workers' right to free expression on a picket line.

Labour leaders, lawyers, and civil libertarians hailed the decision in *Alberta v. UFCW* as a game changer. Alberta Federation of Labour (AFL) president Gil McGowan believed that the ruling represented a substantial victory for workers, stating that it "ensures freedom of expression for working people and their unions ... It's a win for the rights of unions to fully represent workers during labour disputes" (quoted in Cotter 2013). Lawyer Paul Cavalluzzo declared that the court's decision "recognized that the right to strike is a fundamental right under the Charter" (quoted in Gray and Fletcher 2013). Cavalluzzo clearly had his eye on the direct constitutional challenge on the right to strike that was making its way through the courts in Saskatchewan.

The Saskatchewan case arose out of the labour law changes implemented by the right-wing Saskatchewan Party government in 2007. Under the leadership of newly elected premier Brad Wall, one of the provincial government's first acts was to attack labour unions in both the public and private sectors. Wall's labour law changes consisted of Bill 5, the *Public Service Essential Services Act* (*PSESA*), and Bill 6, the *Trade Union Amendment Act*. The *PSESA* created essential service designations for public sector workers, while the *Trade Union Amendment Act* expanded employer speech provisions; ended card check certification procedures, replacing them with a mandatory vote procedure; and raised the numerical threshold for union certification. Combined, Bills 5 and 6 represented a neoliberal restructuring of the province's labour laws in favour of employers (Conway and Conway 2015; Smith 2011).

The impetus for the *PSESA* came from two strikes that seemed to linger in the minds of legislators: the Saskatchewan Government and General Employees Union (SGEU) strike of December 2006 (the so-called snowplough strike) and a Canadian Union of Public Employees (CUPE) strike in 2007 at the University of Saskatchewan, the latter having implications for Royal University Hospital, located on campus (*SFL v. Saskatchewan* 2015, Government of Saskatchewan Respondent Factum, para. 8). Ostensibly, Bill 5 was designed to ensure "that lives are not jeopardized in the process" of a public sector strike (Norris 2008). However, opponents of the bill argued that its true purpose was to weaken the public service unions that were among the government's chief opponents at the bargaining table and in the public sphere (SFL 2008a). Bill 5 was incredibly sweeping, unilaterally withdrawing the right to strike for public sector employees by declaring thousands of workers "essential." In order to counter public sector strikes, the government defined essential services as any work whose absence might create a "danger to life, health or safety; the destruction or serious deterioration of machinery, equipment or premises; serious environmental damage; or disruption of any of the courts of Saskatchewan" (Saskatchewan 2008a, s. 2[c]). The legislation also defined public employers to include the public service, Crown corporations, regional health authorities (including hospitals), municipalities, the universities of Saskatchewan and Regina, the Saskatchewan Institute of Applied Science and Technology, police, and "any other person, agency or body, or class of persons, agencies or bodies, that provides an essential service to the public and is prescribed" (s. 2[i]). In defining such a broad range of public services as "essential," the government's legislation was destined to influence the bargaining capacities of almost all public sector unions in the province.

Under the provisions of the act, the public employer and the union were mandated to negotiate essential service designations. If the union refused to endorse the employer's recommendations, the employer could then unilaterally declare workers "essential" (which could be amended by the employer at any time). In essence, the legislative changes in Bill 5 would allow government employers to unilaterally dictate which employees were essential for collective bargaining purposes and would severely restrict the ability of public sector unions to appeal essential service classifications to an independent body such as the Saskatchewan Labour Relations Board (SLRB). As a result of Bill 5, Saskatchewan had the most restrictive essential services provisions in the entire country. In addition to the essential services legislation, the government introduced Bill 6, *An Act to Amend* The Trade Union Act (Saskatchewan 2008b), which rewrote certain provisions of the *Trade Union Act.* Many of those changes were similar to labour law amendments from other jurisdictions and included expanding management's right to communicate during certification drives and raising the threshold for union certification.

In previous periods, anti-labour legislation such as Bills 5 and 6 would have resulted in labour unrest, political instability, or mass protest. While the province's unions did mount some political resistance in early 2008, the principal tactic was a complaint to the International Labour Organization (ILO), followed by a legal challenge testing the constitutionality of the bills under the Charter. The timing of Premier Wall's actions certainly contributed to labour's strategy: it was the first government assault on the core functions of labour unions since the Supreme Court's decision in *BC Health Services.* In order to build a broad base of support to bolster its legal strategy, the Saskatchewan Federation of Labour (SFL) challenge before the ILO was joined by twenty-one provincial and national labour unions (SFL 2008b; Scott 2008).[5] In its decision, the ILO ruled in favour of the unions, chastising the government for its lack of consultation in introducing both bills and critiquing the government's erosion of the right to strike (ILO, Freedom of Association Committee 2010). Similar to premiers in other provinces, however, Wall's response to the ILO was simply to ignore it. The government defended its labour legislation as "fair and balanced," adding that "the ILO is offering an opinion that's non-binding" (Roth 2010).

Success before the ILO did not prevent internal divisions from arising within the Saskatchewan labour movement over the SFL's legal strategy. Throughout 2009 and 2010, five separate cases were making their way through various tribunals and courts, all designed to test the constitutionality of the provincial government's legislative changes. While the SFL case challenged the constitutionality of both *PSESA,* the essential services law, and the amendments to the *Trade Union Act*, many public sector unions were advancing separate narrower legal challenges concerned only with the essential services law. The Saskatchewan Union of Nurses (SUN), SGEU, CUPE Local 3967, and Service Employees' International Union (SEIU) West had all commenced separate legal challenges to decisions made under the new authority of the *PSESA*. Given competing strategic interests and objectives, the unions were in bitter disagreement over which case should take precedent. In a legal decision on 9 August 2010, Justice Lang of the Saskatchewan Court of Queen's Bench answered that question by joining the challenges and making the SFL case the lead application (*R. v. Saskatchewan Federation of Labour* 2010).

Questions over the relative strength of the various cases and the legitimacy of unilateral judicial action to join them provoked a power struggle within the SFL, culminating in a hotly contested election for the presidency of the federation at its 2010 convention. CUPE Saskatchewan president Tom Graham challenged Larry Hubich, who had been president for eight years, over divisions concerning the ongoing legal challenges. According to media accounts, Graham's challenge arose over internal issues concerning how the union movement should direct its priorities and resources towards political action and working with government (Cowan 2010). However, Graham's candidacy also reflected deep-seated disagreements over the SFL's constitutional challenges, which CUPE saw as problematic – especially the challenge to the *Trade Union Act*. It was no coincidence, for instance, that Graham's candidacy arose shortly after CUPE had lost its legal challenge to Bill 5 at the SLRB (*Canadian Union of Public Employees, Local 3967 v. Regina Qu'Appelle Health Region* 2010). In that decision, the board ruled that the health region's unilateral essential service designation was a relatively open process in which "meaningful negotiations of workplace conditions and the terms of employment had occurred and would, in all likelihood, continue to occur" (para. 111).

Larry Hubich defended the Federation's strategies as providing simultaneous legal and political opposition to the Saskatchewan Party government. In his view, the government "need[s] to respect [that] there is a legitimate and constitutional right under Canada's Charter of

Rights and Freedoms ... to form organizations for the purposes of advancing their cause. As long as the government doesn't believe that's a legitimate right afforded to the citizens under the constitution, then I don't know how you can get beyond that impasse" (quoted in Switzer 2010; ellipses in original). Hubich's convention speech reinforced this point. He emphasized his antagonism towards the Saskatchewan Party government, highlighted the ILO victory, and emphasized the "fight-back" program that he believed was about to bear fruit in the forthcoming Queen's Bench decision (quoted in Chabun 2010). Hubich was re-elected, with 533 votes to Graham's 371. Notwithstanding Hubich's re-election, the relatively slim electoral victory (by union standards) suggested a rift within Saskatchewan's labour movement over the utility of constitutional challenges and, in particular, the SFL's case.

With his renewed mandate, Hubich led the SFL in continuing its challenge in court. A year after the convention dispute, the Court of Queen's Bench finally reached its decision. At the centre of the court decision were several questions: Did *BC Health Services* now require the courts to revisit the labour trilogy? If so, the questions that followed were whether section 2(d) of the Charter now "protect[s] a right to strike, as an essential element of collective bargaining, and to what extent that right can be limited by s. 1 of the Charter to ensure the essential delivery of essential services to the community" (*Saskatchewan v. SFL* 2012, para. 55). In his reading of *BC Health Services,* Justice Dennis Ball took many by surprise by seemingly ignoring the majority's rationale that it was not constitutionalizing a specific model of labour relations.[6] For Ball, collective bargaining could not be easily separated from the ability of workers to withdraw their labour. In short, Ball reasoned that the Wagner/PC 1003 model's protection of the right to strike was now deserving of constitutional protection.

Ball observed that the essential services bill created "substantial interference" for the union to exercise the right to strike (*Saskatchewan v. SFL* 2012, paras. 121–22). Ball also believed that the government's legislation represented a legislative attempt to undermine the capacity of workers to bargain freely (para. 191). While Ball conceded that it might be important for a government to have some form of essential services protection, he argued that the existing bill was too broad in scope and therefore could not pass the Charter's reasonable limits clause in section 1. In his words,

> No other essential services legislation in Canada comes close to prohibiting the right to strike as broadly, and as significantly, as the PSESA Act. No other essential services legislation is as devoid of access to independent, effective dispute resolution processes to address employer designations of essential services workers and, where those designations have the effect of prohibiting meaningful strike action, an independent, efficient, overall dispute mechanism. (para. 205)

In making this final observation, Ball concluded that the *PSESA* transferred *all* the power of designation to the employer, which could not sustain constitutional scrutiny. On the question of Bill 6, Ball did not view the changes to the *Trade Union Act* as a Charter violation. The government quickly appealed the decision to the Saskatchewan Court of Appeal, whose response to Ball's decision was that the Supreme Court had not overturned the 1987 labour trilogy and therefore there continued to be no Charter-based right to strike (*Saskatchewan Federation of Labour v. Saskatchewan* 2013). In arriving at this conclusion, the Court of Appeal built on the Supreme Court's reasoning in *BC Health Services* and *Fraser* that had led to the court's refusal to constitutionalize Canada's specific model of labour relations. The Court of Appeal also borrowed language from the judges in the labour trilogy, concluding that the SFL and its affiliates were asking for constitutional protection for the "modern right to strike" rather than for a historical right with little legal regulation or restrictions. To constitutionalize a freestanding right to strike, the court reasoned, raised dangerous issues for the unions. For instance,

> SFL and the unions do not wish to return to a world where employees can withdraw their labour in concert, but where employers are not obliged to recognize unions, where union representation is based on something other than exclusive majoritarianism, where employers are not required to bargain, or to bargain in good faith, where employees who participate in strikes can be dismissed for

breach of their employment contracts and so forth. The reality is that, in the year 2013, the "right to strike" which the SFL and the unions seek to protect is deeply integrated into, and in many ways can be seen as a function of, a specific statutory system. (para. 63)

The problem for the appellate court was that the Supreme Court had also recognized in *BC Health Services* that the right to collective bargaining predated Canada's acceptance of the Wagner style of collective bargaining (paras. 64–68). There was thus a great deal of ambiguity on the question of constitutional labour rights and the right to strike: Were unions asking for an unfettered right to strike free from statutory limitations? Or were they willing to accept existing limitations on the right (i.e., legal bans on mid-term strikes) but not additional ones? There were no clear answers to these questions. The Court of Appeal struck down Ball's decision and ruled in favour of the government. The issue was then appealed to the Supreme Court.

Perhaps not surprisingly, the case garnered an incredible amount of participation from unions, governments, and employers. In total, twenty-six groups presented arguments before the Supreme Court, including the two principle participants and twenty-four interveners. Those supporting the right to strike included the SFL itself and thirteen interveners, twelve representing labour unions and one from the BC Civil Liberties Association. Of those opposing the right to strike, four groups represented employers and one came from the right-wing libertarian think tank Canadian Centre for Constitutional Freedoms. All seven intervening governments opposed expanding labour rights under the constitution.

For the unions, the central premise of the case was simple: it was "about the freedom to stop working" (*SFL v. Saskatchewan* 2015, UNA and AFL Intervener Factum, para. 1). The Canadian Union of Postal Workers (CUPW) argued that the case was about recognizing that "labour is not a commodity." The ability of workers to freely strike, the union argued, was an essential element of a democratic and free society, and its "absence is a sign of oppression" (CUPW Intervener Factum, para. 5; see similar arguments in CLC Intervener factum, 2014, para. 8). The SFL connected its arguments on the right to strike with the "purposive approach to Charter protection" first highlighted by Chief Justice Dickson in the *Alberta Reference* (SFL Appellant Factum, para. 17; see similar observations in CLC Intervener Factum, para. 6).[7]

The unions argued that the ability to strike was a core principle of labour union activities and, following a contextual approach to freedom of association, was consistent with evolving Charter values. In citing *Alberta v. UFCW,* the SFL argued that the Supreme Court itself had already recognized that freedom of association allowed workers to "enhance their own self-understanding and influence over a core feature of their own lives," thus enhancing the Charter values of democracy and respect for the autonomy of the person at work and in society (*SFL v. Saskatchewan* 2015, SFL Appellant Factum, para. 20). At its roots, the freedom to strike, according to the AFL and the United Nurses of Alberta (UNA), "does not depend on state action for its existence, [rather] workers are free, both individually and collectively, to withdraw their labour, subject only to liability for breach of contract" (UNA and AFL Intervener Factum, para. 7). In short, the right to strike is not a secondary or derivative right of freedom of association but a standalone right (SEIU Intervener Factum, para. 4; SFL Appellant Factum, para. 31; BCTF Intervener Factum, para. 10). In broad terms, the right to strike does not require "positive" action on the part of government because it "is steeped in history" and exists as a by-product of working-class struggles within capitalist labour relations (SUN Intervener Factum, para. 11; see also similar observations in CUPW Intervener Factum, 5–6; see also quotations borrowed from England 1988, 175). According to the BC Teachers' Federation's factum, the proper test to determine a breach of 2(d) was not an arbitrary form of "substantial interference," as suggested in *Dunmore* and *BC Health Services*. Rather, the courts should simply ask if the government's intent is to prevent workers from engaging in collective activity (BCTF Intervener Factum, para. 24).

After providing an overview of the rich history of the freedom to strike in Canada, the unions then turned to the universality of that freedom. On this point, they referenced the broad strike protection in international law, arguing that the ability to strike did not fall to a singular statutory regime, nor did it "guarantee a particular result" (*SFL v. Saskatchewan* 2015, SFL Appellant Factum, paras. 24–26; see similar observations in CUPW Intervener Factum, paras. 6–7). Arguing against the Supreme Court's determination in the labour trilogy that judges should remain neutral in the labour relations context, the unions advanced the idea that the court had slowly opened the door to challenging this determination over the past decade (CUPW Intervener Factum, para. 15). In fact, once the Supreme Court recognized an independent right to union recognition (*Dunmore*) and to collective bargaining (*BC Health Services*), it fell to the court to recognize the constitutionality of the final pillar of labour freedoms: "the freedom of employees to engage in strike activity that would have been lawful in the absence of the Act" (SEIU Intervener Factum, para. 1; see similar observations in SFL Appellant Factum, para. 33). By enacting sweeping legislation that unilaterally withdrew the right of workers to strike, the Saskatchewan government's actions violated the constitutional principles endorsed by *BC Health Services*. Quite simply, the government's refusal to consult with the unions constituted "substantial interference in the ability of unions to strike and to bargain collectively" (SFL Appellant Factum, para. 80).

The SFL and many of the union interveners acknowledged that the freedom to strike was not absolute and could be limited under very narrow circumstances using section 1 of the Charter (*SFL v. Saskatchewan* 2015, SFL Appellant Factum, paras. 81, 90, 95–108; PIPSC Appellant Factum, para. 9). In fact, the SFL conceded that both the Saskatchewan NDP and the Saskatchewan Progressive Conservatives had previously used back-to-work legislation to end legal strikes. The difference between those instances and the current legislation, however, was that past governments accompanied their back-to-work orders with binding interest arbitration to compensate for the loss of the ability to strike (*SFL v. Saskatchewan* 2015, SFL Appellant Factum, para. 39). By not providing third-party interest arbitration or allowing workers to appeal their essential service designation, the government was attempting to alter the balance of power at the bargaining table (PIPSC Appellant Factum, para. 2; PSAC Intervener Factum, paras. 15–24).[8]

Having argued that the government's actions violated the constitutional principles endorsed in *BC Health Services*, the unions turned directly to the legal meaning of the constitutional freedom to strike. On this point, there was some divergence. For example, the Professional

Institute of the Public Service of Canada (PIPSC) assured the court that the constitutional

> freedom to strike under s. 2(d), need not lead to unwarranted fears of labour chaos and unrest. In situations of genuine essential services, it may be a justifiable limit on the rights of workers under s. 2(d) to deny them the freedom to strike, so long as certain key conditions are met. (*SFL v. Saskatchewan* 2015, PIPSC Appellant Factum, para. 16)

Some unions, however, disagreed with such constricted legal arguments. According to the CUPW, the fact that labour unions had accepted limits on the freedom to strike in the Wagner/PC 1003 model did "not detract from the fundamental nature of the freedom" (CUPW Intervener Factum, para. 6; see similar arguments in BCTF Intervener Factum para. 30). The UNA and the Alberta Federation of Labour (AFL) argued that "the fundamental freedom of association protected by s. 2(d) of the Charter encompasses employees' freedom to collectively withdraw their labour for any purpose, not just a collective bargaining purpose" (UNA and AFL Intervener Factum, para. 20). The Air Canada Pilots' Association argued that the right to strike was a protected form of expression that should be interpreted broadly, suggesting that "strikes in the private sector deserve the same constitutional protection as public sector or "political' strikes" (ACPA Intervener Factum, para. 1).

Governments and employers took a very different approach to questions surrounding the constitutional freedom to strike. For governments, the great unanswered question surrounding the appeal was to what extent the court would expand on the "purposive approach" to collective freedoms in *BC Health Services* or continue with the more constrained approach adopted in *Fraser*. Relying almost entirely on *Fraser*, governments argued that a "strike is coercive," thus demonstrating "that a right to strike is incompatible" with the Charter (*SFL v. Saskatchewan* 2015, Government of Saskatchewan Respondent Factum, para. 44; see similar observations in Government of Alberta Intervener Factum, paras. 2, 13–22). The Newfoundland government took the rather straightforward position that the Supreme Court's precedent dating back to the labour trilogy confirmed that section 2(d) did not guarantee the freedom to strike. More importantly, nothing the court had done over the past two decades suggested that there was a "compelling reason to overrule the conclusion in the *Labour Trilogy*" (Government of Newfoundland and Labrador Intervener Factum, para. 11). To constitutionalize these rights in the current context would, in the words of the Government of Saskatchewan, "amount to a change in Canadian labour law of seismic proportions" (Government of Saskatchewan Respondent Factum, para. 2). For its part, the federal government argued that strikes were only "legal" because governments have created statutory regimes to overturn previous common law restrictions on the ability to strike. If the Wagner/ PC 1003 regime ceased to exist, the government argued, employees who acted in concert would be in breach of several of the economic or industrial torts including conspiracy, restraint of trade, intimidation, or breach of contract. Therefore, a stand-alone freedom to strike would not prove useful in resolving disputes between employers and workers (Government of Canada Intervener Factum, para. 12). Put another way, to constitutionalize the freedom to strike would be elevating a "positive" right to a specific statutory framework that would effectively constitutionalize "policy choices" (CCCF Intervener Factum, para. 28).

Government interveners also insisted that *Fraser* demanded a "restrained interpretation" of freedom of association (*SFL v. Saskatchewan* 2015, Government of Saskatchewan Respondent Factum, para. 31; Government of Alberta Intervener Factum, para. 19). The Saskatchewan government and intervening governments took this position for five reasons. First, freedom of association was not simply a labour issue; therefore, the court should not elevate a singular associational activity for a single group. Second, the court should not single out labour unions for associational protection because they are already highly regulated by Canada's Wagner/PC 1003 model. To accept the arguments of the unions would be, in effect, to constitutionalize the Wagner model. Third, to constitutionalize the Wagner/PC 1003 model would make all the limitations of collective freedoms within that regime (i.e., no strike pledges during the life of a collective agreement) vulnerable to further litigation. Fourth, the Charter should provide only a floor, not a ceiling, for associational rights. It was clear that government interveners believed that extensions to the labour relations model in Canada should be a political decision rather than a constitutional one. Finally, the Saskatchewan government called for the Supreme Court to respect the long-held "balance" between organized labour and employers, leaving the complexity of labour relations policy to Parliament and legislatures (Government of Saskatchewan Respondent Factum, paras. 32–36).

Government interveners further argued that rights of association were secondary under the Charter, and because of this, the court should reject the international law arguments made by the unions. The Saskatchewan government argued that international law standards do not compare well with Canada's federal constitutional tradition, where legal sovereignty is divided between the federal and provincial governments. Rather, different levels of governments should be able to preserve the right to craft their own legislation addressing unique labour-management relations in their respective jurisdictions (Government of Saskatchewan Respondent Factum, paras. 50–51; Government of Newfoundland and Labrador Intervener Factum, paras. 51–54; CEC Intervener Factum, para. 4).

The intervening governments and public sector employers also defended Saskatchewan's essential services legislation on the grounds that public sector strikes could endanger public safety. Pointing to the 8,400 nurses who went on strike in the province in 1999 and a CUPE strike in the health sector in 2001, the Saskatchewan Regional Health Authority argued that the "past conduct" of the province's public sector unions warranted a "shift in authority over essential services away from the unions" (*SFL v. Saskatchewan* 2015, SRHA Intervener Factum, para. 33). The Government of Newfoundland and Labrador argued that constitutionalizing the right to strike was particularly dangerous in the public sector, where it was prudent for governments to "promote harmonious relations between employer and employees, achieve labour stability, and recognize the paramount importance of public health, safety and security" (Government of Newfoundland and Labrador Intervener Factum, para. 33).

After hearing these arguments, the Supreme Court reached its long-awaited decision on 30 January 2015, one week after its decision in *MPAO* and *Meredith* (*SFL v. Saskatchewan* 2015). In a 5–2 decision, the court concluded that the Charter includes a stand-alone right to strike.

The court ruled that the *PSESA*'s unilateral withdrawal of the right to strike for public sector workers "amounts to a substantial interference with their right to a meaningful process of collective bargaining" and was therefore unconstitutional (para. 2). Since meaningful collective bargaining can only occur if there is a legitimate threat of workers withdrawing their labour, the majority argued, the right to strike now deserved "constitutional benediction" (para. 2). An important part of that benediction was to rule against the governments' position that strikes are derivative of collective bargaining. Rather, the Supreme Court sided with the unions and determined that the right to strike is a stand-alone right supported by "history, jurisprudence, and by Canada's international obligations" (para. 3). In coming to this conclusion, the court overturned the final elements of the 1987 labour trilogy and ruled that collective bargaining could not occur when government had unilaterally withdrawn a "meaningful dispute resolution mechanism commonly used in labour relations" (para. 25). This conclusion represented a historic reversal and expanded the collective provisions of freedom of association in the Charter. Writing for the majority, Justice Rosalie Abella, a former chair of the Ontario Labour Relations Board, noted that the "judicial arc" with regards to workers' rights was bending "increasingly towards workplace justice" (para. 1).

As had become common in the more recent freedom of association cases, the majority arrived at these lofty conclusions by relying on former Chief Justice Brian Dickson's dissent in the *Alberta Reference* (*SFL v. Saskatchewan* 2015, paras. 32–33). As discussed in Chapter 3, in his dissent, Dickson argued for a more purposive interpretation of freedom of association because of the importance of collective action for workers to challenge the authority of their employers. The only way workers had ever effectively countered the power imbalance between themselves and employers, he argued, was through collective bargaining and the collective withdrawal of labour. Twenty-eight years later, the majority of the Supreme Court agreed with those conclusions.

The Supreme Court proclaimed boldly that "the Charter values of human dignity, equality, liberty, respect for the autonomy of the person and enhancement of democracy" were all enhanced through constitutional protection of bargaining and the right to strike (*SFL v. Saskatchewan*

2015, paras. 53–54). In making this case, Abella noted that strikes were deeply rooted in Canadian history. Yet the actual political and economic details of those strikes were less of a concern to the Supreme Court than the story it wanted to craft: that strikes predated a specific statutory model. Regardless of the legal and often violent state restrictions on workers' ability to strike, the court was able to use this evidence to develop a whiggish history of associational freedoms leading to the adoption of the Wagner/PC 1003 framework in the 1940s. By choosing this model, the court reasoned, governments had attempted to "reduce the frequency of strikes by ensuring a commitment to meaningful collective bargaining" (para. 42). The court majority viewed strikes as a safety valve that occurred infrequently and only to enhance the ability of workers to pursue common workplace goals through meaningful collective bargaining. The court majority argued that together, the right to collective bargaining and the right to strike represented "critical components of the promotion of industrial – and therefore socio-economic – peace" (para. 42).

Having tied the origins of Canada's collective bargaining model to a dispute mechanism process, the court then acknowledged the breadth of this newfound right. In a lengthy discussion, the Supreme Court concluded that the right to strike was firmly endorsed by Canada's international human rights obligations (*SFL v. Saskatchewan* 2015, paras. 62–75). Wrapped within this discussion was the court's clear acceptance of union arguments that the right to strike was closely connected to a free and democratic society. On this point, the court observed that

> the ability to strike thereby allows workers, through collective action, to refuse to work under imposed terms and conditions. This collective action at the moment of impasse is an affirmation of the dignity and autonomy of employees in their working lives. (para. 54)

The power of those words coming from a Supreme Court justice should not be underestimated. Never in its history had the court, as a whole, shown such sympathy for the *collective* actions of workers to further workplace democracy through strike action.

While the majority recognized that the ability to strike did not guarantee a specific outcome, the justices were nevertheless clear that governments did not have the constitutional ability to simply dismiss workers' right to strike. In short, government could not independently determine the rules and outcomes of the labour relations process (*SFL v. Saskatchewan* 2015, para. 81). That said, the Supreme Court was clear that the designations of essential services were "fundamental questions" that certainly could be addressed by government (para. 92). From the court's perspective, the problem with the Saskatchewan government's legislation was that it *unilaterally* withdrew workers' right to strike without designating some sort of independent review process for resolving disputes (para. 96). The court therefore struck down the *PSESA*, giving the government a year to revise the bill. On the constitutional questions surrounding the *Trade Union Amendment Act*, the court simply stated that the law did not interfere with the ability of workers to form associations, a clear loss for the SFL's argument surrounding the transfer of power to employers during the certification process. Nevertheless, the elevation to constitutional status of the right to strike was more than enough for labour leaders to declare victory.

While the majority decision was a strongly worded endorsement of the freedom to strike, it also came with a strong dissent from Justices Rothstein and Wagner. In some ways, this was not surprising. Appointed to the Supreme Court by Prime Minister Stephen Harper in 2006, Rothstein had opposed every Supreme Court decision extending workers' rights.[9] In *SFL v. Saskatchewan*, Rothstein, borrowing the reasoning of the majority from the *Alberta Reference*, stated that the freedom to strike was a modern right (*SFL v. Saskatchewan* 2015, paras. 110–13) and that labour relations should be left to the legislature (paras. 114–24). What was perhaps more surprising was that Rothstein was joined in his dissent by Justice Wagner. In *MPAO*, Wagner had sided with the majority, which appeared to deepen the constitutional right to collective bargaining. How Wagner squared the obvious tension between his endorsement of collective freedoms in *MPAO* and his rejection of those freedoms in *SFL v. Saskatchewan* is unclear.

At the root of Rothstein's dissent in both *MPAO* and *SFL v. Saskatchewan* was his concern with the rights of employers. In *MPAO*, he lamented that the majority's critique of management-dominated associations was slamming the door on "collaborative bargaining" while also claiming that some company-dominated unions "foster representation" (*MPAO* 2015, paras. 190, 197). Rothstein and Wagner believed that the majority, by constitutionalizing the freedom to strike in *SFL v. Saskatchewan,* were really imposing a political (rather than legal) opinion

> that favours the interests of employees over those of employers and even over those of the public. While employees are granted constitutional rights, constitutional obligations are imposed on employers. Employers and the public are equally as entitled to justice as employees – true workplace justice looks at the interests of all implicated parties. (*SFL v. Saskatchewan* 2015, para. 125)

Rothstein and Wagner's reasoning on the balance of power certainly fit well within traditional judicial philosophy with regard to workers' rights. In fact, both justices were channelling the thought process of the majority from the labour trilogy, arguing that "a constitutional right to strike not only upsets this delicate balance [between the interests of the employers, employees, and the public], but also restricts legislatures by denying them the flexibility needed to ensure the balance of interests can be maintained" (*SFL v. Saskatchewan* 2015, para. 125). Interestingly, Justice Abella pointed to this outdated judicial philosophy in her majority decision:

> In essentially attributing equivalence between the power of employees and employers, this reasoning, with respect, turns labour relations on its head, and ignores the fundamental power imbalance which the entire history of modern labour legislation has been scrupulously devoted to rectifying. It drives us inevitably to Anatole France's aphoristic fallacy: "The law, in its majestic equality, forbids the rich as well as the poor to sleep under bridges, to beg in the streets, and to steal bread." (para. 56)

The majority clearly believed that a world view that equates employee and employer power as "balanced" grossly ignores the power differentials of modern workplace relations. That the majority rejected such a deeply entrenched judicial view is what made this case exceptional.

The Aftermath of the New Labour Trilogy

There is little question that this new labour trilogy has the real potential to act as a buffer to protect unions from further attacks by neoliberal governments. In essence, constitutional protection can act as a legal shield to protect labour's existing rights and lay the foundation to grow and expand the labour movement in new ways. Such a view necessarily sees the courts as allies of working people. As Joel Bakan explained,

> As workers' freedom of association is eroded by economic shifts and hostile governments, the judiciary becomes more essential for protecting this fundamental right. It's a classic case – like segregation in the U.S. South, or abortion or sexual orientation equality in Canada – where governments cannot be relied upon to respect constitutional rights and freedoms, so the courts step in (quoted in Fine 2015).

Even prior to the decision in *SFL v. Saskatchewan*, labour law scholars recognized that successful court challenges had the potential to act as tools of legitimation that could reinforce the status and role of unions in Canada (Faraday and Tucker 2014). As Judy Fudge (2012, 16) has argued, constitutional recognition of the right to strike has the potential to assist in "re-establish[ing] a balance between and among civil society organizations and the state by providing constitutional protections to ensure that unions and workers' organizations remain vibrant civil society actors." The Supreme Court's affirmation of a constitutional right to strike will also make it more difficult for government to severely restrain a public sector union from striking without providing some legislative *quid pro quo*. Unions (especially in the public sector) will now be able to legitimize their strikes as protecting Charter values such as democracy, equality, and liberty. By acquiring the ability to equate strikes with Charter values, the labour movement has certainly gained a powerful political, legal, and rhetorical tool. Finally, it is important to remember that the Supreme Court's decision is an important legal and political victory for workers in Saskatchewan, who have not been treated well by the Saskatchewan Party government. In this sense, the SFL and the public sector unions have derailed at least some of the provincial government's anti-labour agenda.

Notwithstanding these important gains, labour's constitutional victory also comes with several drawbacks. As identified by the Supreme Court and the Saskatchewan Court of Appeal, labour has always had a historical right to strike. In fact, it was the postwar Wagner/PC 1003 model of industrial relations that placed restrictions on the ability of workers to strike. In pointing to those limitations, the Supreme Court championed the notion that a legalized, institutionalized collective bargaining process that includes the right to strike actually leads to labour peace (*SFL v. Saskatchewan* 2015, paras. 42–43). Therein, of course, is the fundamental contradiction of labour's constitutional quest: by tying a constitutional right to strike to a meaningful (legalized) collective bargaining process, the court is reinforcing the notion that strikes will be infrequent, apolitical, and narrowly cast. That process is now elevated to constitutional status.

Conclusion
Which Way Forward for Labour?

Over the last three decades, the labour movement has gone from es-
chewing constitutionalized social and economic rights to fully embra-
cing them. In some ways, organized labour's evolving attitude towards
the relationship between workers' rights and the Charter of Rights is
hardly surprising. Forums for constitutional reform such as the 1980–
81 Special Joint Committee on the Canadian Constitution or the 1992
Special Joint Committee on a Renewed Canada have always played an
important role in presenting new conceptions of rights. As a result of
these dialogues, an increasing number of social movements and other
organizations have harnessed the language of rights to press their demands in both the political and judicial arenas. Moreover, human
rights legislation, human rights commissions, and judicial interpretations of the constitution have all fostered broader understandings of
rights. As historian Lynn Hunt (2007, 29) reminds us, "Rights cannot be
defined once and for all, because their emotional basis continues to
shift, in part in reaction to declarations of rights ... The human rights
revolution is by definition unending."

In the wake of landmark Supreme Court decisions in *BC Health Services, MPAO,* and *SFL v. Saskatchewan,* organized labour has clearly become more emboldened to make broader rights-based claims on behalf
of union members and the working class more generally. For example,

in March 2015, the Canadian Union of Postal Workers (CUPW) launched a Charter challenge in an effort to derail Canada Post's decision to end door-to-door mail delivery, arguing that the termination of service discriminates against both the elderly and the disabled (Canadian Press 2015). In May 2015, seventeen federal unions launched a "coordinated" and "comprehensive legal plan" to challenge Bill C-4, the 2013 omnibus budget bill that, among other things, amended the *Public Service Labour Relations Act* in order to make it more difficult for unions to bargain over wages and benefits (May 2015a).[1] The unions' "solidarity pact" included not only coordinated bargaining tactics but also International Labour Organization (ILO) and Charter challenges to defeat the federal Conservative government's unilateral changes. Claude Poirier, president of the Canadian Association of Professional Employees (CAPE), explained that the agreement between the unions "represents a commitment on their part to devote whatever financial and human resources are necessary and to turn to the courts in cases where such action is appropriate" (CAPE 2015). On 29 June 2015, twelve of the unions, led by the Professional Institute of the Public Service of Canada (PIPSC) and CAPE, forged ahead with another Charter challenge to the federal government's budget bill, arguing that the Conservatives' bill was unconstitutional because it sidestepped the collective bargaining process and unduly limited the right to strike in order to impose a new sick leave scheme on the federal public service (May 2015b).

Whereas Canada's judicial system was once considered by the labour movement to be elitist, conservative, and hostile to unions and the working class, a growing number of unions now view the courts as a legitimate and effective avenue to defend and advance workers' collective rights and freedoms. One of the main objectives of this book has been to chart and explain that evolution. Applying a critical institutionalist theoretical approach, we have argued that while unions were initially hostile to constitutionalized labour rights for fear of how they might be interpreted by an unsympathetic judiciary, significant sections of organized labour ultimately retreated back to the legal arena, shed their judicial phobia, and wrapped themselves in the rhetoric of "workers' rights as human rights" as a response to the growing tide of neoliberalism and the crisis in social democratic electoralism in the

1990s. Labour's evolving relationship to the courts and to the Charter was deeply intertwined with struggles to defend existing rights for workers and expand the zone of legal toleration for unions and their members. In this concluding chapter, we interrogate labour's new-found appreciation for the courts and Charter litigation as part of an overall assessment of the contemporary union movement's strategic orientation and political direction in the area of workers' rights.

We have argued throughout the book that increased constitutional protections for workers' collective rights in the areas of association and expression undoubtedly help to expand the zone of legal toleration for organized labour. We have also argued, however, that Charter decisions favouring unions have worked to strengthen the boundaries of legal constraint on workers' collective actions. For example, with the right to collective bargaining comes a reduced legal threshold for what constitutes bargaining in good faith. With the right to secondary picketing comes the Supreme Court's championing of the "wrongful action model" – decades-old economic tort restrictions that severely undermine picketers' collective ability to disrupt business as usual. Finally, with the right to strike comes the expectation that labour disputes will not be initiated for political purposes. In short, Charter victories in the realm of labour law carry important caveats, which simultaneously serve to reinforce the status quo of the labour relations relationship while threatening to undermine class-based political efforts to pursue more radical avenues for transforming the system of labour relations.

Much of our analysis has been built on a critique of the judicialization of labour politics. The courts are not, and never were, the natural place for workers and their unions to pursue their rights. In his stinging critique of Charter-based politics, Mandel (1994) usefully reminds us that the "legalization of politics" through the Charter was fundamentally a conservative project, with the courts having historically overlooked the unequal distribution of social power in society, especially in the realm of labour relations. While labour has certainly come a long way in terms of influencing the court, the imbalance of power between employers and workers is arguably even wider today than when the Charter was enacted in 1982. As we have argued elsewhere, it is difficult to contemplate how judicial decisions alone can fundamentally transform society (Savage 2008; Smith 2012). Recognizing a constitutional right to strike does not necessarily lay the foundation for legislative improvements in the realm of labour rights or lead to a more democratic economy. Under a "labour rights" formula, union victories are reduced to legalistic, judicial-made law that bears little resemblance to workers' everyday struggles. Moreover, elite-driven Charter victories threaten, over time, to depoliticize class-based struggles that have historically advanced the cause of working people. Without a political will or capacity to use their collective rights effectively to strike or organize, especially in the private sector, it is not clear how Supreme Court decisions alone will lead to significant social transformations for workers. The challenge, in our view, is for workers and their unions to transform their legal victories into political victories. To chart a new course forward, the labour movement needs to take stock of the current situation, reconsider the pitfalls inherent in advancing liberal human rights–based arguments, and rediscover its historical take on judicialized politics.

By taking aim at the underlying assumptions and strategic impulses of the chorus of voices within the labour movement and pro-union academic circles calling for labour rights to be elevated to the status of human rights, we are in no way suggesting that the Charter is of no use to organized labour. We have been careful throughout the book not to dismiss entirely the importance of Charter litigation and the broader strategic use of rights discourse in defence of workers' rights. There are persuasive arguments for why workers and their unions should pursue Charter litigation as a defensive strategy to protect their hard-won rights and freedoms. Legal victories do matter insofar as they can help legitimize unions, undo government legislation that is harmful over the long term, and potentially improve the lives of working people. These positives, however, must be weighed against the shortcomings of judicially based strategies for building worker power.

First, because judicially based strategies are necessarily top down and generally only include union lawyers and the labour leadership, such an approach risks demobilizing and ultimately depoliticizing rank-and-file workers, leaving them even more vulnerable to state-led attacks on labour rights. This is not to suggest that unions cannot pursue legal strategies and working-class political mobilizations simultaneously.

Indeed, health care unions in British Columbia did just that in the 2000s. However, a judicial strategy that relies on "joint legal research, communications strategies and financial support on the key cases" (Fudge and Brewin 2005, 83) – as proposed by the National Union of Public and General Employees (NUPGE), for example – does very little to politicize or organize the grassroots in any meaningful way. Instead, such approaches place greater emphasis on lawyers, judges, and elite-driven legal responses to neoliberalism. Moreover, legal strategies risk serving as a substitute for political action. In many ways, the lack of strategic capacity within the Canadian labour movement dictates the use of narrow legal channels rather than rank-and-file mobilization (Panitch and Swartz 2003). This is a particularly worrisome scenario for unions that do not have a strong tradition of militancy or membership mobilization. Members of such unions tend to approve of substituting legal strategies for militant political tactics because a judicial rights-based approach absolves them from having to participate in potentially risky fightback campaigns that may take on unfamiliar dimensions.

From the perspective of the Canadian labour leadership, a Charter challenge or a complaint to the International Labour Organization's Committee on Freedom of Association may serve to pacify the rank-and-file union membership while alleviating pressure to mount an aggressive grassroots counteroffensive. However, the more the labour movement focuses on refining its rights-based legal strategies, the less time and money it has to develop workers' capacities to resist encroachments on rights and freedoms in the political arena. In other words, an overreliance on Charter-based judicial strategies risks atrophying the labour movement's collective political muscle, thus undermining the capacity of unions to build a movement that challenges the boundaries of liberal democracy.

Second, despite recent Charter victories, union power has not demonstrably increased as a result of obtaining a constitutional right to strike or bargain collectively. Overall, union density in Canada continues to decline and the incidences of strikes are near all-time lows. In short, the constitutionalization of labour rights has not led to an increase in the relative strength of organized labour. As Eric Tucker has pointed out, however, capital's "constitutions," in the form of international trade agreements, have clearly helped to increase the power of corporations vis-à-vis organized labour (Tucker 2012b, 355–78). Such neoliberal trade agreements are far more powerful than any labour movement victories in the judicial arena.

It is worth noting that Canada is not the only country in the world to constitutionalize collective workers' rights to bargain and to strike. As the Supreme Court noted in *SFL v. Saskatchewan* (2015, para. 74), Italy, Portugal, Spain, South Africa, and the European Social Charter all recognize the importance of strikes to address bargaining inequalities. In these countries, however, we still see significant encroachments on workers' rights and freedoms, and unions are hardly political power-houses. Constitutionalized labour rights, then, are no panacea. Because neoliberal globalization is a political project promoted by employers and governments, an energized and mobilized political movement is required to combat it effectively.

Third, labour's growing obsession with Charter litigation and its underlying human rights discourse, to borrow a phrase from US labour historian Joseph McCartin (2011, 154), is quickly becoming a "political and rhetorical cul-de-sac." Many of today's "labour rights as human rights" campaigns are narrowly cast as bestowing human rights status on the activities of union members to bargain collectively or to strike (D. Fudge 2012). While we recognize that this approach has some lim-ited normative utility based on the language of rights discourse, it also risks stoking the flames of what Tom Walkom (2010) has called "reverse-class resentment" – the tendency of non-unionized working-class people to misdirect their class antagonism and resentment towards "privileged" union members rather than towards big business and other capitalist interests. Unions that ignore this type of class envy do so at their own peril. The stratification of the working class is not a mirage. If unions are to restore their power, they cannot do so through campaigns that seemingly exclude the vast majority of working-class people; other-wise, many people will justifiably view these actions as self-serving.

Besides the very serious obstacle of reverse-class resentment, asser-tions among labour leaders and union activists that collective bargaining or strike activity ought to be protected on the basis that it is a Char-ter right is ultimately a losing proposition insofar as it leaves labour completely disarmed in the event that the courts interpret the constitution differently in the future. Submitting to the legal expertise of courts in this way is inconsistent with the birth and development of the labour movement, which took place, in many ways, outside the boundaries of the law. It is this tension that underlies both the expansion of the legal zone in which workers' collective freedoms legitimately operate and the parallel boundaries of constraint that are now firmly entrenched in the constitution. While workers were only able to form unions through militant and often illegal strikes, today the so-called freedom to strike is constrained by strict legal (and now constitutional) rules that only recognize legitimate strikes in very narrow circumstances. Thus, the constitutionalization of a right to strike actually predetermines a very narrow ability for workers to challenge the power of government and employers.

Despite the fact that Canadians consistently self-identify with the Charter and demonstrate far greater trust in courts and judges than they do in their elected representatives, contemporary human rights–based judicial strategies for advancing workers' rights are potentially counterproductive for the labour movement. As McCartin (2011) reminds us, anti-union forces are very well equipped to advance rights-based arguments of their own, as evidenced by the litany of right-wing politicians and organized interests calling for – and in some cases, winning – "right-to-work" legislation. The danger, rightly identified by McCartin, of labour's reliance on the language of rights is that it will inevitably trigger counter-rights claims, like the public's right not to have services disrupted by a strike or a worker's individual right to withhold payment of dues.

Admittedly, while it is clear that the Charter has important limitations for labour, the specific political alternatives for defending and expanding workers' rights are not so evident. In terms of parliamentary political action, labour's primary electoral vehicle, the NDP, has proven to be a fair-weather ally, especially when it forms government (Evans 2012; Savage and Smith 2013). The labour movement's newfound faith in political lobbying and experiments with strategic voting in recent years has proven even more disappointing, failing to yield substantive or sustained pro-labour reforms (Savage 2012; Savage and Butovsky 2009).

Some contend that it is time to radically overhaul Canada's Wagner/
PC 1003 labour law regime. Roy Adams (2006) and David Doorey
(2013), for instance, have argued for a complete overhaul or the establishment of a parallel labour law regime to move beyond the Wagner/PC
1003 model. For his part, Adams argues in favour of a new tripartite
human rights–based labour relations framework, underpinned by the
ILO's fundamental freedoms. While Canada's labour relations model
has clearly proven incapable of extending workplace democracy to all
segments of the Canadian workforce, Adams's alternative fails to truly
address the power imbalances that underpin all employment relationships in advanced capitalist democracies like Canada. Adams's co-
determinist and tripartite prescriptions rest on the dubious belief that
employers and unions have compatible economic interests. Stephanie
Ross (2007, 23) critiques Adams's contention that "the government's
failure to promote collective bargaining rights is a failure of political
will – that can be altered voluntarily – rather than a reflection of the
social and political power possessed by certain class forces and expressed through state (in)action." Ross argues that "this lack of political-
economic context results in an overestimation of the power of legislative
change to restore balance to the labour-management relationship, and
an under-specification of the herculean political mobilization required
to win such reforms." Indeed, Adams's specific proposals do not conform to the priorities or political preferences of business, labour, or the
state. The Canadian government, for its part, refuses to sign on to ILO
Convention 98, which protects the right to collective bargaining. Employer groups are openly hostile to Adams's conception of labour rights,
while organized labour is suspicious at best, in particular when it comes
to his outright rejection of Wagner-style labour relations and his support for non-statutory (or minority) unions as a means of extending
workplace democracy to non-unionized workers (Savage 2008, 73).
Moreover, Adams readily admits that influential organizations like Am-
nesty International Canada and the Canadian Civil Liberties Association have largely ignored the perceived human rights gap in Canadian
labour relations (Adams 2008, 61). Overall, while Adams has been
somewhat effective in advancing the notion of workers' rights as human rights as a rhetorical tool, his specific proposals to move towards

a human rights–based model of labour relations have not been operationalized, concretized, or taken up in any meaningful way by the labour movement, let alone by government.

Despite the limitations of the Wagner model of labour relations, and there are many, some unions fear that using the judicial arena to chip away at aspects of Wagner-style labour relations could leave labour worse off (e.g., through the introduction of minority unionism), especially given that unions are so closely connected institutionally to the existing model. But relying on the courts to preserve or enhance the Wagner model is equally dangerous, reinforcing the very zones of legal toleration and boundaries of constraint that keep labour subservient to capital (Tucker 2014). Ultimately, the real problem is not the Supreme Court or how it interprets the Charter but the lack of an effective labour movement that is able to demand rights in the political arena rather than plead for them in court.

The achievement of early labour rights did not occur in courtrooms or through the use of human rights discourse. In the depths of the Great Depression, radical union and political organizers promoted unions as institutions that could elevate working-class people through the spread of workplace democracy. The direct actions and other militant tactics associated with the Congress of Industrial Organizations and the radical movements of the 1930s may provide labour with a roadmap in its quest to restore some of its political and economic power. There is no question that the CIO's willingness to impose significant costs on employers through persistent organizing and strikes helped to build the industrial labour movement. Indeed, the current Wagner/PC 1003 model of labour relations is a product of the labour movement's long history of class struggle against the worst excesses of nineteenth- and twentieth-century capitalism. Moreover, the Wagner/ PC 1003 model's zone of legal toleration exists only because workers were willing to break exploitative laws through civil disobedience, sit-down strikes, and mass protest. The preservation of these capacities had little to do with success in court. On the contrary, courts often used injunctions to limit the ability of unions to challenge employer power. This very class tension led to the long history of labour hostility towards the judiciary.

Admittedly, there is a danger in romanticizing labour strategy from the 1930s without sufficiently acknowledging that society, employers, workers, and the state have all changed dramatically over the past seventy-five years. To be sure, the specific conditions that facilitated certain types of labour movement tactics in the depths of the Great Depression are no longer present. That said, the current era presents its own opportunities for resistance – and ultimately, transformation. Therefore, militant and radical actions that challenge the boundaries of legal constraint should not be dismissed as a political tactic; rather, they should be repackaged to reflect the current context and the strategic possibilities of the moment.

For the last thirty years, the Canadian labour movement has faced unrelenting attacks from both capital and the state. According to the Canadian Foundation for Labour Rights (2016), between 1982 and 2016, federal and provincial governments in Canada adopted 218 laws that have "restricted, suspended or denied collective bargaining rights for Canadian workers." Although legislative interventions undermining union rights have disproportionately impacted the public sector, private sector workers have not been spared the assault on labour rights and freedoms. Union density in the private sector fell from 18.1 percent in 1999 to just 15.2 percent in 2014 (Statistics Canada 2015). Chronically high rates of unemployment, the proliferation of contingent and precarious work arrangements, restricted access to Employment Insurance benefits, and threats of capital flight have created an extremely hostile climate for union organizing. Moreover, unionized private sector workers have demonstrated a reduced propensity to strike and an increased willingness to bargain concessions (Ross et al. 2015, 166). There are exceptions to the rule but they are few and far between, leading some researchers to argue that the need for union renewal in Canada is urgent.

But does legal activism actively contribute to union renewal? The answer is complicated. On one hand, judicial victories have the potential to create openings for unions to expand the zone of legal toleration that extend beyond isolated workplaces. For example, the *SFL* decision yielded a constitutionally recognized right to strike for unions in general. On the other hand, having the right to strike and having the means to win an effective strike are two very different things. In other words, the law may afford greater protection, but it is not the spark that creates militancy, renewal, or victories for workers. Tellingly, the *SFL* decision certainly did not spark any sort of strike wave across the country. In fact, one could argue that it simply reinforced the idea that legal activism, rather than political mobilization, is a better strategic bet. While it is possible that some of the most extreme features of the neoliberal assault on workers' rights will be stayed by recent Charter decisions, none of the substantive challenges facing unions will be overcome through legal activism. Thus, while legal activism is a legitimate strategic weapon for the labour movement, it should not act as a substitute for grassroots political mobilization. Research on social movements has clearly demonstrated that greater member involvement in union affairs and campaigns not only helps to build the collective capacities of workers but also fosters a more robust sense of solidarity between them and, in turn, enhances the legitimacy of the unions' political demands from the perspective of the rank-and-file (Parker and Gruelle 1993; Polletta 2004).

Internal solidarity and mutual support, however, is not enough. The challenge for unions is to reach out beyond their workplaces to build alliances with social movements and the unorganized working class more generally in order to extend the culture of solidarity as broadly as possible. Building sustained alliances is difficult but, on a tactical level, potentially very rewarding. For example, cross-picketing arrangements with other unions, workers' centres, student associations, or community groups, wherein activists picket someone else's workplace, could potentially allow unions to side-step important legal constraints of the Wagner model of labour relations that would prevent workers from picketing their own workplace while a collective agreement was still in force. Clawson (2013, 34) explains the logic of such a tactic:

> Integral to neoliberalism is corporations' use of subcontractors to avoid legal liability (and often even public relations blame): "We had no idea those goods were made by sweated labor, it's not our fault, we'll stop using that subcontractor." Perhaps our unions can do the same: make a grant to an independent group that happens to be organizing protests, even (we'd be "shocked, shocked" to discover) militant disruptive protests.

Of course, this type of disruptive tactic would require a high level of co-ordination and, more importantly, solidarity between unions and other social movements. However, the shared sense of struggle that would result would also have the effect of forging the types of long-term alliances that are required to foster a truly transformative political project.

The case of the 2012 Quebec student strike is instructive here. In the words of Clawson (2013, 34), the strike "did not declare moral victory after a day or week or month; its sustained power led to a change of government and complete repeal of the proposed tuition increases ... For any movement facing a seemingly impregnable power structure, the challenge appears impossible – until the movement develops a winning strategy and new tactics." The mobilization of student groups against the Quebec government's proposed tuition hikes and, in turn, its repressive law restricting freedom of assembly led to Canada's largest ever display of civil disobedience. During the dramatic and controversial maple spring demonstrations in 2012, Quebec's student movement, rather than uncritically embrace Charter rights to association and expression, toyed with a number of strategies to deal with "the law," from outright defiance to an ironic embrace. Student leaders, correctly in our view, understood the law as a contested terrain that could be stretched, changed, and even broken (Nadeau-Dubois 2015).

While the legal obstacles facing the labour movement are admittedly more significant than those facing Quebec students, so too is the transformative potential of organized labour. The labour movement is one of the only political forces in society that has the potential collective strength and resource capacity to organize the plethora of social movement organizations committed to resisting neoliberalism and, ultimately, building an alternative society. However, pursuing a transformative political strategy requires workers and union leaders to think outside the narrow and defensive scope of Charter politics. It requires flexible and participatory long-term planning and alliance building that is open, democratic, and sustained. The emergence of a transformative political project for the labour movement would also require unions to devote more resources towards radical labour education and solidaristic political initiatives in support of social movement partners, community groups, and other workers' organizations, both unionized and non-unionized. It would seek to build worker capacities around what Jane McAlevey (2014, 15) has described as "whole worker organizing," which seeks to "bring community organizing techniques right into the shop floor while moving labour organizing techniques into the community." In short, unions would need to transcend their sectional interests in pursuit of a broader working-class agenda.

These prescriptions will require a significant change in the current politics of the Canadian labour movement insofar as they challenge many of the political practices and legal frames traditionally associated with unions. Part of the problem, as described by Gindin (2006), is that "the political choices we confront today are not real choices because we don't in fact have the political capacity to implement them and – more distressing – we haven't figured out a way of developing such capacities." This sober assessment of the Canadian labour movement's ability to adopt new ways of thinking and acting politically leads us back to the specific issue of Charter litigation.

When a union spends time and resources on implementing a legal strategy, there is an expectation that the union will also refrain from criticizing the very judicial system it looks to for support. To do otherwise would undermine the instrumental logic of Charter litigation and defeat the purpose of launching Charter challenges in the first place. This leads some unions to overlook the limitations of the Supreme Court or the Charter. If labour farms out its key social and economic demands to lawyers and judges to be filtered into neatly crafted legal arguments, how does labour's vision for an alternative society based on principles of social justice and economic equality ever gain a toehold in the minds of rank-and-file union members? Organized labour incrementally loses the capacity and the imagination to act as a truly transformative movement every time unions embrace the liberal individualist notions that have traditionally been a cornerstone of rights-based Charter litigation. More importantly, because tactical shifts have an educative effect on the union rank-and-file, and thus help validate ideological shifts over time, union-sponsored Charter challenges – whether motivated by anger, fear, instrumentalism, or a combination of all three – threaten to depoliticize the labour movement over time, making it increasingly difficult for workers and their unions to mount the political resistance necessary to challenge and ultimately overcome neoliberalism.

It is unclear whether the labour movement's thirty-year ride on what Eric Tucker (2012a, 42) calls the "Charter rollercoaster" is in for another round of ascents or descents. Given the stunning decisions produced by the Supreme Court in the field of labour law since the turn of the century, it would be foolhardy to predict how Charter jurisprudence in this area will continue to evolve. That said, our analysis does not hinge on a specific case or set of decisions. The Canadian judiciary is unlikely to ever interpret the Charter in a way that facilitates transformational political change for organized labour. At best, the Charter is an incredibly unreliable and expensive shield for the labour movement. At worst, it can be used as an anti-union sword, wielded by employers intent on dismantling workers' rights and freedoms. The labour movement will not be saved by one Charter victory or even by a string of successful legal challenges; organized labour cannot transform labour law without tackling much larger political issues related to structural inequality and growing wealth disparity, not only between the super-rich and the rest of society but between union members and non-organized segments of the working class. Confronting those larger issues will inevitably mean staking out positions and engaging a different type of labour politics that will no doubt make some union leaders uncomfortable, but it could also lead to a resurgence of labour's political activism, strongly influenced by the energy and vision of a new generation of union activists.

Notes

Introduction: Law, Workers, and Courts

1 There are, of course, exceptions. For example, US-based labour historians; McCartin 2005; Lichtenstein 2013) have convincingly argued that rights-based approaches to advancing workers' interests undermine labour militancy and foster a sense of individualism in workers rather than the sense of collective worker power required to transform society. Consistent with this theme, some historically focused work in Canada has challenged the traditional liberal interpretations of Canada's early judicial rulings with regard to workers' collective rights (Fudge and Tucker 2001; Panitch and Swartz 2003).

2 Admittedly, political scientists have not completely ignored organized labour. In their influential "Court Party" critique of social movement influence on Charter interpretation, F.L. Morton and Rainer Knopff (2000) argue that labour unions – separate and apart from post-materialist, identity-focused social movements – were part of the "old economic left" that were critical of using courts and judges "as an instrument for economic leveling" (66). Matt James has critiqued Morton and Knopff's argument that the Canadian labour movement, as the principal agent of "old economic left," did not view constitutional reform throughout the twentieth century as central to its material well being (2006). James's work convincingly demonstrates that labour unions in the immediate postwar period were very much interested in questions of human rights as part of a larger commitment to social democracy. However, he is probably overly generous in his assessment of labour's attitude toward the courts, and constitutional politics more generally, as avenues for advancing workers' material interests, underemphasizing the level of antagonism that labour sustained for the pro-employer biases of courts and judges.

Chapter 1: Labour Rights in the Pre-Charter Era

1   Stockpiling often occurs in the final weeks of a contract. In these cases, employers intensify production and store the commodities produced in locations away from the workplace. If a strike occurs, employers are free to continue to sell their products. Yellow-dog contracts are those signed by company unions requiring, as a condition of employment, that employees do not join *bona fide* labour unions.

2   Section 98 of the *Criminal Code* was passed by the federal Parliament after the 1919 Winnipeg General Strike. The law banned any association that sought to bring about "industrial or economic change within Canada by use of force, violence or physical injury to person or property" (Berger 1981, 132).The provisions were used to limit the ability of communist-inspired unions to organize in the 1920s and 1930s (Endicott 2012).

3   Inspired by the social doctrines of the Catholic Church, the CCCL, which was founded in 1921, rejected socialism, communism, and even the idea of class struggle. Instead, it focused on the "harmony of capital and labour and the right to national autonomy" (Denis 1979, 86). Suspicious of Americans, international unions, and foreign capital, the CCCL in many ways represented a reaction to industrialization's threat to traditional French Canadian values.

4   PC 7307 contained a provision allowing the minister of labour to determine who was eligible to participate in a strike vote. At times, the minister included foremen and clerical staff who, under the American Wagner model, were not considered part of bargaining units. This decision made it more difficult for unions to strike legally. PC 7307 also required that a strike be approved by a majority of all those entitled to vote rather than a simple majority of those participating in the vote. Although PC 7307 was erased from the statute books after the implementation of PC 1003, these voting procedures formed an important component of many postwar labour codes in the provinces.

5   After the Rand decision, union security clauses came to include six forms: (1) the Closed Shop: an agreement where all employees in the bargaining unit are required to become members of the union as a condition of employment; (2) the Union Shop: an agreement that requires all employees to become members of the union but gives no direction to the employer on who to hire; (3) the Modified Union Shop: exempts workers from compulsory membership who are not members at the time the agreement comes into force, but requires that all new employees to join the union; (4) Maintenance of Membership: workers are under no obligation to join the union, but those who do must, as a condition of employment, maintain their membership throughout the life of a contract; (5) the Optional Clause: requires employees who are not members of a union either to join or pay dues; (6) Preferential Hiring: the employer gives preference to members of the contracting union when hiring employees. Depending on the form of contract, a security clause was revocable, but this rarely occurred during the life of an agreement. For

those unions able to win a security clause in collective agreements, the most common were the voluntary revocable plan (where the individual worker requests the check-off) or a compulsory plan (where participation was mandatory).

6 In *Re Sisters of Charity, Providence Hospital and Labour Relations Board et al.* [1951] D.L.R. 735., the court stated that the board was performing its function in a manner that favoured labour at the expense of the people of Saskatchewan. It also argued that the board "not only intended to expeditiously determine legal disputes but, by full inquiry into the facts, for the discovery of which extensive powers have been conferred upon the board, it should bring them to an amicable settlement." In this case, three women workers from the Textile Workers were dismissed from their jobs at a private charitable hospital because of alleged union activity. In the course of its investigation, the board ruled that this was a violation of the act and ordered the women reinstated. The hospital appealed the decision to the court on the grounds that the board lacked jurisdiction and held an improper hearing into the affairs at the hospital. The hospital also alleged that the conduct of the board demonstrated bias in favour of the union. The court concluded that the board had acted improperly and overturned the order.

7 Bora Laskin made this observation much earlier, admitting that the concept of "jurisdiction" became "the convenient umbrella under which the provincial courts have chosen to justify their continual assertions of a reviewing power" (Laskin 1952, 990).

8 Archives of Ontario (hereafter AO), Ministry of Labour Legislation and Regulation Files, RG 7-3-0-12, Box 1, Canadian Manufacture's Association (Ontario Division), Rejoinder: Circular No. 6–59, 13 February 1959, 1.

9 AO, RG 49–138, Proceedings of the Select Committee on Labour Relations (hereafter PSCLR), Box C 90, "Testimony of the Ontario Federation of Labour," 1 October 1957, 4807–8.

10 AO, Proceedings of the Royal Commission Inquiry Into Labour Disputes (hereafter PRCILD), RG 18–152, Box 3 B227098, Testimony of the Toronto and District Labour Council, 19 January 1967, 644.

11 AO, PRCILD, RG 18–152, Box 3 B227098, Submission of the Canadian Labour Congress, January 1967, 15.

12 AO, PRCILD, RG 18–152, Box 3 B227098, Submission of the Canadian Labour Congress, January 1967, 19.

13 AO, PSCLR, RG 49–138 Box C90, Testimony of the International Union, United Automobile, Aircraft, and Agricultural Implement Workers of America (UAW), 15 October 1957, 2748. In 1967, the system of industrial relations was extended to the federal public service (Albo 1990; Jenson 1989).

14 The constitutional power of disallowance gives the federal government power to overturn (or disallow) provincial statutes. Although the federal power of disallowance was used frequently after confederation, it has largely fallen into disuse.

Chapter 2: Disorganized Labour and the Charter of Rights

1 Translated by authors: "cette Constitution ... n'est pas, ne peu pas être et ne sera jamais la nôtre."

Chapter 3: Canadian Labour and the First Era of Charter Challenges

1 Translated literaly, *quia timet* means "because he or she fears." Under the common law, an employer can apply for a *quia timet* injunction if he or she fears that a potential action might violate one of the established economic or nominate torts. In short, the injunction can be used to stop a collective action before it actually occurs.

2 McIntyre's three final variations were: (4) that freedom of association protects all collective activities that are fundamental to Canadian culture and traditions, (5) that freedom of association protects all activities that are fundamental to the lawful objectives of the association and (6) the extension of full collective rights to associations subject to their limitations under the law and the reasonable limits clause of the constitution.

3 Because neither the Ontario courts nor the Supreme Court of Canada took much interest in the freedom of expression claims raised by Lavigne and his lawyers, we will not address these arguments here.

Chapter 4: A Legal Response to Neoliberalism

1 There were also two certifications pending at another mushroom farm and a poultry facility (Fudge 2004, 436n58).

2 The LICC, a coalition of agriculture and horticulture employers, was formed in the early 1990s to oppose legislative changes improving labour conditions on the farms. For instance, the LICC opposed improved health and safety regulations on the farms and was strongly opposed to the *ALRA*.

3 It is worth noting that all three Quebec justices – for very different reasons – voted to support the mandatory unionization law.

4 In 1999, NAPE changed its name to Newfoundland and Labrador Association of Public and Private Employees.

Chapter 5: The Possibilities and Limitations of Constitutional Labour Rights

1 That article reads as follows:
   Article 23.
   (1) Everyone has the right to work, to free choice of employment, to just and favourable conditions of work and to protection against unemployment.
   (2) Everyone, without any discrimination, has the right to equal pay for equal work.
   (3) Everyone who works has the right to just and favourable remuneration ensuring for himself and his family an existence worthy of human dignity, and supplemented, if necessary, by other means of social protection.

(4) Everyone has the right to form and to join trade unions for the protection of his interests.

2 Among the other unions in the health services field were the BC Government and Service Employees' Union, CUPE, and the Health Sciences Association.

3 In the same weekend sitting, the Liberals also passed Bill 27, the *Education Services Collective Agreement Act*, and Bill 28, the *Public Education Flexibility and Choice Act*. These bills designated education in the province an essential service, eliminating the ability of teachers to strike. Teachers were also forbidden from bargaining for numerous workplace conditions, including class sizes, workplace assignments, and the allocation of professional development and vacation time.

4 Although unions have repeatedly attempted to use the section 15 equality provision to expand labour rights under the Charter, it has never been addressed by the courts. Although the constitutional arguments are interesting and worthy of scholarly attention, we will not concentrate on those arguments here.

5 The court has recently recognized the inequality of bargaining power in non-union, non-Charter related areas. For example, in *Potter v. New Brunswick Legal Aid Services Commission* (2015), the Supreme Court ruled that there is a duty of good faith and honesty in the negotiation of a contract with employees.

6 "Labour Organizations in Canada 2015," Government of Canada, Labour Program. http://www.labour.gc.ca/eng/resources/info/publications/union_coverage/union_coverage.shtml.

7 The three agricultural workers were Xin Yuan Liu, Julia McGorman, and Billie-Jo Church. Michael Fraser represented these workers as president of United Food and Commercial Workers.

Chapter 6: A New Era of Constitutional Labour Rights

1 "Court of Queen's Bench Rules Alberta Labour Laws Violate Charter," Alberta Union of Provincial Employees, 4 February 2015. http://www.aupe.org/news/court-of-queens-bench-rules-alberta-labour-laws-violate-charter-of-rights/.

2 Members also created a not-for-profit Members' Legal Fund (MLF). The MLF was funded by voluntary membership dues and provided legal assistance to members in any work-related issue. Although not at the centre of this appeal, the MLF intervened in the case on the side of management, arguing that the current system facilitated "a process of good faith consultation and dialogue between RCMP members and management in respect of workplace issues" (*MPAO* 2015, Mounted Police Members' Legal Fund Intervener Factum, para. 4).

3 The court reasoned that relevant considerations in gauging "independence" would include "the freedom to amend the association's constitution and rules, the freedom to elect the association's representatives, control over financial administration and control over the activities the association chooses to pursue" (*MPAO* 2015, para. 89).

4 Justice Abella disagreed with this conclusion. She would have struck down the *ERA* on the grounds that it substantially interfered with RCMP members' ability to engage in meaningful collective bargaining. She even addressed the substantive nature of bargaining, suggesting that "ensuring fair wage increases is among the key purposes" of this right (*Meredith v. Canada* 2015, para. 53).

5 Those unions were the Advance Employees' Association; Canadian Office and Professional Employees' Union local 397; Canadian Union of Public Employees; Communications, Energy, and Paper Workers' Union of Canada; Construction and General Workers Union local 180; Grain Services Union Health Science Association of Saskatchewan; International Alliance of Theatrical Stage Employees, Moving Picture Technicians, Artists and Allied Crafts of the United States, Its Territories and Canada; International Association of Bridge, Structural, Ornamental and Reinforcing Ironworkers; International Association of Heat and Frost Insulators and Allied Workers; International Brotherhood of Electrical Workers, Locals 2038, 2067, 529; International Longshore and Warehouse Union; Public Service Alliance of Canada; Saskatchewan Joint Board Retail, Wholesale and Department Store Union; Saskatchewan Union of Nurses; Teamsters' Canada Rail Conference; Saskatchewan Legislative Board; United Association of Journeymen Fitters, Welders, Plumbers and Apprentices of the United States and Canada, Local 179; United Brotherhood of Carpenters and Joiners of America 1985, 1021; United Mine Workers of America, Local 7606; United Steel, Paper and Forestry, Rubber, Manufacturing, Energy, Allied Industrial and Service Workers International Union and its locals; and the University of Regina Faculty Association.

6 It is somewhat ironic that prior to his appointment to the Court of Queen's Bench, Dennis Ball was chair of the Saskatchewan Labour Relations Board. Ball was appointed chair by Conservative premier Grant Devine.

7 The SFL's factum contained detailed legal arguments over the constitutionality of Bills 5 and 6. However, since no court ruled in favour of the SFL's Bill 6 challenge, those arguments will not be covered here.

8 There was some disagreement on this point. The Alberta Union of Provincial Employees argued that its experience with compulsory interest arbitration as a replacement for the right to strike had not been positive. From the union's perspective, compulsory arbitration "takes the decision-making power away from both employees and employer, and replaces their contractual freedom with a state proscribed mechanism of dispute resolution in the form of an apparently neutral third-party decision-maker. As a policy choice, it avoids the perceived negative consequences of strike action in the event of a bargaining impasse, presumably social and economic disruption or high wage increases" (*SFL v. Saskatchewan* 2015, Intervener Factum, para. 12).

9 Rothstein's first case dealing with workers' constitutional rights was in the 2011 *Fraser* case (he did not participate in *BC Health Services*), where he argued forcefully for a reversal of *BC Health Services* after four short years. Then in *MPAO*,

Rothstein lamented the fact that his colleagues were too cavalier with overturning precedent from the 1980s and argued for a more restrictive interpretation of workers' collective freedoms (*MPAO* 2015, paras. 171–75).

Conclusion

1 The unions that signed the solidarity pact are the following: Association of Canadian Financial Officers; Association of Justice Counsel; Canadian Air Traffic Control Association, Unifor, Local 5454; Canadian Association of Professional Employees; Canadian Federal Pilots Association; Canadian Merchant Service Guild; Canadian Military Colleges Faculty Association; Coast Guard Marine Communications Officers, Unifor Local 2182; Unifor Local 588-G, Federal Government Dockyards Chargehands Association; Federal Government Dockyards Trades and Labour Council (East); Federal Government Dockyards Trades and Labour Council (West); International Brotherhood of Electrical Workers, Local 2228; Professional Association of Foreign Service Workers; Professional Institute of the Public Service of Canada; Public Service Alliance of Canada; Research Council employees' Association; Union of Canadian Correctional Officers-CSN. "Federal Public Service Unions United in Defense of Collective Bargaining Rights," *CNW*, 15 May 2015. http://www.newswire.ca/en/story/1537761/federal-public-service-unions -united-to-defend-collective-bargaining-rights-file-complaint-with-international- labour-organization-ilo.

References

Books and Articles

Abella, Irving. 1973. *Nationalism, Communism, and Canadian Labour: The CIO, the Communist Party and the Canadian Congress of Labour, 1935–1956*. Toronto: University of Toronto Press.

–. 1974. *On Strike: Six Key Labour Struggles in Canada, 1919–1949*. Toronto: James Lewis and Samuel.

Adell, Bernard. 2003. "Secondary Picketing After *Pepsi-Cola*: What's Clear, and What Isn't?" *Canadian Labour and Employment Law Journal* 10: 135–59.

Adams, Roy. 2003. "The Revolutionary Potential of *Dunmore*." *Canadian Labour and Employment Law Journal* 10: 117–34.

–. 2005. "Organizing Wal-Mart: The Canadian Campaign." *Just Labour* 6–7: 1–11.

–. 2006. *Labour Left Out: Canada's Failure to Protect and Promote Collective Bargaining as a Human Right*. Ottawa: Canadian Centre for Policy Alternatives.

–. 2008. "From Statutory Right to Human Right: The Evolution and Current Status of Collective Bargaining." *Just Labour* 12: 48–67.

–. 2009a. "*Fraser v. Ontario* and International Human Rights: A Comment." *Canadian Labour and Employment Law Journal* 14: 379–94.

–. 2009b. "Prospects for Labour's Right to Bargain Collectively after B.C. Health Services." *University of New Brunswick Law Journal* 59: 85–94.

Akyeampong, Ernest B. 2001. "Time Lost Due to Industrial Disputes." *Perspectives on Labour and Income* (August). http://www.statcan.gc.ca/pub/75-001-x/00801/5881-eng.html.

–. 2004. "The Union Movement in Transition." *Perspectives* (August), 5. http://www.statcan.gc.ca/pub/75-001-x/10804/7011-eng.pdf.

Albo, Gregory. 1990. "The New Realism and Canadian Workers." In *Canadian Politics: An Introduction to the Discipline*, eds Alain Gagnon and James Bickerton, 471-504. Toronto: Broadview.

Anderson, Fiona. 2007. "Ruling May Impact Other Contracts; Decision Could Undo All Liberal Legislation That Wiped Out Agreements." *Vancouver Sun*, 9 June.

Arthurs, Harry. 1963. "Labour Law – Secondary Picketing – Per Se Illegality – Public Policy." *Canadian Bar Review* 41: 573–86.

–. 1985. "Understanding Labour Law: The Debate over 'Industrial Pluralism.'" *Current Legal Problems* 38: 83–116.

–. 1988. "'The Right to Golf': Reflections on the Future of Workers, Unions, and the Rest of Us under the *Charter*." *Queen's Law Journal* 13: 17–31.

–. 2007. "Labour and the 'Real' Constitution." *Les Cahiers de droit* 48 (1–2): 43–64. http://dx.doi.org/10.7202/043922ar.

–. 2009. "Constitutionalizing the Right of Workers to Organize, Bargain and Strike: The Sight of One Shoulder Shrugging." *Canadian Labour and Employment Law Journal* 15: 373–87.

Barrett, Steven. 2003. "Dunmore v. Ontario (Attorney General): Freedom of Association at the Crossroads." *Canadian Journal of Labour and Employment Law* 10: 83–116.

Barrett, Steven, and Benjamin Oliphant. 2013–14. "The Trilogy Strikes Back: Reconsidering Constitutional Protection for the Freedom to Strike." *Ottawa Law Review* 45(2): 201–45.

Barrett, Steven, and Ethan Poskanzer. 2012. "What Fraser Means for Labour Rights in Canada." In *Constitutional Labour Rights in Canada: Farm Workers and the Fraser Case*, ed. Fay Faraday, Judy Fudge, and Eric Tucker, 190–233. Toronto: Irwin.

Bartholomew, Amy, and Susan Boyd. 1987. "Toward a Political Economy of Law." In *The New Canadian Political Economy*, ed. Wallace Clement and Glen Williams, 212–39. Montreal and Kingston: McGill-Queen's University Press.

Bartkiw, Timothy J. 2009. "Proceed with Caution, or Stop Wherever Possible? Ongoing Paradoxes in Legalized Labour Politics." *Canadian Labour and Employment Law Journal* 15: 77–100.

Bateman, Thomas M.J. 1998. "Rights Application Doctrine and the Clash of Constitutionalisms in Canada." *Canadian Journal of Political Science* 31(1): 3–29. http://dx.doi.org/10.1017/S0008423900008660.

BC Liberal Party. 2001. *A New Era for British Columbia*. Vancouver: BC Liberals.

BCFL (BC Federation of Labour). 1981. Presentation to the Special Joint Committee of the Constitution of Canada. 8 January.

Beatty, David M. 1987. *Putting the Charter to Work: Designing a Constitutional Labour Code*. Montreal and Kingston: McGill-Queen's University Press.

Beatty, Jim, and Craig McInnes. 2002. "Government Rescinds NDP-Era Deals with Thousands of Workers." *Vancouver Sun*, 26 January.

Bernstein, Irving. 1970. *The Turbulent Years: The History of the American Worker, 1933–1941*. Boston: Houghton Mifflin.

Berger, Thomas R. 1981. *Fragile Freedoms: Human Rights and Dissent in Canada*. Toronto: Clarke, Irwin.

Bilson, Beth. 2009. "Enter Stage Right: Players and Roles in a Post–B.C. Health Services World." *University of New Brunswick Law Journal* 59: 67–84.

–. 2010. "Developments in Labour Law: The 2009-2010 Term." *Supreme Court Law Review* 52 (2d): 281–309.

Bindman, Stephen. 1987. "Labor Vows to Fight Anti-strike Ruling." *Ottawa Citizen*, 10 April.

Black, Edwin. 1975. *Divided Loyalties: Canadian Concepts of Federalism*. Montreal and Kingston: McGill-Queen's University Press.

Black, Simon. 2012. "Community Unionism and the Canadian Labour Movement." In Ross and Savage, *Rethining the Politics of Labour in Canada*, 146–58.

Blackett, Adelle. 2009. "Mutual Promise: International Labour Law and *B.C. Health Services.*" *Supreme Court Review* 48: 365–407.

Blakeney, Allan. 2008. *An Honourable Calling: Political Memoirs*. Toronto: University of Toronto Press.

Braley, Alison. 2011. "'I Will Not Give You a Penny More Than You Deserve': *Ontario v. Fraser* and the (Uncertain) Right to Collectively Bargain in Canada." *McGill Law Journal / Revue de droit de McGill* 57(2): 351–74. http://dx.doi.org/10.7202/1007819ar.

Braley-Rattai, Alison. 2013. "Harnessing the Possibilities of Minority Unionism in Canada." *Labor Studies Journal* 38(4): 321–40. http://dx.doi.org/10.1177/016044 9X14530706.

Brethour, Patrick, and Laura Drake. 2007. "Unions Hail Ruling as 'Tremendous Victory.'" *Globe and Mail*, 9 June.

Briskin, Linda. 2007. "From Person-Days Lost to Labour Militancy: A New Look at the Canadian Work Stoppage Data." *Relations industrielles / Industrial Relations* 62(1): 31–65. http://dx.doi.org/10.7202/015797ar.

Brodie, Ian. 2002. *Friends of the Court: The Privileging of Interest Group Litigants in Canada*. Albany: State University of New York Press.

Brym, Robert, Louise Birdsell Bauer, and Mitch McIvor. 2013. "Is Industrial Unrest Reviving in Canada? Strike Duration in the Early Twenty-First Century." *Canadian Review of Sociology* 50(2): 227–38. http://dx.doi.org/10.1111/cars.12013.

Byers, Barb. 2002. "Applying the Lessons to the Canadian Experience: Barb Byers, President, Saskatchewan Federation of Labour." In *Labour and Social Democracy: International Perspectives*, ed P. Leduc Browne, 75–78. Ottawa: Canadian Centre for Policy Alternatives.

Bula, Frances. 1987. "Ruling Dismays Unionists." *Vancouver Sun*, 10 April.

Cadigan, Sean T. 2015. "Newfoundland and Labrador, 1979–2011: Contradiction and Continuity in a Neoliberal Era." In Evans and Smith, *Transforming Provincial Politics*, 21–48.

Cako, Stephen. 1971. "Labour Struggle for Union Security: The Ford of Canada Strike." Master's thesis, University of Guelph, Ontario.

Cameron, J.C., and F.J.L. Young. 1960. *The Status of Trade Unions in Canada*. Kingston: Centre of Industrial Relations, Queen's University.

Camfield, David. 2006. "Neoliberalism and Working-Class Resistance in British Columbia: The Hospital Employees' Union Struggle, 2002–2004." *Labour/Le Travail* 57: 9–41.

–. 2007. "CUPE's Sympathy Strikes in British Columbia, October 2005: Raising the Bar for Solidarity." *Just Labour* 11: 35–42.

Campbell, Charles. 1984. "The Canadian Left and the Charter of Rights." *Socialist Studies* 2: 30–45.

Canada. 1981. Special Joint Committee on the Constitution of Canada: Record of Proceedings, Vol. 43.

Canada. Department of Labour. 1925. "Report of the Executive Council." *Labour Gazette* (September): 893–95.

–. 1926. "Summary re Briefs Presented February, 1925." *Labour Gazette* (April): 337–38.

–. 1929a. "Proposed Amendment to British North America Act." *Labour Gazette* (September): 1014–15.

–. 1929b. "Report of the Executive Board." *Labour Gazette* (December): 1360–66.

–. 1940. "Unemployment Insurance." *Labour Gazette* (June): 549–50.

–. 1946. "Award on Issue of Union Security in Ford Dispute." *Labour Gazette* (January): 123–31.

–. 1950. "Legislative Proposals of Labour Organizations." *Labour Gazette* (January–December): 637–43.

–. 1951. "Security Provisions in Collective Agreements, Manufacturing Industry." *Labour Gazette* (October): 1360.

–. 1954. "Union Security Clauses in Collective Agreements." *Labour Gazette* (September): 1140–41.

Canada. Task Force on Canadian Unity. 1979. *A Future Together: Observations and Recommendations*. Ottawa: Privy Council Office.

Canada. 1968. *Canadian Industrial Relations: Report on the Task Force on Labour Relations (Woods Commision)*. Ottawa: Privy Council Office.

Canadian Bar Association. 1978. *Towards a New Canada*. Ottawa: Canadian Bar Association, Committee on the Constitution.

Canadian Foundation for Labour Rights. 2015. *New Labour Trilogy: Canadian foundations for Labour Rights Forum Report*. http://www.labourrights.ca/sites/labour rights.ca/files/documents/cflr_new_labour_trilogy_forum.pdf.

–. 2016. "Restrictive Labour Laws in Canada." *Canadian Federation for Labour Rights*. http://labourrights.ca/issues/restrictive-labour-laws-canada.

Canadian Press. 1980. "Quebecers Ponder CLC Restructuring." *Montreal Gazette*, 5 May.

–. 2007. "Seasonal Workers to Gain Bargaining Rights, Benefits." *Globe and Mail*, 1 December.

–. 2015. "Postal Workers Union Says Ending Home Delivery Is Unconstitutional." *CTV News*, 4 March. http://www.ctvnews.ca/business/postal-workers-union-says-ending-home-delivery-is-unconstitutional-1.2263433.

CAPE (Canadian Association of Professional Employees). 2015. "Union Solidarity on a Large Scale." *CAPE*. http://www.acep-cape.ca/en/resources/publications/professional-dialogue/union-solidarity-on-a-large-scale/.

Caplan, Gerald. 1973. *The Dilemma of Canadian Socialism: The CCF in Ontario*. Toronto: McClelland and Stewart.

Carr, Shirley G.E. 1987. Letter to Ray Hnatyshyn re: interventions before the Supreme Court of Canada in Charter cases, 26 May. CLC Archives.

Carroll, William K., and R.S. Ratner. 2005. "The NDP Regime in British Columbia, 1991–2001: A Post-Mortem." *Canadian Review of Sociology* 42(2): 167–96. http://dx.doi.org/10.1111/j.1755-618X.2005.tb02460.x.

Carrothers, A.W.E., E.E. Palmer, and W.B. Rayner. 1986. *Collective Bargaining Law in Canada*. 2nd ed. Toronto: Butterworths.

Carter, Donald D., et al. 2002. *Labour Law in Canada*. 5th ed. Markham: Butterworths.

Cavalluzzo, P. 1986. "Freedom of Association and the Right to Bargain Collectively." In *Litigating the Values of a Nation*, ed. J.M. Weiler and R.M. Elliot, 245–60. Toronto: Carswell.

–. 2012. "The *Fraser* Case: A Wrong Turn in a Fog of Judicial Deference." In *Constitutional Labour Rights in Canada: Farm Workers and the Fraser Case*, ed. Fay Faraday, Judy Fudge, and Eric Tucker, 155–89. Toronto: Irwin.

CBC (Canadian Broadcasting Corporation). 1987. "NDP Tops Polls under Broadbent." http://www.cbc.ca/archives/categories/politics/parties-leaders/ed-broadbent/ndp-tops-the-polls.html.

Chabun, Will. 2010. "Hubich slams Sask. Government; SFL convention also sees campaigning for president." *Regina Leader Post*, 28 September.

Chaykowski, Richard P. 2011. "Canadian Labour Policy in the Aftermath of Fraser." *Canadian Labour and Employment Law Journal* 16: 291–312.

Clancy, James, Wayne Roberts, David Spence, and John Ward. 1985. *All for One: Arguments from the Labour Trial of the Century on the Real Meaning of Unionism*. Toronto: Ontario Public Service Employees Union.

Clawson, Dan. 2013. "Faculty Unions at the Crossroads: Why Playing Defense Is a Losing Strategy." *New Labor Forum* 22: 29–35.

CLC (Canadian Labour Congress). 1960. Minutes of Proceedings and Evidence of the Canadian Labour Congress, Presentation to the House of Commons Special Committee on Human Rights and Fundamental Freedoms. No. 3, 19 July.

–. 1978a. Annual Convention Document, Quebec, 3–7 April.

–. 1978b. Proceedings of the 1978 Annual Convention, Quebec, 3–7 April. Canadian Labour Congress Library.

–. 1980a. Executive Council minutes, 15 September.

–. 1980b. Executive Council minutes, 9–11 December.

–. 1981. Executive Committee minutes, 9 March.

–. 1987. Discussion paper on the Charter of Rights and Freedoms, 6 May.

–. 1989. Position of the CLC on the Meech Lake Accord, 5 September, Appendix, 1.

–. 1990a. Executive Committee 10 April.

–. 1990b. Executive minutes, 4 December.

–. 1991a. Executive minutes, 4 April.

–. 1991b. Sub-committee of the Executive Committee on the Canadian Constitution, Principles Guiding Labour's View of Constitutional Issues, 8 April.

–. 1992a. Executive Council minutes, 31 August.

–. 1992b Executive Council minutes, 15–16 September.

–. 1992c. "Make Your Vote Count." 30 September.

"CLC Decides to Fight Charter Challenges of Labour Union Rights." 1985. *Ottawa Citizen,* 11 September.

Clément, Dominique. 2008. *Canada's Rights Revolution: Social Movements and Social Change, 1937–82.* Vancouver: UBC Press.

Cohen, Marcy. 1994. "British Columbia: Playing Safe Is a Dangerous Game." *Studies in Political Economy* 43(1): 149–59. http://dx.doi.org/10.1080/19187033.1994.11675393.

–. 2006. "The Privatization of Health Care Cleaning Services in Southwestern British Columbia, Canada: Union Responses to Unprecedented Government Actions." *Antipode* 38(3): 626–44. http://dx.doi.org/10.1111/j.0066-4812.2006.00599.x.

Conway, Aiden, and John Conway. 2015. "Saskatchewan: From Cradle of Social Democracy to Neoliberalism's Sandbox." In Evans and Smith, *Transforming Provincial Politics,* 226–54.

Cotler, Irwin. 1981. "Freedom of Assembly, Association, Conscience and Religion." In *The Canadian Charter of Rights and Freedoms: Commentary,* ed. Walter Tarnopolsky and Gerald-A. Beaudoin, 123–211. Toronto: Carswell.

Cotter, John. 2013. "Alberta's Personal Information Protection Act Struck Down by Supreme Court of Canada." *Huff Post Alberta,* 15 November. http://www.huffingtonpost.ca/2013/11/15/alberta-personal-information-protection-act-struck-down_n_4282055.html.

Coulter, Kendra. 2012. "Anti-Poverty Work: Unions, Poor Workers and Collective Action in Canada." In Ross and Savage, *Rethining the Politics of Labour in Canada,* 146–58.

Cowan, Pamela. 2010. "Hubich Re-elected as SFL President." *Star Phoenix,* 1 November.

Cox, Kevin. 1991. "Nfld. Budget Slashes Jobs, Salaries Frozen, 360 Beds Closed." *Globe and Mail,* 8 March.

Craig, John D.R., and Henry Dinsdale. 2003. "A 'New Trilogy' or the Same Old Story?" *Canadian Labour and Employment Law Journal* 83: 59–82.

Craven, Paul. 1980. *An Impartial Umpire: Industrial Relations and the Canadian State, 1900–11*. Toronto: University of Toronto Press.

–. 1984. "Workers' Conspiracies in Toronto, 1854–1872." *Labour/Le Travail* 14: 49–70. http://dx.doi.org/10.2307/25140481.

Crosariol, Beppi. 1985. "Labor Movement Threatened by Power Given to Judges under New Charter of Rights." *Kingston Whig-Standard*, 10 October.

Cruikshank, Douglas, and Gregory S. Kealey. 1987. "Strikes in Canada, 1891–1950." *Labour/Le Travail* 20: 85–145.

CUPE (Canadian Union of Public Employees). 1985. "Charter of Rights: Will It Protect Collective As Well As Individual Freedom?" *The Facts* 7(6): 8–9.

D'Aoust, Claude, and François Delorme. 1981. "The Origin of the Freedom of Association and the Right to Strike in Canada: A Historical Perspective." *Relations industrielles/Industrial Relations* 36(4): 894–921. http://dx.doi.org/10.7202/029209ar.

Déclaration Conjointe. 1982. Canadian Labour Congress Library. 11 December.

Denis, Roch. 1979. *Lutte de classes et question nationale au Quebec: 1948-1968*. Montreal: Presses Socialistes Internationales.

Denis, Roch, and Serge Denis. 1992. *Les syndicats face au pouvoir: Syndicalisme et politique au Quebec de 1960 à 1992*. Ottawa: Vermillion.

Deverall, John. 1987. "Unions Fear Charter Ruling Will Restrict Right to Strike." *Toronto Star*, 10 April.

Dinsdale, Henry, and Dan Awrey. 2003–4. "Secondary Picketing in Canada: Thoughts for the Pepsi Generation." *Queen's Law Journal* 29: 789–808.

Doorey, David J. 2010. "Union Access to Workers during Organizing Campaigns: A New Look through the Lens of *B.C. Health Services*." *Canadian Labour and Employment Law Journal* 15: 1–49.

–. 2012. "The Charter and the Law of Work: A Beginner's Guide." Unpublished paper. http://papers.ssrn.com/sol3/papers.cfm?abstract_id=2150279.

–. 2013. "Graduated Freedom of Association: Worker Voice beyond the Wagner Model." *Queen's Law Journal* 28: 515–48.

Drache, Daniel, and Harry Glasbeek. 1992. *The Changing Workplace: Reshaping Canada's Industrial Relations System*. Toronto: Lorimer.

Elder, David. 2013. "No Dice: Supreme Court Declares Alberta Privacy Law Unconstitutional in Palace Casino Case." *Canadian Technology and IP Law*. 31 November. http://www.canadiantechnologyiplaw.com/2013/11/articles/privacy/no-dice-supreme-court-declares-alberta-privacy-law-unconstitutional-in-palace-casino-case/.

Endicott, Stephen. 2012. *Raising the Workers' Flag: The Workers' Unity League of Canada, 1930–1936*. Toronto: University of Toronto Press.

England, Geoffrey. 1988. "Some Thoughts on Constitutionalizing the Right to Strike." *Queen's Law Journal* 13: 168–213.

Etherington, B. 1987. "Freedom of Association and Compulsory Union Dues: Towards a Purposive Conception of a Freedom Not to Associate." *Ottawa Law Review* 19: 1–48.

–. 1991. "Lavigne v OPSEU: Moving Toward or Away from a Freedom to Not Associate?" *Ottawa Law Review* 23: 533–52.

–. 1992. "An Assessment of Judicial Review of Labour Laws under the Charter: Of Realists, Romantics, and Pragmatists." *Ottawa Law Review* 24: 685–732.

–. 2009. "The B.C. Health Services and Support Decision – The Constitutionalization of a Right to Bargain Collectively in Canada: Where Did It Come from and Where Will It Lead?" *Comparative Labor Law and Policy Journal* 30: 715–49.

–. 2010. "Does Freedom of Association under the *Charter* Include the Right to Strike after *B.C. Health*? Prognosis, Problems and Concerns." *Canadian Labour and Employment Law Journal* 15: 315–32.

Evans, Bryan. 2012. "The New Democratic Party in the Era of Neoliberalism." In *Rethinking the Politics of Labour in Canada*, ed. Stephanie Ross and Larry Savage, 48–61. Halifax: Fernwood Publishing.

Evans, Bryan, and Charles W. Smith. 2015. *Transforming Provincial Politics: The Political Economy of Canada's Provinces and Territories in the Neoliberal Era.* Toronto: University of Toronto Press.

Faraday, Fay, and Eric Tucker. 2014. "Who Owns Charter Values? A Mobilization Strategy for the Labour Movement." In *Unions Matter: Advancing Democracy, Economic Equality, and Social Justice*, ed. Matthew Behrens, 125–38. Toronto: Between the Lines.

Fine, Sean. 2015. "Canadian Workers Have Fundamental Right to Strike, Top Court Rules." *Globe and Mail,* 30 January.

Fudge, Derek. 2012. "Labour Rights: A Democratic Counterweight to Growing Income Inequality in Canada." In *Constitutional Labour Rights in Canada: Farm Workers and the Fraser Case*, ed. Fay Faraday, Judy Fudge, and Eric Tucker, 234–60. Toronto: Irwin.

Fudge, Derek, and John Brewin. 2005. *Free Collective Bargaining in Canada: Human Right or Canadian Illusion?* Nepean: National Union of Public and General Employees and United Food and Commercial Workers.

Fudge, Judy. 1988. "Labour, the New Constitution and Old Style Liberalism." *Queen's Law Journal* 13: 61–111.

–. 2004. "'Labour Is Not a Commodity': The Supreme Court of Canada and the Freedom of Association." *Saskatchewan Law Review* 67: 425–52.

–. 2007a. "The New Discourse of Labour Rights: From Social to Fundamental Rights?" *Comparative Labor Law and Policy Journal* 29: 29–66.

–. 2007b. "Substantive Equality, the Supreme Court of Canada, and the Limits to Redistribution." *South African Journal on Human Rights* 23: 245–52.

–. 2008a. "Conceptualizing Collective Bargaining under the Charter: The Enduring Problem of Substantive Equality." *Supreme Court Review* 42: 213–47.

–. 2008b. "The Supreme Court of Canada and the Right to Bargain Collectively: The Implications of the Health Services and Support Case in Canada and Beyond." *Industrial Law Journal* 37(1): 25–48. http://dx.doi.org/10.1093/indlaw/dwm038.

–. 2010. "Brave New Words: Labour, the Courts and the Canadian Charter of Rights and Freedoms." *Windsor Yearbook of Access to Justice* 28: 23–52.

–. 2012. "Farm Workers, Collective Bargaining Rights, and the Meaning of Constitutional Protection." In *Constitutional Labour Rights in Canada: Farm Workers and the Fraser Case*, ed. Fay Faraday, Judy Fudge, and Eric Tucker, 1–29. Toronto: Irwin.

Fudge, Judy, and Eric Tucker. 2001. *Labour before the Law: The Regulation of Workers' Collective Action in Canada, 1900–1945*. Toronto: Oxford University Press.

–. 2010. "The Freedom to Strike in Canada: A Brief Legal History." *Canadian Labour and Employment Law Journal* 15: 333–53.

Fudge, Judy, and Harry Glasbeek. 1992a. "Alberta Nurses v. A Contemptuous Supreme Court of Canada." *Constitutional Forum* 4: 1–5.

–. 1992b. "The Politics of Rights: A Politics with Little Class." *Social and Legal Studies* 1(1): 45–70. http://dx.doi.org/10.1177/096466399200100104.

Gindin, Sam. 1995. *The Canadian Auto Workers: The Birth and Transformation of a Union*. Toronto: James Lorimer.

–. 2006. "Towards a New Politics? After the CAW-NDP Divorce." *Socialist Project*. E-Bulletin 27. 14 July. http://www.socialistproject.ca/bullet/bullet027.html.

Glasbeek, Harry. 1985. "Law: Real and Ideological Constraints on the Working Class." In *Law in a Cynical Society? Opinion and Law in the 1980s*, ed. Dale Gibson and Janet K. Baldwin, 282–301. Calgary: Carswell.

–. 1990. "Contempt for Workers." *Osgoode Hall Law Journal* 28: 1–52.

Godard, John. 2011. "What Has Happened to Strikes?" *British Journal of Industrial Relations* 49(2): 282–305. http://dx.doi.org/10.1111/j.1467-8543.2011.00853.x.

Gray, Jeff, and Jordan Fletcher. 2013. "Union Can Videotape Picket Line, Supreme Court Rules in Privacy Case." *Globe and Mail,* 23 November.

Greene, Ian. 2014. *The Charter of Rights and Freedoms*. 2nd ed. Toronto: Lorimer.

Gupta, A. 2013. "The Walmart Working Class." In *Registering Class: Socialist Register 2014*, ed. Leo Panitch, Gregory Albo, and Vivek Chibber, 1–39. London: Merlin.

Harcourt, Mark, and Peter Haynes. 2001. "Accommodating Minority Unionism: Does the New Zealand Experience Provide Options for Canadian Law Reform?" *Canadian Labour and Employment Law Journal* 16: 51–79.

Harder, Lois, and Steve Patten. 2015. "Looking Back on Patriation and Its Consequences." In *Patriation and Its Consequences: Constitution Making in Canada*, ed. Lois Harder and Steve Patten, 3–24. Vancouver: UBC Press.

Hardisty, Rand. 1987. "Labor Vows Fight for the Right to Strike." *Edmonton Journal,* 10 April.

Hargrove, Buzz. 2009. "Striking a Collective Bargain: The Supreme Court Decision in B.C. Health Services." *University of New Brunswick Law Journal* 59: 41–47.

Harrison, Robert. 1872. "Letter in the Globe." *The Globe,* 30 March.

Hay, Colin. 2002. *Political Analysis: A Critical Introduction*. New York: Palgrave.

Hein, Gregory. 2001. "Interest Group Litigation and Canadian Democracy." In *Judicial Power and Canadian Democracy*, ed Paul Howe and Peter H. Russell, 214–54. Montreal and Kingston: McGill-Queen's University Press.

Heron, Craig. 1996. *The Canadian Labour Movement: A Short History*. 2nd ed. Toronto: Lorimer.

Hill, Sharon. 2011. "Supreme Court Denies Right of Farm Workers to Unionize." *Postmedia News*, 29 April.

Hodgetts, J.E. 2000. *The Sound of One Voice: Eugene Forsey and His Letters to the Press*. Toronto: University of Toronto Press.

Hogg, Peter W. 1987. "The Dolphin Delivery Case: The Application of the Charter to Private Action." *Saskatchewan Law Review* 51: 273–80.

–. 2011. *Constitutional Law of Canada, 2011*. Student ed. Toronto: Carswell.

Hollander, Taylor. 2001. "Making Reform Happen: The Passage of Canada's Collective-Bargaining Policy, 1943–1944." *Journal of Policy History* 13(3): 299–328. http://dx.doi.org/10.1353/jph.2001.0008.

Hoogers, Evert. 1978. "A Report from Convention." *Canadian Dimension*, August/September 13: 19.

Horwitz, Morton J. 1974. "The Historical Foundations of Modern Contract Law." *Harvard Law Review* 87(5): 917–56. http://dx.doi.org/10.2307/1340045.

Hoxie, Robert. 1914. "Trade Unionism in the United States: General Character and Types." *Journal of Political Economy* 22(3): 201–17.

Hughes, Patricia. 2003. "Dumore v. Ontario (Attorney General): Waiting for the Other Shoe." *Canadian Journal of Labour and Employment Law* 10: 27–58.

Hunt, Lynn. 2007. *Inventing Human Rights*. New York: W.W. Norton.

Hutchinson, Allan C., and Patrick J. Monahan. 1984. "Law, Politics, and the Critical Legal Scholars: The Unfolding Drama of American Legal Thought." *Stanford Law Review* 36(1–2): 199–245. http://dx.doi.org/10.2307/1228683.

–. 2001. "Democracy and the Rule of Law." In *Law and Morality: Readings in Legal Philosophy*, ed. David Dyzenhaus and Arthur Ripstein, 340–67. Toronto: University of Toronto Press.

Hutchinson, Allan C., and Andrew Petter. 1988. "Private Rights/Public Wrongs: The Liberal Lie of the Charter." *University of Toronto Law Journal* 38(3): 278–97. http://dx.doi.org/10.2307/825787.

James, Matt. 2000. "Misrecognized Materialists: Social Movements in Canadian Constitutional Politics, 1938–1992." PhD diss., University of British Columbia, Vancouver.

–. 2006. *Misrecognized Materialists: Social Movements in Canadian Constitutional Politics*. Vancouver: UBC Press.

Jamieson, Stuart. 1968. *Times of Trouble: Labour Unrest and Industrial Conflict in Canada, 1900–66*. Ottawa: Information Canada.

–. 1973. *Industrial Relations in Canada*. Toronto: MacMillan.

Jane Jenson. 1989. "'Different' but not 'exceptional': Canada's Permeable Fordism." *Canadian Review of Sociology* 26(1): 69–94.

Johnston, Richard. 1996. *The Challenge of Direct Democracy: The 1992 Canadian Referendum*. Montreal and Kingston: McGill-Queen's University Press.

Kaplan, William. 2009. *Canadian Maverick: The Life and Times of Ivan C. Rand*. Toronto: University of Toronto Press.

Kealey, Gregory K. 1980. *Toronto Workers Respond to Industrial Capitalism 1867–1892*. Toronto: University of Toronto Press.

–. 1995. "The Canadian State's Attempt to Manage Class Conflict, 1900–1948." In *Workers and Canadian History*, ed. Gregory Kealey, 419–40. Montreal and Kingston: McGill-Queen's University Press.

Kershaw, Anne. 1985. "The State and the Union: Setting Limit to the Charter." *Kingston Whig-Standard*, 8 July.

Klare, Karl. 1981. "Labor Law as Ideology: Toward a New Historiography of Collective Bargaining Law." *Industrial Relations Law Journal* 4: 450–82.

Kumar, Pradeep, and Dennis Ryan, eds. 1988. *Canadian Union Movement in the 1980s: Perspectives from Union Leaders*. Kingston: Queen's University, Industrial Relations Centre.

Kumar, Pradeep, and Gregor Murray. 2006. "Innovation in Canadian Unions: Patterns, Causes and Consequences." In *Paths to Union Renewal: Canadian Experiences*, ed. Pradeep Kumar and Chris Schenk, 79–102. Peterborough: Broadview Press.

Kumar, Pradeep, and Chris Schenk, eds. 2006. *Paths to Union Renewal: Canadian Experiences*. Peterborough: Broadview Press.

"Labor to Fight Court Ruling on Union Dues." 1986. *Ottawa Citizen*, 8 July.

Lajoie, Don. 1991. "Unions Laud 'Dues' Ruling" *Windsor Star*, 28 June.

Langille, Brian. 2009. "The Freedom of Association Mess: How We Got into It and How We Can Get out of It." *McGill Law Journal/Revue de droit de McGill* 54(1): 177–212. http://dx.doi.org/10.7202/038181ar.

–. 2010a. "Is There a Constitutional Right to Strike in Canada?" *Canadian Labour and Employment Law Journal* 15: 129–32.

–. 2010b. "Why Are Canadian Judges Drafting Labour Codes – and Constitutionalizing the Wagner Act Model?" *Canadian Labour and Employment Law Journal* 15: 101–28.

–. 2011. "Labour Law's Theory of Justice." In *The Idea of Labour Law*, ed. Guy Davidov and Brian Langille, 101–19. Oxford: Oxford University Press.

Laskin, Bora. 1952. "Certiorari to Labour Boards: The Apparent Futility of Privative Clauses." *Canadian Bar Review* 30: 986–1003.

Leclerc, André. 1978. "Quebec's 'Radical' Unionists." *Canadian Dimension* 13: 34–36.

Leier, Mark. 2013. *Rebel Life: The Life and Times of Robert Gosden*. Vancouver: New Star Books.

Lemieux, Matthews, and Steven Barrett. 2007. "Charter Protection Extended to Collective Bargaining – How Far Does It Reach?" *Canadian Centre for Policy Alternatives Review Labour Notes*, December.

Lewis, David, and Frank Scott. 1943. *Make This Your Canada: A Review of C.C.F. History and Policy*. Toronto: Central Canada Publishing Co.

Lichtenstein, Nelson. 2002. *State of the Union: A Century of American Labor*. Princeton: Princeton University Press.

–. 2008. "How Wal-Mart Fights Unions." *Minnesota Law Review* 92: 1462–1501.

–. 2010. *The Retail Revolution: How Wal-Mart Created a Brave New World of Business*. New York: Picador.

–. 2006. *Wal-Mart: The Face of Twenty-First-Century Capitalism*. New York: New Press.

–. 2013. *State of the Union: A Century of American Labor*. 2nd ed. Princeton: Princeton University Press.

List, Wilfred. 1977. "Self-Determination for Quebec? OFL Won't Take Stand." *Globe and Mail*, 30 November.

–. 1978. "Morris Puts Union Ahead of Unity." *Globe and Mail*, 3 April.

–. 1985. "Labor Movement Discovers Charter Is a Two-Edged Sword." *Globe and Mail*, 29 July.

Logan, H.A. 1956. *State Intervention and Assistance in Collective Bargaining: The Canadian Experience, 1943–1954*. Toronto: University of Toronto Press.

Lougheed, Peter. 1998. "Why a Notwithstanding Clause?" Points of View No. 6. Centre for Constitutional Studies. https://ualawccsprod.srv.ualberta.ca/images/points-of-view/Lougheed.pdf.

MacCharles, Tonda. 2001. "Ontario Farm Labour Law Struck Down." *Toronto Star*, 21 December.

MacIvor, Heather. 2013. *Canadian Politics and Government in the Charter Era*. 2nd ed. Don Mills: Oxford University Press.

MacNeil, Michael. 2010. "Freedom of Association in a Free Enterprise System: Wal-Mart in Jonquière." *Canadian Labour and Employment Law Journal* 15: 495–540.

–. 2011. "Collective Bargaining in the Shadow of the Charter Cathedral: Union Strategies in a Post–BC Health Services World." *Dalhousie Law Journal* 34: 19–50.

Makin, Kirk. 1987. "Charter of Rights Puts Labor Law in the Dark Ages, Group Agrees." *Globe and Mail*, 30 March.

–. 2007. "Collective Bargaining Is a Right, Top Court Rules." *Globe and Mail*, 9 June.

Mandel, Michael. 1994. *The Charter of Rights and the Legalization of Politics*. 2nd ed. Toronto: Thompson Educational Publishing.

Matheson, David. 1989. "The Canadian Working Class and Industrial Legality." Master's thesis, Queen's University, Kingston, Ontario.

May, Kathryn. 2015a. "Public Sector Unions Turn to Legal Action over Bargaining Rights." *Ottawa Citizen*, 15 May. http://ottawacitizen.com/news/politics/ps-unions-turn-to-legal-action-over-bargaining-rights.

–. 2015b. "Unions File Charter Challenge on Government's Right to Determine Sick Leave Deal." *Ottawa Citizen,* 30 June. http://ottawacitizen.com/news/politics/unions-file-charter-challenge-on-governments-right-to-determine-sick-leave-deal?hootPostID=bb129b8c81af9e416af289dd9f06f960.

McAdam, Doug, John D. McCarthy, and Mayer N. Zald, eds. 1996. *Comparative Perspectives on Social Movements: Opportunities, Mobilizing Structures, and Cultural Framings.* Cambridge, UK: Cambridge University Press. http://dx.doi.org/10.1017/CBO9780511803987.

McAlevey, Jane. 2014. *Raising Expectations (and Raising Hell): My Decade Fighting for the Labor Movement.* London: Verso.

McBride, Stephen. 2001. *Paradigm Shift: Globalization and the Canadian State.* Halifax: Fernwood.

McCartin, Jospeh. 2005. "Democratizing the Demand for Workers' Rights: Toward a Reframing of Labour's Argument." *Dissent* 52(1): 61–71. http://dx.doi.org/10.1353/dss.2005.0010.

–. 2011. "Probing the Limits of Rights Discourse in the Obama Era: A Crossroads for Labor and Liberalism." *International Labor and Working Class History* 80(1): 148–60. http://dx.doi.org/10.1017/S0147547911000111.

McCormick, Peter J. 2015. *The End of the Charter Revolution: Looking Back from the New Normal.* Toronto: University of Toronto Press.

McEvoy, John P. 2009. "B.C. Health Services: The Legacy after Eighteen Months." *University of New Brunswick Law Journal* 59: 48.

McGrane, David. 2014. *Remaining Loyal: Social Democracy in Quebec and Saskatchewan.* Montreal and Kingston: McGill-Queen's University Press.

McInnis, Peter S. 2002. *Harnessing Labour Confrontation: Shaping the Postwar Settlement in Canada, 1943–1950.* Toronto: University of Toronto Press.

–. 2012. "Hothead Troubles: Sixties Era Wildcat Strikes in Canada." In *Debating Dissent: Canada and the Sixties,* ed. Lara Campbell, Dominique Clément, and Gregory S. Kealey, 155–70. Toronto: University of Toronto Press.

McIntosh, Tom. 1989. *Labouring under the Charter: Trade Unions and the Recovery of the Canadian Labour Regime.* Kingston: Queen's University, Industrial Relations Centre.

McRoberts, Kenneth. 1997. *Misconceiving Canada: The Struggle for National Unity.* Toronto: Oxford University Press.

Melnitzer, Julius. 2011. "Fraser Decision Reveals Judicial Debate over Bargaining Rights." *Financial Post,* 3 May.

Milligan, Frank. 2004. *Eugene A. Forsey: An Intellectual Biography.* Calgary: University of Calgary Press.

Moorcroft, Lois. 2005. "Newfoundland Women Want Pay Equity Too." *Canadian Dimension* 39(2). https://canadiandimension.com/articles/view/newfoundland-women-want-pay-equity-too.

Morton, Desmond. 2007. *Working People: An Illustrated History of the Canadian Labour Movement*. 5th ed. Montreal and Kingston: McGill-Queen's University Press.

Morton, Desmond. 1998. Working People: An Illustrated History of the Canadian Labour Movement 4th ed. Montreal and Kingston: McGill-Queen's University Press.

Morton, F.L. and Ranier Knopff. 2000. *The Charter Revolution and the Court Party*. Peterborough: Broadview Press.

Mosher, Peter. 1976. "Wage, Price Scheme Ruled Constitutional." *Globe and Mail*, 13 July.

Moulton, David. 1974. "Ford Strike 1945." In *On Strike: Six Key Labour Struggles in Canada, 1919–1949*, ed. Irving Abella, 129–62. Toronto: Lorimer.

Nadeau-Dubois, Gabriel. 2015. *In Defiance*. Toronto: Between the Lines.

Napier, Jo Ann. 1987. "Right to Strike 'Not Buried' Yet." *Halifax Chronicle-Herald*, 1 and 18 April.

Norman, Ken. 2004. "ILO Freedom of Association Principles as Basic Canadian Human Rights: Promises to Keep." *Saskatchewan Law Review* 67: 591–608.

Norris, Rob. 2008. "Bill No. 5 – The Public Service Essential Services Act." *First Session – Twenty-Sixth Legislature of the Legislative Assembly of Saskatchewan: Debates and Proceedings*. Hansard. N.S. Vol. 50, No. 10A, 11 March, 267.

O'Neil, Peter. 2007. "Collective Bargaining Protected by Charter; Supreme Court Rules." *National Post*, 9 June.

Ontario. 1968. *Royal Commission Inquiry into Labour Disputes*. Toronto: Queen's Printer.

Ostry, Bernard. 1960. "Conservatives, Liberals and Labour in the 1870s." *Canadian Historical Review* 41(2): 93–127. http://dx.doi.org/10.3138/CHR-041-02-01.

Palmer, Bryan. 1992. *Working Class Experience: Rethinking the History of Canadian Labour, 1800–1991*. 2nd ed. Toronto: McClelland and Stewart.

–. 2003. "What's Law Got To Do With It? Historical Considerations on Class Struggle, Boundaries of Constraint, and Capitalist Authority." *Osgoode Hall Law Journal* 41: 465–90.

–. 2009. *Canada's 1960s: The Ironies of Identity in a Rebellious Era*. Toronto: University of Toronto Press.

Palmer, Vaughn. 2008. "Liberals, Health Unions Reach Agreement – at Point of Judicial Gun." *Vancouver Sun*, 29 January.

Panitch, Leo. 1995. "Elites, Classes, and Power in Canada." In *Canadian Politics in the 1990s*, ed. Michael Whittington and Glen Williams, 152–75. Toronto: Nelson.

Panitch, Leo, and Donald Swartz. 2003. *From Consent to Coercion: The Assault on Trade Union Freedoms*. Toronto: Garamond.

–. 2013. "The Continuing Assault on Public Sector Unions." In *Public Sector Unions in the Age of Austerity*, ed. Stephanie Ross and Larry Savage, 38–40. Halifax: Fernwood Publishing.

Parker, Mike, and Martha Gruelle. 1993. *Democracy Is Power: Rebuilding Unions from the Bottom Up*. Detroit: Labor Notes.

Parrot, Jean-Claude. 2005. *My Union, My Life: Jean-Claude Parrot and the Canadian Union of Postal Workers*. Halifax: Fernwood Publishing.

Parti Québécois. 1978. *Official Program of the Parti Québécois*. Montreal: Parti Québécois.

Patrias, Carmela. 2011. *Jobs and Justice: Fighting Discrimination in Wartime Canada, 1939–1945*. Toronto: University of Toronto Press.

Peirce, Jon. 2003. *Canadian Industrial Relations*. 2nd ed. Toronto: Prentice Hall.

Pentland, H.C. 1979. "The Canadian Industrial Relations System: Some Formative Factors." *Labour/Le Travail* 4: 9–23. http://dx.doi.org/10.2307/25139922.

Petter, Andrew. 1986. "The Politics of the Charter." *Supreme Court Review* 8: 473–505.

–. 2010. *The Politics of the Charter: The Illusive Promise of Constitutional Rights*. Toronto: University of Toronto Press.

Pilon, Dennis. 2013. *Wrestling with Democracy: Voting Systems as Politics in the Twentieth-Century West*. Toronto: University of Toronto Press.

–. 2015a. "British Columbia: Right-Wing Coalition Politics and Neoliberalism." In *Transforming Provincial Politics: The Political Economy of Canada's Provinces and Territories in a Neoliberal Era*, ed. Bryan Evans and Charles W. Smith, 284–312. Toronto: University of Toronto Press.

–. 2015b. "Critical Institutionalism: Recovering the Lost Social Core of Institutionalism." Paper prepared for the Association for Institutional Thought at the 57th Annual Western Social Science Conference, Portland, Oregon, 8–11 April 2015.

"Political Use of Union Dues Violates Charter." 1986. *Montreal Gazette*, 8 July.

Polletta, Francesca. 2004. *Freedom Is an Endless Meeting: Democracy in American Social Movements*. Chicago: University of Chicago Press.

PSAC (Public Service Alliance of Canada). 1987. Presentation to the 1987 Special Joint Committee, No. 6, 12 August.

QFL (Quebec Federation of Labour). 1980. Mémoire présenté par la Féderation des travailleurs du Quebec au gouvernement de Quebec. December.

–. 1981. Mémoire de la FTQ a la commission de la présidence du conseil et de la constitution relativement au project de résolution du gouvernement federal concernant la constitution, Quebec. 5 February.

Reed, Louis. S. 1966. *The Labor Philosophy of Samuel Gompers*. Port Washington, NY: Kennikat.

Robinson, Ian. 2000. "Neoliberal Restructuring and US Unions: Towards Social Movement Unionism?" *Critical Sociology* 26(1–2): 109–38. http://dx.doi.org/10.1177/08969205000260010701.

Rose, Joseph B. 2004. "Public Sector Bargaining: From Retrenchment to Consolidation." *Relations industrielles/Industrial Relations* 59 (2): 271–74. http://dx.doi.org/10.7202/009542ar.

Ross, Stephanie. 2005. "The Making of CUPE: Structure, Democracy, and Class Formation." PhD diss., York University.

–. 2007. "Book Review: Labour Left Out: Canada's Failure to Protect and Promote Collective Bargaining as a Human Right." *Social Studies* 3(2): 121–23.

–. 2012. "Business Unionism and Social Unionism in Theory and Practice." In *Rethinking the Politics of Labour in Canada*, ed. Stephanie Ross and Larry Savage, 33–46. Halifax: Fernwood Publishing.

Ross, Stephanie, Larry Savage, Errol Black, and Jim Silver. 2015. *Building a Better World: An Introduction to the Canadian Labour Movement*. 3rd ed. Halifax: Fernwood Publishing.

Roth, Pamela. 2010. "ILO Finds Province's Labour Laws Lacking; UN Body Suggests New Trade Union Act." *Star Phoenix*, 30 March.

Rouillard, Jacques. 2004. *Le syndicalisme Québécois: Deux siécles d'histoire*. Montréal: Boréal.

Russell, Bob. 1990. *Back to Work? Labour, State, and Industrial Relations in Canada*. Toronto: Nelson.

–. 1995. "Labour's Magna Carta? Wagnerism in Canada at Fifty." In *Labour Gains, Labour Pains: FIfty Years of PC 1003*, ed. Cy Gonick, Paul Phillips, and Jesse Vorst, 177–92. Halifax: Fernwood Publishing.

Russell, Peter H. 1977. "The *Anti-inflation* Case: The Anatomy of a Constitutional Decision." *Canadian Public Administration* 20(4): 632–65. http://dx.doi.org/10.1111/j.1754-7121.1977.tb01741.x.

–. 2004. *Constitutional Odyssey: Can Canadians Become a Sovereign People?* 3rd ed. Toronto: University of Toronto Press.

Sangster, Joan. 2004. "'We No Longer Respect the Law': The Tilco Strike, Labour Injunctions, and the State." *Labour / Le Travail* 53: 47–87. http://dx.doi.org/10.2307/25149446.

–. 2010. *Transforming Labour: Women and Work in Postwar Canada*. Toronto: University of Toronto Press.

Saskatchewan. 2008a. *Bill No. 5: An Act Respecting Essential Public Services.* http://www.qp.gov.sk.ca/documents/english/FirstRead/2007-08/Bill-5.pdf.

–. 2008b. *Bill No. 6: An Act to Amend* The Trade Union Act. http://www.qp.gov.sk.ca/documents/english/FirstRead/2007-08/Bill-6.pdf.

Savage, Larry. 2007. "Organized Labour and the Canadian Charter of Rights and Freedoms." *Supreme Court Review* 36: 175–99.

–. 2008. "Labour Rights as Human Rights? A Response to Roy Adams." *Just Labour* 12: 68–75.

–. 2009. "Workers Rights as Human Rights: Organized Labour and Rights Discourse in Canada." *Labor Studies Journal* 34(1): 8–20. http://dx.doi.org/10.1177/0160449X08328889.

–. 2010. "Contemporary Party-Union Relations in Canada." *Labor Studies Journal* 35: 8–26.

–. 2012. "Organized Labour and the Politics of Strategic Voting." In *Rethinking the Politics of Labour in Canada*, ed. Stephanie Ross and Larry Savage, 75–87. Winnipeg: Fernwood Publishing.

Savage, Larry, and Jonah Butovsky. 2009. "A Federal Anti-scab Law for Canada? The Debate over Bill C-257." *Just Labour* 13: 15–28.

Savage, Larry, and Charles Smith. 2013. "Public Sector Unions and Electoral Politics in Canada." In *Public Sector Unions in the Age of Austerity,* ed. Stephanie Ross and Larry Savage, 45–46. Winnipeg: Fernwood Publishing.

Schmitz, Cristin. 2011. "SCC Reins in Labour Rights Protection." *Lawyers Weekly,* 12 May.

Scott, Neil. 2008. "Labour Groups File Complaint." *Leader Post,* 4 September.

Sefton MacDowell, Laurel. 1978. "The Formation of the Canadian Industrial Relations System during World War II." *Labour/Le Travail* 3: 175–96.

SFL (Saskatchewan Federation of Labour). 2008a. *Brief to Minister Norris – Bill 5, The Public Service Essential Services Act and Bill 6, An Act to Amend the* Trade Union Act. 15 February. http://www.sfl.sk.ca/public/images/documents/Bill%205%20 and%206%20brief.pdf.

–. 2008b. *Statement of Evidence in Support of the Complaint of the National Union of Provincial Government Employees to the International Labour Organization.* August. http://www.sfl.sk.ca/public/images/documents/ILO%20Support%20Complaint%20(Sep%208%20edit).pdf.

SGEU (Saskatchewan Government Employees Union). 1985. "The Charter of Rights: What's It Worth?" *Implications for Collective Bargaining* 3, 16 April.

Sharpe, Robert, and Kent Roach. 2003. *Brian Dickson: A Judge's Journey.* Toronto: University of Toronto Press.

–. 2009. *The Charter of Rights and Freedoms.* 4th ed. Toronto: Irwin.

Sheppard, Robert, and Michael Valpy. 1982. *The National Deal: The Fight for a Canadian Constitution.* Toronto: Fleet.

Sigurdson, Richard. 1993. "Left- and Right-Wing Charterphobia in Canada: A Critique of the Critics." *International Journal of Canadian Studies* 7–8: 95–115.

–. 1997. "The British Columbia New Democratic Party: Does It Make a Difference?" In *Politics, Policy and Government in British Columbia,* ed. R.K. Carty, 310–38. Vancouver: UBC Press.

Simeon, Richard, and Ian Robinson. 1990. *State, Society and the Development of Canadian Federalism.* Toronto: University of Toronto Press.

Slattery, Brian. 1987. "The Charter's Relevance to Private Litigation: Does Dolphin Deliver?" *McGill Law Journal/Revue de droit de McGill* 32: 905–23.

Slinn, Sara. 2011. "Structuring Reality So That the Law Will Follow: British Columbia Teachers' Quest for Collective Rights." *Labour/Le Travail* 68: 35–77.

Slotnick, Lorne. 1985a. "Charter Challenge on Use of Dues Worries Unions – Pro Business Group Backs Teacher's Fight." *Globe and Mail,* 18 December.

–. 1985b. "Labor Leader Takes Aim at Coalition Anti-unionists Using Charter, OFL Says." *Globe and Mail,* 11 November.

Smith, Charles W. 2008. "The Politics of the Ontario Labour Relations Act: Business, Labour, and Government in the Consolidation of Post-War Industrial Relations, 1949–1961." *Labour/Le Travail* 62: 109–51.

–. 2009. "Fairness and Balance? The Politics of Ontario's Labour Relations Regime, 1949-1963." PhD diss., York University.

–. 2011. "The 'New Normal' in Saskatchewan: Neoliberalism and the Challenge to Workers' Rights." In *New Directions in Saskatchewan Public Policy*, ed. David McGrane, 121–52. Regina: University of Regina Press.

–. 2012. "Labour, Courts and the Erosion of Workers' Rights in Canada." In *Rethinking the Politics of Labour in Canada*, ed. Stephanie Ross and Larry Savage, 184–97. Halifax: Fernwood Publishing.

–. 2014. "'We Didn't Want to Totally Break the Law': Industrial Legality, the Pepsi Strike, and Workers' Collective Rights in Canada." *Labour/Le Travail* 74 (Fall): 89–121.

Smith, Miriam. 1999. *Lesbian and Gay Rights in Canada: Social Movements and Equality Seeking, 1971–1995*. Toronto: University of Toronto Press.

–. 2002. "Ghosts of the Judicial Committee of the Privy Council: Group Politics and Charter Litigation in Canadian Political Science." *Canadian Journal of Political Science* 35: 3–29.

–. 2005. *A Civil Society? Collective Actors in Canadian Political Life*. Toronto: Broadview.

–. 2014. "Identity and Opportunity: The Lesbian, Gay, Bisexual, and Transgender Movement." In *Group Politics and Social Movements in Canada*, ed. Miriam Smith, 179–200. Toronto: University of Toronto Press.

Special Joint Committee. 1987. Minutes of the Special Joint Committee on the 1987 Constitutional Accord. 20 August.

Stanford, Jim. 2001. "Social Democratic Policy and Economic Reality: The Canadian Experience." In *The Economics of the Third Way: Experiences from around the World*, ed. Philip Arestis and Malcolm Sawyer, 79–105. Cheltenham: Edward Elgar. http://dx.doi.org/10.4337/9781843762836.00012.

Statistics Canada. 2015. "Unionization Rates Falling." *Statistics Canada.* http://www.statcan.gc.ca/pub/11-630-x/11-630-x2015005-eng.htm.

Steed, Judy. 1989. *Ed Broadbent: The Pursuit of Power*. Markham: Penguin.

Steffenhagen, Janet. 2003. "Labour Lauds UN Slap at Liberals." *Vancouver Sun*, 28 March.

Stevenson, Garth. 2004. *Unfulfilled Union: Canadian Federalism and National Unity*. 4th ed. Montreal and Kingston: McGill-Queen's University Press.

Strayer, B.L. 1963. "The Concept of 'Jurisdiction in Review of Labour Relations Board Decisions.'" *Saskatchewan Law Review* 28: 157–67.

Swimmer, Gene. 1984. "Six and Five: Part Grandstanding and Part Grand Plan." In *How Ottawa Spends, 1984: The New Agenda,* ed. A. Maslove, 240–81. Toronto: Methuen.

Switzer, Tim. 2010. "SFL Candidates Differ on Province." *Regina Leader-Post*, 30 October.

Tarrow, Sidney. 1998. *Power in Movement: Social Movements and Contentious Politics*. 2nd ed. Cambridge, UK: Cambridge University Press. http://dx.doi.org/10.1017/CBO9780511813245.

Teeple, Gary. 2004. *The Riddle of Human Rights*. Toronto: Garamond.

–. 2000. *Globalization and the Decline of Social Reform: Into the Twenty-First Century*. Aurora: Garamond.

Thompson, Elizabeth. 2001. "Labour Peace at Stake: Union Obligation Is a Reasonable Restriction." *Montreal Gazette*, 20 October.

Thompson, Mark, and Brian Bemmels. 2003. "British Columbia: The Parties Match the Mountains." In *Beyond the National Divide: Regional Dimensions of Industrial Relations*, ed. Mark Thompson, Joseph B. Rose, and Anthony E. Smith, 108–9. Montreal and Kingston: McGill-Queen's University Press.

Tomlins, Christopher. 1985. "The New Deal, Collective Bargaining, and the Triumph of Industrial Pluralism." *Industrial and Labor Relations Review* 39(1): 19–34. http://dx.doi.org/10.1177/001979398503900103.

Tracey, Tyler. 2007. "Top Court Protects Bargaining; Supreme Court Reverses Itself in Landmark Ruling Hailed as 'Victory for Workers' from Coast to Coast." *Toronto Star*, 9 June.

Tucker, Eric. 1991a. "Industry and Humanity Revisited: Everything Old Is New Again." *McGill Law Journal / Revue de droit de McGill* 36: 1483–93.

–. 1991b. "'That Indefinite Area of Toleration': Criminal Conspiracy and Trade Unions in Ontario, 1837–77." *Labour/Le Travail* 27: 15–54. http://dx.doi.org/10.2307/25130244.

–. 2005. "Wal-Mart and the Remaking of Ontario Labour Law." *International Union Rights* 12: 10–11.

–. 2006. "Will the Vicious Circle of Precariousness Be Unbroken? The Exclusion of Ontario Farm Workers from the Occupational Health and Safety Act." In *Precarious Employment: Understanding Labour Market Insecurity in Canada*, ed. Leah Vosko, 256–76. Montreal and Kingston: McGill-Queen's University Press.

–. 2008. "The Constitutional Right to Bargain Collectively: The Ironies of Labour History in the Supreme Court of Canada." *Labour/Le Travail* 61: 151–80.

–. 2010. "*Hersees of Woodstock Ltd. v. Goldstein*: How a Small Town Case Made It Big." In *Work on Trial: Canadian Labour Law Struggles*, ed. Judy Fudge and Eric Tucker, 217–48. Toronto: Irwin.

–. 2012a. "Farm Worker Exceptionalism: Past, Present, and the Post-Fraser Future." In *Constitutional Labour Rights in Canada: Farm Workers and the Fraser Case*, ed. Fay Faraday, Judy Fudge, and Eric Tucker, 30–56. Toronto: Irwin.

–. 2012b. "Labour's Many Constitutions (and Capital's Too)." *Comparative Labor Law and Policy Journal* 33: 101–23.

–. 2014. "Shall Wagnerism Have No Dominion?" *Just Labour* 21: 1–27.

Tucker, Eric, and Judy Fudge. 1996. "Forging Responsible Unions: Metal Workers and the Rise of the Labour Injunction in Canada." *Labour/Le Travail* 37: 81–120. http://dx.doi.org/10.2307/25144036.

UAW (United Auto Workers) Local 444. 1970. *Presentation to the Special Joint Committee of the Constitution of Canada* 23: 8. 12 October.

UEW (United Electrical, Radio and Machine Workers of Canada). 1987. Presentation to the 1987 Special Joint Committee, No. 10, 20 August.

Vallée, Émile 1991. Memo to CLC President Shirley Carr, 13 May.

Vienneau, David. 1991. "Top Court Gives Labor Freedom on Union Dues." *Toronto Star,* 28 June.

Villeneuve, Nobel. 1995. As cited in Ontario *Legislative Assembly of Ontario Debates (Hansard),* 23 October http://hansardindex.ontla.on.ca/hansardeissue/36-1/l014.htm.

Walchuk, Bradley. 2009. "Ontario's Agricultural Workers and Collective Bargaining: A History of Struggle." *Just Labour* 14: 150–63.

–. 2011. "Union Democracy and Labour Rights: A Cautionary Tale." *Global Labour Journal* 2: 106–24.

Walkom, Thomas. 2010. "The Art of Reverse Class Resentment." *Toronto Star,* 27 February.

–. 1994. *Rae Days: The Rise And Follies Of The NDP.* Toronto: Key Porter.

Warnock, John. 2005. "The CCF–NDP in Saskatchewan: From Populist Social Democracy to Neo-Liberalism." In *Challenges and Perils: Social Democracy in Neoliberal Times,* ed. William Carroll and Robert Ratner, 82–102. Halifax: Fernwood Publishing.

Webber, Jeremy. 1986. "The Malaise of Compulsory Conciliation: Strike Prevention in Canada during World War II." In *The Character of Class Struggle: Essays in Canadian Working Class History,* ed. Bryan D. Palmer, 138–59. Toronto: McClelland and Stewart.

Weiler, Joseph M. 1986. "The Regulation of Strikes and Picketing under the Charter." In *Litigating the Values of the Nation: The Charter of Rights and Freedoms,* ed. Joseph Weiler and Robin M. Elliot, 211–44. Toronto: Carswell.

Weiler, Paul C. 1971. "The 'Slippery Slope' of Judicial Intervention: The Supreme Court and Canadian Labour Relations, 1950–1970." *Osgoode Hall Law Journal* 9: 1–80.

–. 1980. *Reconcilable Differences: New Directions in Canadian Labour Law.* Toronto: Carswell.

–. 1990. "The *Charter* at Work: Reflections on the Constitutionalizing of Labour and Employment Law." *University of Toronto Law Journal* 40(2): 117–212. http://dx.doi.org/10.2307/825781.

Wells, Don. 1995. "The Impact of the Postwar Compromise on Canadian Unionism: The Formation of an Auto Worker Local in the 1950s." *Labour/Le Travail* 36: 147–73. http://dx.doi.org/10.2307/25143977.

Whitaker, Reg, Gregory S. Kealey, and Andrew Parnaby. 2012. *Secret Service: Political Policing in Canada from the Fenians to Fortress America.* Toronto: University of Toronto Press.

Whitaker, Reginald, and Gary Marcuse. 1994. *Cold War Canada: The Making of a National Insecurity State, 1945–1957.* Toronto: University of Toronto Press.

York, Geoffrey. 1991. "Union Wins Six-Year Battle on Spending Members' Dues." *Globe and Mail,* 28 June.

Yussuff, Hassan. 2015. "With the Right to Strike, the Supreme Court Returns Balance to the Workplace." *Globe and Mail,* 30 January.

Cases

Alberta (Information and Privacy Commissioner) v. United Food and Commercial Workers, Local 401, [2013] S.C.R. 733.

Alberta Union of Provincial Employees (AUPE) v. Alberta, (2015), court file number 140300279.

Allsco Bldg. Prods. Ltd. v. UFCW Local 1288P, [1999] 2 S.C.R. 1136.

Arlington Crane Service Ltd. v. Ontario (Minister of Labour), [1988] O.J. No. 2060.

Baldwin v. B.C.G.E.U., [1986] 28 DLR (4th), 301.

B.C.G.E.U. v. British Columbia (Attorney General), [1988] 2 S.C.R. 214.

Bhindi v. BC Projectionists' Local 348 of Int. Alliance of Picture Machine Operators of U.S. and Can. (B.C.C.A.), [1986] 29 DLR (4th) 47.

British Columbia Teachers' Federation v. British Columbia Public School Employers' Assn., 2009 BCCA 39.

Canada (A.G.) v. Ontario (A.G) [1937] UKPC 6, [1937] A.C. 326.

Canadian Egg Marketing Agency v. Richardson, [1998] 3 S.C.R. 157.

Canadian Union of Public Employees, Local 301 v. Montreal (City), [1997] 1 S.C.R. 793.

Canadian Union of Public Employees, Local 3967 v. Regina Qu'Appelle Health Region, 2010 CanLII 5199 (SK LRB).

Chaoulli v. Quebec (Attorney General), [2005], 1 SCR 791, 2005 SCC 35.

Delisle v. Canada (Deputy Attorney General), [1999] 2 S.C.R. 989.

Desbiens v. Wal-Mart Canada Corp., [2009] 3 S.C.R. 540.

Dolphin Delivery Ltd. v. Retail, Wholesale and Department Store Union, Local 580, [1984] B.C.J. No. 4.

Dunmore v. Ontario (Attorney General), 1997, 12214 (ON SC).

Dunmore v. Ontario (Attorney General), [2001] 3 S.C.R. 1016, 2001 SCC 94.

Fraser v. Ontario (Attorney General), [2006] O.J. No. 45.

Fraser v. Ontario (Attorney General), [2008] 92 O.R. (3d) 481.

Harrison v. Carswell, [1976] 2. S.C.R. 200.

Health Services and Support – Facilities Subsector Bargaining Assn. v. Her Majesty the Queen et al. (2003) BCSC 1379.

Health Services and Support – Facilities Subsector Bargaining Assn. v. British Columbia, (2004) BCCA, 377.

Health Services and Support – Facilities Subsector Bargaining Assn. v. British Columbia, [2007] 2 S.C.R. 391.

Hersees v. Goldstein, 1963, 38 D.L.R. (2d) 449.

Hunter et al. v. Southam Inc., [1984] 2 S.C.R. 145.

ILO (International Labour Organization). Freedom of Association Committee. 2003. Case 2180 (in conjunction with Case 2173), para 304, http://www.ilo.org/dyn/normlex/en/f?p=1000:20060:0::NO:20060.

–. 2010. Case 2654, March 2010, http://www.ilo.org/dyn/normlex/en/f?p=1000:20060:0::NO:20060.

International Longshoremen's and Warehousemen's Union – Canada Area Local 500 v. Canada, [1994] 1 S.C.R. 150.

Lavigne v. Ontario Public Employees Union, (1989), 67 O.R. (2d) 536, 56 D.L.R. (4th) 474.

Lavigne v. Ontario Public Service Employees Union, [1991] 2 S.C.R. 211.

McKinney v. University of Guelph, [1990] 3 S.C.R. 229.

Meredith v. Canada (Attorney General), 2015 SCC 2, [2015] 1 S.C.R. 125.

Metropolitan Stores (MTS) Ltd. v. Manitoba Food and Commercial Workers, Local 832, [1990] W.W.R. 373 (MB CA).

Mounted Police Association of Ontario v. Canada (Attorney General), 2015 SCC 1, [2015] 1 S.C.R. 3.

Newfoundland (Attorney General) v. N.A.P.E., [1988] 2 S.C.R. 204.

Newfoundland (Treasury Board) v. N.A.P.E., [2004] 3 S.C.R. 381.

Plourde v. Wal-Mart Canada Corp., [2009] 3 S.C.R. 465.

Professional Institute of the Public Service of Canada v. Northwest Territories (Commissioner), [1990] 2 S.C.R. 367.

Pruden Building Ltd. v. Construction and General Workers' Union, Local 92, [1985] 13 DLR (4th), 584.

Potter v. New Brunswick Legal Aid Services Commission, [2015] 1 S.C.R. 500.

PSAC v. Canada, [1984] 2 F.C. 880, 11 D.L.R. (4th) 387.

PSAC v. Canada, [1987] 1 S.C.R. 424.

R. v. Advance Cutting and Coring Ltd., [2001] 3 S.C.R. 209.

R. v. Big M Drug Mart Ltd., [1985] 1 S.C.R. 295.

R. v. Edwards Books and Art Ltd., [1986] 2 S.C.R. 713.

R. v. Saskatchewan Federation of Labour, [2010] SKQB 286.

R. v. Skinner, [1990] 1 S.C.R. 1235.

Ramsden v. Peterborough (City), [1993] 2 S.C.R. 1084.

Re: Canada Assistance Plan (B.C.), [1991] 2. S.C.R. 525.

Re: Anti-Inflation Act, [1976] 2 S.C.R. 373.

Re: Judicature Act, [1984] ABCA 354; 16 DLR (4th) 359.

Re Lavigne and Ontario Public Service Employees Union et al., [1986] O.J. No. 659.

Re Lavigne and Ontario Public Service Employees Union et al., (No. 2) [1987] O.J. No. 653.

Re: Objection by Quebec to a Resolution to Amend the Constitution, [1982] 2 S.C.R. 793.

Re: Resolution to Amend the Constitution, [1981] 1 S.C.R. 753.

Re Service Employees' International Union, Local 204 and Broadway Manor Nursing Home et al., (1983) 44 O.R. (2d) 392 4 D.L.R (4th) 231.

Re Sisters of Charity, Providence Hospital and Labour Relations Board et al. [1951] D.L.R. 735.

Reference re Public Service Employee Relations Act (Alta.), [1987] 1 S.C.R. 313.

Retail, Wholesale and Department Store Union v. Saskatchewan, [1987] 1 S.C.R. 460.

Retail, Wholesale and Department Store Union, Local 544 v. Saskatchewan, (1985) 19 D.L.R. 609.

Retail, Wholesale and Department Store Union, Local 558 v. Pepsi-Cola Canada Beverages (West) Ltd., [2002] 1 S.C.R. 156.

Retail, Wholesale and Department Store Union, Local 580 v. Dolphin Delivery Ltd., [1986] 2 S.C.R. 573.

Rocket v. Royal College of Dental Surgeons of Ontario, [1990] 2 S.C.R. 232.

Saskatchewan v. Saskatchewan Federation of Labour, 2012 SKQB 662.

Saskatchewan Federation of Labour v. Saskatchewan, 2013 SKCA 43.

Saskatchewan Federation of Labour v. Saskatchewan, 2015 SCC 4, [2015] 1 S.C.R. 245.

Saskatchewan (Labour Relations Board) v. John East Iron Works Ltd. 947, [1948] 1 W.W.R. 81, [1948] 1 D.L.R. 652.

Saskatchewan (Labour Relations Board) v. John East Iron Works Ltd., [1948] 2 W.W.R. 1055, [1948] 4 D.L.R. 673, [1949] A.C. 134, [1949] L.J.R. 66, 92 S.J. 704.

Slaight Communications Inc. v. Davidson, [1989] 1 S.C.R. 1038.

St. Anne Nackawic Pulp and Paper v. CPU, [1986] 1 S.C.R. 704.

Toronto Electric Commissioners v. Snider, [1925] A.C. 396, [1925] 2 D.L.R. 5, [1925] 1 W.W.R. 785 (P.C.).

U.F.C.W., Local 1518 v. KMart Canada Ltd., [1999], 2 S.C.R. 1083.

United Food and Commercial Workers v. Kmart Canada Ltd., 1995 CanLII 1849, 14 BCLR (3d) 162.

United Food and Commercial Workers International Union v. Highline Produce Ltd., [1995] OLRB Rep. June 803.

United Nurses of Alberta v. Alberta (Attorney General), [1992] 1 S.C.R. 901.

Wallace v. United Grain Growers Ltd., [1997] 3 S.C.R. 701.

Factums

Delisle v. Canada (Deputy AG), [1999] 2 S.C.R. 989. Delisle Appellant Factum.

–. OTF (Ontario Teachers' Federation) Intervener Factum.

Dunmore v. Ontario (Attorney General), [2001] 3 S.C.R. 1016, 2001 SCC 94. Dunmore Appellant Factum.

–. Government of Ontario Respondent Factum.

. LICC (Labour Issues Coordinating Committee) Intervener Factum.

Health Services and Support – Facilities Subsector Bargaining Assn. v. British Columbia, [2007] 2 S.C.R. 391. Appellants' Factum, Public Copy.

BCTF (British Columbia Teachers' Federation) Intervener Factum.

–. CLC (Canadian Labour Congress) Intervener Factum.

–. CSN (Confédération des syndicats nationaux) Intervener Factum.

–. Health Services and Support – Facilities Subsector Bargaining Association et al., Public Factum.

Health Services and Support-Facilities Subsector Bargaining Association, et al., Reply Factum.

–. Government of Alberta Intervener Factum.

–. Government of British Columbia Respondent's Factum.

–. Government of New Brunswick Intervener Factum.

–. Government of Ontario Intervener Factum.

Lavigne v. Ontario Public Service Employees Union, [1991] 2 S.C.R. 211. CCLA (Canadian Civil Liberties Association) Intervener Factum.

–. CLC/OFL (Canadian Labour Congress/Ontario Federation of Labour) Intervener Factum.

–. Government of Canada Intervener Factum.

–. Government of Ontario Intervener Factum.

–. Government of Quebec Intervener Factum.

–. Lavigne Appellant Factum.

–. NUPGE (National Union of Public and General Employees) Respondent Factum.

–. OPSEU (Ontario Public Service Employees Union) Respondent Factum.

Ontario (Attorney General) v. Fraser, [2011] 2 S.C.R. 3. Government of Alberta Intervener Factum.

–. Government of British Columbia Intervener Factum.

–. Government of Canada Intervener Factum.

–. Government of Ontario Appellant Factum.

–. Michael Fraser Respondent Factum.

Mounted Police Association of Ontario v. Canada (Attorney General), 2015 SCC 1, [2015] 1 S.C.R. 3. CLC (Canadian Labour Congress) Intervener Factum.

–. Government of Alberta Intervener Factum.

–.Government of Canada Respondent Factum.

–. Government of Ontario Intervener Factum.

–. Government of Saskatchewan Intervener Factum.

–. MPAO (Mounted Police Association of Ontario) Appellant Factum.

Newfoundland (Treasury Board) v. N.A.P.E., [2004] 3 S.C.R. 381, 2004 SCC 66. Government of British Columbia Intervener Factum.

–. Government of Newfoundland and Labrador Respondent Factum.

–. NAPE (Newfoundland and Labrador Association of Public and Private Employees) Appellant Factum.

–. WLAF (Women's Legal Action Fund) Intervener Factum.

Plourde v. Wal-Mart Canada Corp., [2009] 3 S.C.R. 465. CBCB (Coalition of BC Businesses) Intervener Factum.

–. CCC (Canadian Chamber of Commerce) Intervener Factum.

–. Gaétan Plourde Appellant Factum.

–. Walmart Canada Respondent Factum.

Professional Institute of the Public Service of Canada v. Northwest Territories (Commissioner), [1990] 2 S.C.R. 367. Government of NWT Respondent Factum.

–. PIPSC (Professional Institute of the Public Service of Canada) Appellant Factum.

Reference re Public Service Employee Relations Act (Alta.), [1987] 1 S.C.R. 313. AUPE (Alberta Union of Provincial Employees) Appellant Factum.

–. CUPE (Canadian Union of Public Employees) Appellant Factum.

–. Government of Alberta Respondent Factum.

–. Government of Canada Intervener Factum.

–. Government of Manitoba Intervener Factum.

–. Government of Newfoundland and Labrador Intervener Factum.

–. Government of Ontario Intervener Factum.

–. Government of PEI Intervener Factum.

–. Government of Saskatchewan Intervener Factum.

RWDSU v. Dolphin Delivery Ltd., [1986] 2 S.C.R. 573. Dolphin Delivery Ltd. Respondent Factum.

–. Government of Alberta Intervener Factum.

–. Government of Canada Intervener Factum.

–. RWDSU (Retail, Wholesale, and Department Store Union) Appellant Factum.

R.W.D.S.U., Local 558 v. Pepsi-Cola Canada Beverages (West) Ltd., [2002] 1 S.C.R. 156. Government of Alberta Intervener Factum.

–. Pepsi Appellant Factum.

–. RWDSU (Retail Wholesale and Department Store Union) Respondent Factum.

Saskatchewan Federation of Labour v. Saskatchewan, 2015 SCC 4, [2015] 1 S.C.R. 245. ACPA (Air Canada Pilots' Association) Intervener Factum.

–. BCTF (British Columbia Teachers' Federation) Intervener Factum.

–. CCCF (Canadian Centre for Constitutional Freedoms) Intervener Factum.

–. CEC (Canadian Employers Council) Intervener Factum.

–. CLC (Canadian Labour Congress) Intervener Factum.

–. CUPW (Canadian Union of Postal Workers) Intervener Factum.

–. Government of Alberta Intervener Factum.

–. Government of Canada Intervener Factum.

–. Government of Newfoundland and Labrador Intervener Factum.

–. Government of Saskatchewan Respondent Factum.

–. PIPSC (Professional Institute of the Public Service of Canada) Appellant Factum.

–. PSAC (Public Service Alliance of Canada) Intervener Factum.

–. SEIU (Service Employees International Union) Intervener Factum.

–. SFL (Saskatchewan Federation of Labour), Appellant Factum.

–. SRHA (Saskatchewan Regional Health Authority) Intervener Factum.

–. SUN (Saskatchewan Union of Nurses) Intervener Factum.

–. UNA (United Nurses of Alberta) and AFL (Alberta Federation of Labour) Intervener Factum.

U.F.C.W., Local 1518 v. KMart Canada, [1999] 2 S.C.R. 1083. CBCB (Coalition of BC Businesses) Intervener Factum.

–. CLC (Canadian Labour Congress) Intervener Factum.

–. Government of BC Intervener Factum.

–. Kmart Respondent Factum.

–. Pepsi Intervener Factum.

–. UFCW (United Food and Commercial Workers) Local 1518 Respondent Factum.

Index

Allyson Lunny
Debating Hate Crime: Language, Legislatures, and the Law in Canada
(2017)

George Pavlich, and Matthew P. Unger, eds.
Accusation: Creating Criminals (2016)

Michael Weinrath
*Behind the Walls: Inmates and Correctional Officers on the State
of Canadian Prisons* (2016)

Dimitrios Panagos
*Uncertain Accommodation: Aboriginal Identity and Group Rights in the
Supreme Court of Canada* (2016)

Wes Pue
Lawyers' Empire: Legal Professionals and Cultural Authority, 1780-1950
(2016)

Sarah Turnbull
Parole in Canada: Gender and Diversity in the Federal System (2016)

Amanda Nettelbeck, Russell Smandych, Louis A. Knafla,
and Robert Foster
*Fragile Settlements: Aboriginal Peoples, Law, and Resistance in South-West
Australia and Prairie Canada* (2016)

Adam Dodek and Alice Woolley (eds.)
In Search of the Ethical Lawyer: Stories from the Canadian Legal Profession
(2016)

David R. Boyd
Cleaner, Greener, Healthier: A Prescription for Stronger Canadian Environmental Laws and Policies (2015)

Margaret E. Beare, Nathalie Des Rosiers, and Abby Deshman (eds.)
Putting the State on Trial: The Policing of Protest during the G20 Summit (2015)

Dale Brawn
Paths to the Bench: The Judicial Appointment Process in Manitoba, 1870–1950 (2014)

Dominique Clément
Equality Deferred: Sex Discrimination and British Columbia's Human Rights State, 1953–84 (2014)

Irvin Studin
The Strategic Constitution: Understanding Canadian Power in the World (2014)

Elizabeth A. Sheehy
Defending Battered Women on Trial: Lessons from the Transcripts (2014)

Carmela Murdocca
To Right Historical Wrongs: Race, Gender, and Sentencing in Canada (2013)

Donn Short
"Don't Be So Gay!" Queers, Bullying, and Making Schools Safe (2013)